the cinema of HAL HARTLEY

DIRECTORS' CUTS

Other selected titles in the Directors' Cuts series:

the cinema of ROBERT ALTMAN: *hollywood maverick*
ROBERT NIEMI

the cinema of SEAN PENN: *in and out of place*
DEANE WILLIAMS

the cinema of CHRISTOPHER NOLAN: *imagining the impossible*
JACQUELINE FURBY & STUART JOY (eds)

the cinema of THE COEN BROTHERS: *hardboiled entertainments*
JEFFREY ADAMS

the cinema of CLINT EASTWOOD: *chronicles of america*
DAVID STERRITT

the cinema of ISTVÁN SZABÓ: *visions of europe*
JOHN CUNNINGHAM

the cinema of AGNÈS VARDA: *resistance and eclecticism*
DELPHINE BÉNÉZET

the cinema of ALEXANDER SOKUROV: *figures of paradox*
JEREMI SZANIAWSKI

the cinema of MICHAEL WINTERBOTTOM: *borders, intimacy, terror*
BRUCE BENNETT

the cinema of RAÚL RUIZ: *impossible cartographies*
MICHAEL GODDARD

the cinema of MICHAEL MANN: *vice and vindication*
JONATHAN RAYNER

the cinema of AKI KAURISMÄKI: *authorship, bohemia, nostalgia, nation*
ANDREW NESTINGEN

the cinema of RICHARD LINKLATER: *walk, don't run*
ROB STONE

the cinema of BÉLA TARR: *the circle closes*
ANDRÁS BÁLINT KOVÁCS

the cinema of STEVEN SODERBERGH: *indie sex, corporate lies, and digital videotape*
ANDREW DE WAARD & R. COLIN TATE

the cinema of TERRY GILLIAM: *it's a mad world*
JEFF BIRKENSTEIN, ANNA FROULA & KAREN RANDELL (eds)

the cinema of THE DARDENNE BROTHERS: *responsible realism*
PHILIP MOSLEY

the cinema of MICHAEL HANEKE: *europe utopia*
BEN McCANN & DAVID SORFA (eds)

the cinema of SALLY POTTER: *a politics of love*
SOPHIE MAYER

the cinema of DAVID CRONENBERG: *from baron of blood to cultural hero*
ERNEST MATHIJS

the cinema of JAN SVANKMAJER: *dark alchemy*
PETER HAMES (ed.)

the cinema of LARS VON TRIER: *authenticity and artifice*
CAROLINE BAINBRIDGE

the cinema of WERNER HERZOG: *aesthetic ecstasy and truth*
BRAD PRAGER

the cinema of TERRENCE MALICK: *poetic visions of america (second edition)*
HANNAH PATTERSON (ed.)

the cinema of ANG LEE: *the other side of the screen (second edition)*
WHITNEY CROTHERS DILLEY

the cinema of STEVEN SPIELBERG: *empire of light*
NIGEL MORRIS

the cinema of TODD HAYNES: *all that heaven allows*
JAMES MORRISON (ed.)

the cinema of DAVID LYNCH: *american dreams, nightmare visions*
ERICA SHEEN & ANNETTE DAVISON (eds)

the cinema of KRZYSZTOF KIESLOWSKI: *variations on destiny and chance*
MAREK HALTOF

the cinema of GEORGE A. ROMERO: *knight of the living dead (second edition)*
TONY WILLIAMS

the cinema of KATHRYN BIGELOW: *hollywood transgressor*
DEBORAH JERMYN & SEAN REDMOND (eds)

the cinema of
HAL HARTLEY

flirting with formalism

edited by Steven Rybin

A Wallflower Press Book
Published by
Columbia University Press
Publishers Since 1893
New York • Chichester, West Sussex
cup.columbia.edu

Copyright © 2017 Columbia University Press
All rights reserved

Wallflower Press® is a registered trademark of Columbia University Press

A complete CIP record is available from the Library of Congress

ISBN 978-0-231-17616-3 (cloth : alk. paper)
ISBN 978-0-231-17617-0 (pbk. : alk. paper)
ISBN 978-0-231-85084-1 (e-book)

Columbia University Press books are printed on permanent
and durable acid-free paper.
Printed in the United States of America

Series design by Rob Bowden Design
Cover image of Hal Hartley courtesy of Photofest (www.photofestnyc.com)

CONTENTS

Acknowledgements vii
Notes on Contributors ix

Introduction: Hal Hartley: A Quality of Attention   *Steven Rybin*   1

1   Up Close and Impersonal: Hal Hartley and the Persistence of Tradition
    David Bordwell   13
2   'Young. Middle-Class. College-Educated. Unskilled.': Hal Hartley in 1991
    Mark L. Berrettini   30
3   'Some Things Shouldn't Be Fixed': Frameworks of Critical Reception and the
    Early Career of Hal Hartley   *Jason Davids Scott*   43
4   The Locality of Hal Hartley: The Aesthetics and Business of Smallness
    Steven Rawle   60
5   Hal Hartley's Romantic Comedy   *Sebastian Manley*   77
6   A New Man: The Logic of the Break in Hal Hartley's *Amateur*
    Daniel Varndell   94
7   Not Getting It: *Flirt* as Anti-Puzzle Film   *Steven Rybin*   109
8   Poiesis and Media in *The Book of Life* and *No Such Thing*
    Fernando Gabriel Pagnoni Berns   121
9   Bodies, Space and Theatre in *The Unbelievable Truth* (and its American
    Precursors)   *Zachary Tavlin*   132
10 Parker Posey as Hal Hartley's 'Captive Actress'   *Jennifer O'Meara*   144
11 The Figure Who Writes: On the *Henry Fool* Trilogy   *Steven Rybin*   159

Filmography   175
Bibliography   181
Index   193

ACKNOWLEDGEMENTS

The editor would like to thank Yoram Allon, Commissioning Editor at Wallflower Press, for his enthusiastic support of this project from its beginning, as well as all of the contributors for their excellent work and keen insight on Hal Hartley's films. Thanks also to everyone at Columbia University Press, in particular Jennifer Crewe, Justine Evans and Miriam Grossman. Thanks also to my family and to Jessica Belser for her tireless encouragement of all of my endeavours and obsessions.

NOTES ON CONTRIBUTORS

Mark L. Berrettini is Professor of Film Studies and the Director of the School of Theater + Film at Portland State University, where he teaches in film history, theory, genre and screenwriting. He is the author of *Hal Hartley* (2011), part of the Contemporary Film Directors Series at the University of Illinois Press.

Fernando Gabriel Pagnoni Berns currently works at Universidad de Buenos Aires (UBA) – Facultad de Filosofía y Letras, as a Graduate Teaching Assistant of 'Estética del Cine y Teorías Cinematográficas'. He has published articles in the collections *Undead in the West* (Scarecrow Press, 2013), *Horrofílmico: Aproximaciones al Cine de Terror en Latinoamerica y el Caribe* (Editorial Isla Negra, 2012), *The Culture and Philosophy of Ridley Scott* (Lexington Books, 2013), *To See the Saw Movies: Essays on Torture Porn and Post 9/11 Horror* (McFarland, 2013), *The Ages of Wonder Woman: Essays on the Amazon Princess in Changing Times* (McFarland, 2014) and *Reading Richard Matheson: A Critical Survey* (Rowman & Littlefield, 2014).

David Bordwell is Jacques Ledoux Professor Emeritus of Film Studies at the University of Wisconsin-Madison. His books include *The Films of Carl Theodor Dreyer* (University of California Press, 1981), *Narration in the Fiction Film* (University of Wisconsin Press, 1985), *Ozu and the Poetics of Cinema* (Princeton University Press, 1988), *Making Meaning: Inference and Rhetoric in the Interpretation of Cinema* (Harvard University Press, 1989), *The Cinema of Eisenstein* (Harvard University Press, 1993), *On the History of Film Style* (Harvard University Press, 1997), *Planet Hong Kong: Popular Cinema and the Art of Entertainment* (Harvard University Press, 2000), *Figures Traced in Light: On Cinematic Staging* (University of California Press, 2005), *The Way Hollywood Tells It: Story and Style in Modern Movies* (University of California Press, 2006) and *The Poetics of Cinema* (Routledge, 2008). He has won a University Distinguished Teaching Award and was awarded an honorary degree by the University of Copenhagen.

Sebastian Manley completed a PhD in film studies at the University of East Anglia in 2011. He is the author of *The Cinema of Hal Hartley* (Bloomsbury, 2013) and the co-editor of *Lives Beyond Us: Poems and Essays on the Film Reality of Animals* (Sidekick Books, 2015).

Jennifer O'Meara holds a PhD in Film Studies from Trinity College Dublin. She is currently a lecturer in Film Studies at Maynooth University, Ireland. Her publications include contributions on sound, performance and dialogue to *Frames*

Cinema Journal, *The New Soundtrack*, *Cinema Journal*, *The Cine-files* and *The Soundtrack*. She is in the process of completing a monograph on engaging dialogue in contemporary independent US cinema.

Steven Rawle is a lecturer in film studies at York St. John University. He holds a PhD and an MLitt from the University of Aberdeen. He has previously published on repetition in the work of Hal Hartley in *Film Criticism*, and other publications have appeared in *The Journal of Japanese and Korean Cinema* and *Asian Cinema*. He is the author of *Performance in the Cinema of Hal Hartley* (Cambria Press, 2011).

Steven Rybin is Assistant Professor of Film Studies at Minnesota State University, Mankato. He is the author of *Gestures of Love: Romancing Performance in Classical Hollywood Cinema* (SUNY Press, 2017). He is also co-editor, with Will Scheibel, of *Lonely Places, Dangerous Ground: Nicholas Ray in American Cinema* (SUNY Press, 2014) and author of *Michael Mann: Crime Auteur* (Scarecrow Press, 2013), *Terrence Malick and the Thought of Film* (Lexington Books, 2011) and various book chapters and journal articles.

Jason Davids Scott is an Assistant Professor at Arizona State University's School of Film, Dance and Theatre, where he teaches courses in film and theatre history. He has published in the Mid-Atlantic Almanack and the Journal of Popular Culture, and currently edits *Response: The Digital Journal of Popular Culture Scholarship*. His work appears in the *Cambridge Encyclopedia of Stage Actors and Acting*, and he has a chapters in the collections *Robert Downey, Jr., from Brat to Icon: Essays on the Film Career* (McFarland, 2014) and *The Films of Wes Anderson: Critical Essays on an Indiewood Icon* (Palgrave, 2014), and wrote the author profiles for *Monologues for Latino/a Actors* (Smith and Kraus, 2014).

Zachary Tavlin is a PhD candidate in English at the University of Washington. His areas of research include American literature, critical theory, the history of philosophy, and film. He has published essays in several venues, including *Language & Psychoanalysis*, *The Comparatist* and *Theoretical Practice*, and has a number of book chapters and articles forthcoming on topics ranging from Jazz Age fiction to phenomenology.

Daniel Varndell is Programme Leader and Lecturer in English Literature at The University of Winchester. His first book, *Hollywood Remakes, Deleuze and the Grandfather Paradox* (Palgrave, 2014) looks philosophically at repetition and difference in Hollywood remakes, sequels and reboots. He is currently working on a new monograph on the subject of faith and faithfulness in literary adaptations and visual culture.

INTRODUCTION

Hal Hartley: A Quality of Attention

Steven Rybin

Hal Hartley's 2014 film *My America* consists of a series of monologues written by notable playwrights and performed by several actors from independent film and theatre. Each monologue – some delivered in direct address to the camera, others to imaginary, offscreen interlocutors – addresses the broad question of what it means to live and think in America in the second decade of the twenty-first century. For auteurists, though, the most curious quality of *My America* is its status as 'a film by Hal Hartley'. The stories told by the speakers are not Hartley's own. Neither written nor conceived by the director (the project originated in Baltimore's Center Stage Theater prior to the auteur's involvement), salient signs of his authorship are prevalent only around its edges. Hartley devotees might glimpse the director's signature in the occasional canted camera position from which the monologues are filmed, a stylistic device seen in some of his films, most memorably in *Fay Grim* (2006). Shades of Hartley's sensibility are also found in the delivery of monologues by two figures familiar from several Hartley films, Thomas Jay Ryan (*Henry Fool* [1997], *Fay Grim*, *Ned Rifle* [2014]) and DJ Mendel (*The Book of Life* [1998], *No Such Thing* [2001], *The Girl from Monday* [2005], *Meanwhile* [2011]). The construction of the soundtrack recalls Hartley's previous work, with its uses of slices of offscreen sound and dispersive music playfully evoking an imagined space prompted by the words of each speaker. Yet in its serial presentation of twenty-one monologues written by a diverse selection of voices, *My America* will likely strike many Hartley fans – those who, in particular, highly value his early cycle of cinematic triumphs, such as *The Unbelievable Truth* (1989), *Trust* (1990), *Simple Men* (1992) (these first three films forming the director's 'Long Island Trilogy'), *Amateur* (1994) and *Flirt* (1995) – as a minor work, a footnote in a career otherwise known for its remarkably (and perhaps even stubbornly) consistent aesthetic.

In another sense, however, *My America* is thoroughly in keeping with Hartley's work on the margins of American independent cinema. Unquestionably an 'art film' aimed at a very small audience of Hartley devotees – *My America* received no theatrical release, premiering instead on the boutique cinephile website Fandor – the film finds Hartley where he is perhaps most comfortable: on the outer limits of the independent film scene, where he is as likely to attempt another film in the style of *Henry Fool* as he is to create a non-narrative or experimental one-off. In contrast to figures such as Wes Anderson, Neil LaBute, Richard Linklater and Steven Soderbergh – all filmmakers who have worked comfortably within the commercial film industry, even as each has successfully cultivated a reputation within independent cinema – Hal Hartley remains a decidedly and, by all accounts, contentedly liminal figure, one whose works are consistently at one remove from the mainstream of film discourse and reception. Of course, Hartley and his films have flirted with (if not finally ever committing to) the commercial film industry at certain junctures in his career. Shunning overtures from Hollywood after the 'buzz' generated around his first three films – *The Unbelievable Truth*, *Trust* and *Simple Men* – in the early nineties, Hartley, in films as varied as *Amateur*, *Henry Fool* and *No Such Thing*, nevertheless plays with the conventions of traditional genres (in *Amateur*, the crime film; *Henry Fool*, the epic; *No Such Thing*, the monster movie). And his films are sometimes financed or distributed by companies with direct connections to Hollywood studios (*Henry Fool*, distributed by Sony Pictures Classics; *No Such Thing* with a budget of $3 million, and distribution by MGM; *Fay Grim* with distribution by HDNet Films, a side project of billionaire Mark Cuban). Yet, as the small-scale *My America* suggests, Hartley continues to remain productively detached from the tides of popular culture and the centres of both commercial and independent moviemaking.

Perhaps more surprisingly, Hartley is also somewhat distanced from the culture of cinephilia itself. In contemporary cinephile circles – in the writings of film critics and on the film festival circuit, as well as in discussions about film on blogs and Facebook – Hartley's name does not come up much anymore. This is perhaps partially because of Hartley's own relatively marginal position in the world of independent filmmaking. But it is also a consequence of the director's own detachment from cinephile culture. As early as 1993, Hartley, who has never overtly engaged with the kind of postmodernist play with film-historical reference points evident in the films of, for example, Quentin Tarantino, publicly questioned 'whether I've ever been obsessed with movies' (Fuller 1994: xx). Hartley's passion for cinema, of course, cannot be doubted – but it is a passion for *making* films, for the craft and precision of the frame, and for the design and meticulousness of the soundtrack, that drives his work, not an obsessive cinephilia. Hartley is, indeed, something more than a film director, even if that remains his primary profession. He is also an accomplished photographer (as a limited edition collection of stills entitled *The Heart is a Muscle* attests), a talented sketch artist (evident in a published anthology of his drawings, *From Here to the Station*), and an admirable musician (Hartley, often under the pseudonym 'Ned Rifle', scores the music to many of his films, which places him in a lineage of composer-directors including John Carpenter, Charlie Chaplin, Clint Eastwood, David Lynch and Satyajit Ray). With the exception of occasional references (in interviews, or in the films themselves) to the films of Jean-Luc Godard, Howard Hawks and Robert

Bresson, Hartley's works make very few explicit references to other films, or indeed to few works of popular culture, literature or music. (This even as his films are themselves cinematic and literate, and often quite musical, in their sensibility.) In this sense, the conversation about the politics of Madonna undertaken by the characters in *Simple Men* – a scene that is something of a distant cousin to Tarantino's opening sequence in *Reservoir Dogs* (1992), full of tough-guy talk about popular music – is the exception rather than the rule in Hartley's self-contained universe. In contrast to the work of more film-obsessed filmmakers, his works operate according to a formal logic and sensibility that is informed by film tradition but which exudes no particular desire to show off its knowledge or wear that tradition on its sleeve. Hartley's cinema, in this sense, is less akin to Tarantino and more reminiscent of the films of Mark Rappaport. Hartley's work, like Rappaport's, grows out of the larger tradition and history of movies but uses that knowledge as the energy source for a different kind of cinema – images, gestures and rhythms that are clearly informed by tradition but which seek autonomy from the circulation and commodification of cinephile culture on display in the films of Tarantino, Soderbergh, Sofia Coppola and others.[1]

However, if Hartley's work has a kind of independence – a position or posture that separates it from both Hollywood as well as a more explicitly cinephilic cinema – this is not an independence defined solely in terms of financing, aesthetics or social position. Hartley has at various moments in his career relied on major distributors for the exhibition of his work and the financing of its production, and his formal approach to cinema, while unique among his contemporaries and while avoiding overt cinephilic reference, nevertheless has its roots in European art cinema and even in certain strains of the Classical Hollywood cinema. Rather than assuming a singular shape, Hartley's independence perpetually reasserts itself, with each new film, as a peculiar and distinctive kind of emotional and intellectual force that pushes lightly against certain prevailing contexts of reference. These contexts are various. They include the refiguration of genre in Hartley's early films, which revise the tradition of romantic and screwball comedy in their stories of awkward loners searching for some kind of connection amidst vaguely threatening and stiflingly conservative political landscapes. Many of Hartley's films, too, work against the notion that the performer in cinema must be seen as a delivery device for character psychology fully sketched out in the screenplay; the independence of Hartley's work might very well be seen in the striking way in which figures such as Robert John Burke, Martin Donovan, Parker Posey, Thomas Jay Ryan and Adrienne Shelly move across, into and out of the frame, a lightly mannered form of cinematic choreography that gives Hartley's characters unique breath and life. (Steven Rawle has studied this aspect of performance in several key works of scholarship; see Rawle 2011 and 2013.) So too has Hartley, in his later films, pushed against the idea that digital cinema must mimic the look of 35mm film, for in work such as *The Book of Life* and *Fay Grim* the director instead highlights the painterly and textural qualities of the image possible through digital recording. And sometimes these contexts of reference that Hartley's works push against are his own previous films: *Fay Grim*, a screwball espionage tale, darts away from expectations his own viewers might have of a sequel to his celebrated *Henry Fool*.

Yet even as much of Hartley's force as an independent auteur comes through his resistance to certain prevailing forms (whether these be genres, traditional means of performance, accepted means of image capture or his own established cultural reputation as a film auteur), much of the emotional and cerebral punch of his cinema arrives not through any negative or wholly ironic relation to conventional approaches to moviemaking but rather through a more vital energy that emerges in his films with surprising stealth. Think of, for example, the musical numbers in *Simple Men* and *Surviving Desire* (1991) – sudden bursts of choreographic energy which are only ostensibly ironic variations on the traditional movie musical number; the wrenching ending of *Henry Fool*, which denies narrative closure even as it more powerfully overwhelms us as the touching relationship between two very different writers comes to a (temporary) close; and Hartley's monster movie, *No Such Thing*, a film that positions its viewer to critique conventional forms of media consumption even as it moves us, through both narrative and aesthetic means, to care about the central relationship in its story of awkward love between cerebral beauty and thoughtful, tortured beast.

The complexity of Hartley's status as an independent filmmaker, then, precludes any sort of global definition of precisely what distinguishes his work from so-called 'dependent' cinema (films dependent upon mainstream forms of financing, or reliant upon commercial imperatives in their making). Instead, the approaches taken by the authors in this collection are varied, looking at Hartley's distinctive filmmaking through diverse lenses. Topics include his grounding in film tradition, the cultural discourse surrounding his works, his playful revisions of genre, and his memorable work with performers. Of course, each of the authors brings a unique perspective and method to Hartley's work. But collectively, the concerns of the writers in this book might be broadly mapped using three different terms: *authorship*, *history* and *reception*. Before briefly introducing the individual pieces, I want to reflect on how these three terms might offer a kind of overarching framework for understanding Hartley's contribution to cinema and the approaches to his work taken in this volume.

Hartley as Author

One way to understand Hartley's work is through the prism of authorship, and one way to understand Hartley as a film director with a personal style – an 'auteur' – is to consider how his aesthetics grow out of a general resistance to mainstream forms of moviemaking, even as this ironic resistance makes room for a particular kind of emotional engagement. Like certain directors in the modernist film tradition, such as Godard and Bresson, Hartley remains a staunch anti-realist, which is perhaps another reason for his liminal position in an American film culture which remains steadfastly grounded (even in its most self-reflexive, allusive or postmodern forms) in a tradition of narrative realism. Despite their varying levels of independence, and despite certain occasional textual strategies which draw attention to cinematic or intertextual references in their films, filmmakers such as David O. Russell and Steven Soderbergh remain generally committed to a recognisably realist cinema driven by narrative and genre conventions and viewer empathy and identification with character. Even in the heavily stylised mise-en-scène of a filmmaker like Wes Anderson, for example, viewers are given recognisable points of empathic identification (the familiar voice of George Clooney, for example, indicates which wild animal the viewer aligns her sympathies with in the fantasy world of *Fantastic Mr. Fox* [2009]). Hartley, by contrast, makes easygoing identification with character and conventional consumption of narrative information difficult. His sensibility as a film author is partially grounded in the tradition of modernist cinema and strategies of Brechtian estrangement, and as such it would seem he works to appeal to a viewer's intellectual engagement prior to (if not, it should be said, instead of) their emotional response.

In the years preceding the release of this collection, several fine authorship studies on Hartley's films have found publication, all by film scholars who appear later in these pages with new work on the director. All of them generally concur on Hartley's status as an anti-realist filmmaker as a key ingredient in understanding what constitutes his authorship. Mark L. Berrettini offers a persuasive view of Hartley as a filmmaker who 'draws upon estrangement precisely as [Fredric] Jameson describes it: as a way to look differently and as a way to suggest change', attempting 'to reveal the *construction* of reality within narrative films' (2011: 3). Sebastian Manley, likewise, locates certain formal innovations in Hartley's films that work to position him outside mainstream commercial cinema, textual aspects 'which take the form of various narrative strategies (the somewhat "open" endings of *The Unbelievable Truth*, *Henry Fool* and other films), cinematographic devices (the two-shots in which the two conversing characters face the camera in *Amateur*) and musical practices (the melancholy, repetitive scores in the Long Island series and other films)' (2013: 8). Finally, in his discussion of performance in Hartley's films, Steven Rawle highlights his 'gestural modes of performance, where the camera abstracts and isolates units of potential meaning, where context and style supplement and frame other possible meanings' (2011: 11). These three immensely valuable studies, each focusing on a particular set of concerns (Berrettini, with Hartley's style; Manley, with the director's sense of landscape and place; and Rawle, with performance in Hartley's films), all tend to agree that Hartley is a filmmaker who is invested in critiquing normative modes of narrative consumption and conventional styles of filmmaking practice. Berrettini, Manley and Rawle each offer a persuasive and complementary view of Hartley as an anti-realist. Indeed, their scholarly work, when placed into dialogue, suggests how scholars might approach Hartley's 'independence' through the prism of authorship, that is, through his commitment to an aesthetic that avoids the realism of both Hollywood and more mainstream independent films.

Of course, this ironic relation of Hartley to the mainstream film industry – and using this negative relation as a means of identifying his status as an independent auteur – should not obscure our understanding of the potential and positive emotional impact Hartley's films have on viewers. As Sophie Wise demonstrates in a remarkable article entitled 'What I Like About Hal Hartley, or rather, What Hal Hartley Likes About Me' (1999), Hartley's films have the potential to *move* viewers in sometimes startling ways – or, perhaps more accurately, Hartley's films encourage viewers to work to develop complicated emotional relationships to them. As Wise writes, 'Hartley's films offer a detached model for identification which paradoxically coaxes the spectator into an attachment. By being made part of the process I felt as integral as an actor or director. The work I perform as a spectator, or perhaps what we could call a spect(actor), is what seems to make his films work' (1999: 246). For Wise, the viewer is an important part of Hartley's aesthetic signature precisely because she becomes a performer alongside the films, working to forge a unique affective bond through an intimacy with the film as a performative object. This affective bond is not *sui generis*; as Wise acknowledges, what makes intimacy with Hartley's works possible is the intellectual work the films themselves demand viewers perform, a demand that is itself a negation of the escapism of mainstream Hollywood product. Nevertheless, the intimate space created between viewer and film is a positive force emerging contingently, every time a spectator with the 'right' sensibility – perhaps a sensibility that in some sense 'matches' that of Hartley's own as an *auteur* – views a Hartley film. This performance of the Hartley viewer, so touched by one or more of his films, results – for Wise in her writing and for many of the authors in this book – in the Hartley viewer becoming a *writer*, seeking the page as a means to make sense of what is felt in an intimate bond with his authorship. This paratextual space – the space created by Hartley's viewers who are sparked to write upon viewing his films – is as crucial to understanding the significance of Hartley's work as author as the films are themselves, as the existence of this book partially attests. (I will discuss this idea further when I consider the third word in my critical map, *reception*.)

Hartley as a Historical Figure

Hartley, now in the later stages of his career, can also be considered a historically situated independent auteur. His own history as a filmmaker ebbs and flows with the history and changing discursive meaning of 'independent filmmaking' itself. The word 'independent' is a vexed one in film studies, largely because there is no global or essential meaning to the term. As with all forms of discourse, what constitutes independence at any given moment changes over time. Further, Hartley, as a filmmaker, is himself informed by certain traditions in film history (for more on this, see David Bordwell's invaluable contribution in this volume).

In many ways, the sensibility of Hartley as a filmmaker recalls the American independent filmmaking of the late 1970s and early 1980s, which was marked by a heavily European inflection. Writing in 1981, Annette Insdorf characterises independent films as those which counter 'big stars with fresh faces, big deals with intimate canvases, and big studios with regional authenticity, [treating] inherently American concerns with a primarily European style' (2005: 29). While other scholars writing in the 1970s and 1980s privilege a broader definition of independent that includes exploitation and genre films as well as alternative cinemas created by subaltern groups, certain elements of Insdorf's definition seems relevant to Hartley's own film practice, at least in its broad outlines – particularly its combination of American settings and narratives within a style (and even in some cases a diegesis, as in the case of *Flirt*, *No Such Thing* and *Fay Grim*, which all take place, in part, beyond the confines of American borders) that is often marked as in some sense 'European'. Insdorf's proposed connection between American independent film and an 'authentic' set of inherently American themes echoes what Janet Staiger notes as the tendency to 'see historical linkage of what is now being called indie cinema with the 1961 New American Cinema Group's project' (2012: 19) – a project that involved, among other things, a commitment to 'personal cinema' free of interference from mainstream studios and investors. For her own part, Staiger proposes American independent film as a discrete 'film practice' with its own history, and its own conventions of production and reception, that might be compared with similar practices in other national cinemas (2012: 23). This goes some way to reducing emphasis on aspects of independent films that may be in one way or another 'intrinsically' American, instead highlighting larger historical and aesthetic features that connect indie filmmakers together as practitioners. It is a valuable framework for thinking about Hartley's films, which are grounded at least in part in a global film tradition (and, in the latter half of his career, are set in a variety of global locations).

Recent scholarship on American independent cinema echoes Staiger's interest in defining the historical contours of indie film as a discrete practice but in ways that return in some senses to the 'American-ness' of the practice, situating American indie cinema as an industry discourse rather than only a set of filmmaking strategies. Yannis Tzioumakis, in his critique of 'ideal' definitions of independent film which take 'low-budget' and 'anti-Hollywood' as essential features, encourages us to approach 'American independent cinema as a discourse that expands and contracts when socially authorised institutions (filmmakers, industry practitioners, trade publications, academics, film critics, and so on) contribute towards its definition at different periods in this history of American cinema' (2006: 11). Such a point-of-view is useful for considering Hartley's work, which is only rarely 'anti-Hollywood' in any forthright way and which at times becomes relatively high-budget as Hartley moves closer to the indiewood sector, with *Henry Fool* and *No Such Thing*, at the midpoint of his career in the late 1990s and early 2000s. His films, as previously mentioned, forego explicit citation (in either approving or disapproving terms) of other movies and prefer instead to intervene in the discourse of independent filmmaking implicitly and through varying relationships to funding sources tied to the mainstream of the film industry. Geoff King echoes this call to situate American independent film as a historically evolving discourse, focusing on those films 'marked as sufficiently different from the Hollywood mainstream' in order 'to qualify as independent' (2006: 2) while acknowledging that both 'mainstream' and 'independent' are terms subject to formal, economic and cultural variation at different moments in history. King's ideas here are useful for understanding Hartley, too, given the fluctuation of his work in relation to 'mainstream' and 'independent' discourses: Hartley's experimental and relatively obscure short films such as *Opera No. 1* (1994) and *The Sisters of Mercy* (2004, a recut version of a music video Hartley directed in 1994) remain further away from the capitalistic centres of American moviemaking than the more recent *Ned Rifle*, for example, which, despite its status as a project funded through Kickstarter, features popular television and indiewood actor Aubrey Plaza in a central role.

These historical works of scholarship on American independent cinema thus leave us with at least two intersecting conceptions of Hartley's place in both film history and the history of discourse on independent film. On the one hand, there is the shifting history of American independent film itself which, as this very brief overview of some key scholarship in the field suggests, has never been stable (even as some scholars have called for its understanding as a 'discrete practice'). As the tectonic plates of the film industry shift, Hartley's films find different means of distribution (a trajectory studied in great depth by Manley 2013; see especially 91–8): his early cycle of films, through *Flirt*, which are made before and during the sale of independent studios such as Miramax and New Line to major Hollywood conglomerates; his middle period, which includes *Henry Fool* and *No Such Thing*, two films distributed by major studios (respectively, Sony Pictures Classics, the independent wing of Sony; and MGM); and his late period, which relies on a mix of overseas financing as well as more economical means of digital filmmaking. These shifts, in turn, have impacted his aesthetic: the initial celluloid-based approach of the first film in the *Henry Fool* trilogy, an 'indie epic' originally produced and projected on 35mm film, has given way to the smaller-scale, lower-budget, digitally-shot *Ned Rifle*, which concludes the trilogy with a different style and sensibility determined in part through a different economic and technological context.

Hartley's films are, of course, thoroughly grounded in a larger history of filmmaking that goes beyond the various historical shifts of contemporary independent film. Nevertheless, it will be difficult for the neophyte viewer to 'spot' the references in Hartley's works (apart from occasional explicit citations of Godard in his early films) because his films, as suggested earlier, refuse to wear that knowledge and passion for cinema on their sleeve. Hartley is after something else: a devotion to craft that will bestow upon his subjects in front of the camera, in his words, a 'quality of attention' (see Fuller 1995: 56) that responds to their figural and performative vitality in the present moment, rather than their place in a web of reference apart from how Hartley frames them in the here and now. This does not remove Hartley's films from history or tradition – as many of the essays explore in some detail, Hartley's work is immersed in and informed by the history of cinema and its forms. But that history, for Hartley, is inspiration rather than obsession, an energy source rather than the content of his precise, lean, angular style of filmmaking, which always strives to put the viewer in a position to see, think and feel through and finally beyond conventional and received modes of seeing, thinking and feeling about cinema.

Receiving Hartley's Films
And this leads me to the final term in this map for approaching Hartley's work, one which I have begun to explore earlier: the matter of *reception*. Here it is important to again consider the director's postmodern revisions of certain categories of filmmaking recognisable from earlier cycles of films, for these genres potentially form a point of departure for our reception of Hartley's films: the screwball or romantic comedy; the monster movie; the espionage caper. Another possible genre in which to place Hartley – one which might better describe the critic's reception of his work rather than the filmmaker's own creative points of departure – is the larger category of 'smart cinema'. As defined by Jeffrey Sconce in a seminal article in *Screen* (2002), 'smart cinema'

originally referred to a cycle of films that symbolically positioned themselves against the imagined ideology of mainstream Hollywood movies, largely through a collective (if paradoxically disparate) tone or sensibility marked by ironic detachment, dark humour, postmodern variations of traditional genres and frameworks, and cultural scepticism (but nonetheless avoiding, for the most part, the formal experimentation of earlier generations of independent filmmaking, experimental film and European 'high' modernism). In her book on the subject, Claire Perkins makes the persuasive argument that, at this stage in its critical history, the term 'smart cinema' might be seized less as a fixed type or category of films but rather as an 'affective force' open to multiple situations of viewing. Perkins builds upon Sconce's characterisation of 'smart cinema' as ironically detached and disengaged by suggesting that this sort of irony is potentially itself a kind of path to emotional engagement, albeit a kind of engagement far different than that mobilised by commercial or mainstream independent filmmaking. Citing the poststructuralist critique of irony by philosopher Gilles Deleuze, Perkins reminds us that one potential drawback of irony as a critical or aesthetic position is 'its movement or "ascent" toward a unified principle or position of judgment' (2012: 15), a hierarchal position of superiority that stands above the vitality of life itself – a vitality that, for Deleuze, is the source for all ideas, including irony. As Perkins writes, 'Ideas, for Deleuze, do not exist *above* life as ideal forms but come *from* life as a flow of forces and desires ... All of Deleuze's concepts – including irony itself – are founded upon multiplicity in this way' (ibid.). This conception of irony as a force that emerges *from* life rather than *above* it allows Perkins to understand 'the smart film not as an expression of judgment or disengagement but as a pluralising, *affective* force' (2012: 16).

The approach Perkins takes to understanding smart cinema not only as a genre but also as a mode of reception, I suggest, has the virtue of removing the 'smart' or 'ironic' viewer from the top or most distinctive position of a hierarchy, a position that is perhaps too far removed from the life and vitality of cinema broadly speaking. One need not position oneself 'against' (either symbolically or ideologically) the mainstream cinema in order to enjoy Hartley's films; the peculiar enjoyment they offer (and the ironic stances his films sometimes take) is, for most viewers, part of a larger cinephilia that understands Hartley as one important film director among many. And his films are not disengaged from those 'lower' or somehow more 'primitive' forms of film reception: as David Martin-Jones shows in a recent essay on bodily humour in Hartley's films (2013), this director's works often inspire bawdy laughter in a manner that is perhaps closer to the gross-out comedy than it is to other works of smart cinema. But most importantly, Perkins' approach returns Hartley's cinema to the flux and flow of life. It is not finally productive to position oneself as a viewer of Hartley's films in order to achieve distinction relative to other kinds of viewers or to place his films at a remove from other kinds of films. The 'affective force' coursing through his cinema might indeed originate from the 'periphery' of independent filmmaking (as suggested by Perkins 2012: 28–9), but where this force takes his viewers (in their lives as cinephiles or writers on film) is potentially quite unpredictable. This idea of a peripheral or liminal 'affective force' is also an idea that helps us understand the peculiarly appealing nature of Hartley's characters in the films themselves. Although the director rejects the empathetic identification key to the emotional satisfactions of many Hollywood films, his characters (in part because of the range of distinctively appealing 'indie' actors Hartley casts in his films) nevertheless move us to thought. Our active engagement with the carefully choreographed moving body in Hartley's cinema is itself one potential point of origin of the kind of sharp force Perkins claims we can find, on the level of reception, in the smart cinema cycle.

The essays in this book, then, might be understood as different ways of receiving Hartley's cinema: as part of a larger historical film tradition; as a crucial node in cultural discourse; as objects created and circulated within a complex economic context; as creative works of mise-en-scène focused on the staging of the human body; as collaborative films made in tandem with highly creative actors; and finally as highly *written* works, films that engage our minds and senses through a unique 'quality of attention' inspiring thought.

Exploring Hartley's Films
The book's first essay serves as a prelude to the contributions which follow it. In his revised and updated version of the previously published work 'Up Close and Impersonal: Hal Hartley and the Persistence of Tradition', David Bordwell explores Hartley's filmmaking using the historical poetics approach, situating the director's distinctive style in a larger history that in some cases transcends the category of independent filmmaking itself. Bordwell's characteristically eloquent and insightful essay focuses on narrative and staging strategies in Hartley's early work, particularly *Simple Men*, situating the director in a tradition of filmmaking informed by European modernism as much as American independent films.

The next three go on to look at Hartley's work in the context of economics and cultural discourse. The second essay, '"Young. Middle-Class. College-Educated. Unskilled.": Hal Hartley in 1991', by Mark L. Berrettini, takes a sharp and detailed look at three of Hartley's early short features, *Theory of Achievement*, *Ambition* and *Surviving Desire*. Berrettini shows how these early short works pose challenges to viewers through their formal experimentation with form and style, and how they '[incorporate] low-budget economics into the creative process as a valuable way to challenge mainstream practices within film, art, and music'. The third essay, '"Some Things Shouldn't Be Fixed": Frameworks of Critical Reception and the Early Career of Hal Hartley', by Jason Davids Scott, shifts the discussion to critical discourse on Hartley's early work and the consequences of this critical reputation for our understanding of Hartley's later films. Showing how the critical response to Hartley's early work shifted the perceived value of the films over the course of the first few years of his career, Scott incorporates discussion of his own past experience working for a public relations firm which connected independent filmmakers with influential journalists and editors. His perspective offers an important picture of how public discourse about a film author shapes a shifting understanding of the films and their participation in a surrounding context. In the fourth essay, 'The Locality of Hal Hartley: The Aesthetics and Business of Smallness', Steven Rawle looks at the importance of the idea of 'the local' to understanding both the economics and aesthetics of Hartley's films, using this valuable approach to understanding Hartley's status as, in Rawle's words, 'a guardedly (perhaps obsessively) independent filmmaker'.

The following four essays find creative and thoughtful ways to analyse Hartley's interventions into genre. In 'Hal Hartley's Romantic Comedy', Sebastian Manley ably shows how Hartley takes the template of the romantic comedy, as established by Hollywood, and opens it up to vivid new kinds of representation through a more poetic and less conventional approach to the genre. The sixth essay, Daniel Varndell's 'A New Man: The Logic of the Break in Hal Hartley's *Amateur*', looks at Hartley's creative appropriation of genre in order to perform a 'break' from previous forms – a break that is mirrored, as Varndell eloquently shows, in the film's own narrative, which involves 'an act of breaking' that takes its characters in unexpected new directions. The seventh essay is the first of two contributions by the editor of this book. In 'Not Getting It: *Flirt* as Anti-Puzzle Film', I use theories of flirtation from the work of author Adam Phillips in order to map Hartley's distinctive variation on (or, perhaps, outright rejection of) the idea of the 'puzzle' film. Concluding this second section of the book is the eighth essay, by Fernando Gabriel Pagnoni Berns, entitled 'Poiesis and Media in *The Book of Life* and *No Such Thing*'. Berns sets the concept of 'poetic' creativity against the instrumental and destructive tendencies of modern, corporate media, a frame providing a provocative new reading of Hartley's work in a category of films that prefigure human apocalypse.

The third and final section focuses on Hartley's strategies of staging bodies in action and on his work with performers. The ninth essay, 'Bodies, Space and Theatre in *The Unbelievable Truth* (and its American Precursors)', by Zachary Tavlin, intriguingly situates Hartley's debut feature *The Unbelievable Truth*, and its strategies for staging performers in space, into a larger aesthetic lineage including filmmakers such as Robert Altman and John Cassavetes. The tenth essay, by Jennifer O'Meara, focuses specifically on Hartley's work with one actor. In 'Parker Posey as Hal Hartley's "Captive Actress"', O'Meara analyses both the text and paratext of 'the Hartley/Posey dynamic', examining both discourse about the creative partnership as well as its onscreen results, offering precise and thought-provoking descriptions of Posey's performances with Hartley, particularly Posey's sharp use of vocal performance. The eleventh and final essay, 'The Figure Who Writes: On the *Henry Fool* Trilogy', is my second contribution to the collection. Here I look at how acts of writing and reading in *Henry Fool, Fay Grim* and *Ned Rifle* propel characters through narrative and physical space, exploring the charge carried by the written and read word in Hartley's cinematic universe – a charge that is echoed, as all of the thought-provoking essays in this collection show, in our own reception of the films.

This anthology was put together in the belief that Hartley continues to be relevant and potentially inspiring to a new generation of film scholars and filmmakers. At a time when numerous indie movies have conformed to an aesthetic that is at times only superficially distinctive from mainstream films, the essays in this volume work to show how Hartley's path offers a model for new filmmakers seeking to craft identities of 'independence' that meaningfully diverge from both Hollywood and the typical economies of the independent circuit. It is especially hoped that young scholars and cinephiles, perhaps mostly or entirely unfamiliar with Hartley's work, will derive pleasure and discovery not only from these pieces on the films in the pages to follow but also from the films themselves.

Note
1   I thank Adrian Martin, in a personal correspondence, for pointing out to me a parallel between Hartley's style and Rappaport's.

CHAPTER ONE

Up Close and Impersonal: Hal Hartley and the Persistence of Tradition

David Bordwell

In typical run-through histories of English-language film studies, at least one chapter casts *Screen* in a starring role during the 1970s. The British Film Institute quarterly, we are told, was largely responsible for introducing semiotics, Lacanian and Althusserian theory, and other post-Structuralist tendencies into the Anglo-American conversation. During the same years, however, a much less-discussed journal was at least as important.

Edited by Thomas Elsaesser, *Monogram* was no less ambitious than *Screen*, as its first issue in spring of 1971 made clear. The new magazine would carry on the line of enquiry that the editors had launched in *The Brighton Film Review*. It would 'investigate the main cinematic tradition as we see it, and to define at least one possible approach to the cinema as a whole, by a careful attention to the actual films being made today, whether commercial or independent, and to re-assess outstanding or interesting works of the past' ('Editorial': April 1971). Tradition? *One* possible approach (and not the approach we *must* take)? Re-*assess* (that is, make explicit value judgements, and on artistic grounds)? In 1971 this enterprise probably seemed far too cautious.

Author's note: This essay was originally published in a *festschrift* in honour of film scholar Thomas Elsaesser.[1] The current version retains the discussion of Elsaesser's career for the sake of readers who might not be familiar with the journal *Monogram* and its place in the history of film studies. Elsaesser's and *Monogram*'s commitment to studying films and their artistic traditions still seems to me valid for our understanding of Hartley's achievements.

The tradition referred to was, unapologetically, that of Hollywood, then being widely condemned as ideologically oppressive. In France, *Cinéthique* and *Cahiers du cinéma* had forged a radical perspective during 1969–1970, and *Screen* was about to publish Christopher Williams' essay presenting Godard as 'an important link between the American-dominated cinema of the past and the politicized cinema of the future' (1971/2: 7). As if in anticipation, the *Monogram* editorial continued: 'We are not a theoretical magazine, nor are we persuaded that a particular political commitment will necessarily dispose of, or resolve, certain fundamental aesthetic problems' ('Editorial': April 1971). The waiver is too modest (many *Monogram* essays were deeply theoretical), but the emphasis is clear. Aesthetics still mattered, and the problems it posed were to be tackled in ways different from *Screen*'s version of High Theory.

Yet the journal would also avoid the main alternative, that Leavisian attachment to moral, not to say moralising, psychological realism most visible in the work of Robin Wood. 'The cinema,' the editorial asserts, 'derives its complexity and richness not only from its relation to felt and experienced "life" – a difficult quality to assess at best – but also from the internal relation to the development and history of the medium' (ibid.).

Monogram would steer a new course between Parisian theory and Cambridge Great Tradition realism. As a methodological first step, its writers would posit that the history of Hollywood cinema – 'classical cinema', as the editorial calls it – is central to any adequate account of how films in many traditions tell stories.

These views, controversial to this day, seem to me still well founded. I can scarcely imagine my own conceptions of film research without the powerful essays published across the five or so years of *Monogram*'s life. In particular, the idea that we may analyse any instance of cinematic expression in relation to formal and stylistic traditions has been a guiding premise for me, and I owe to *Monogram*, and particularly Thomas Elsaesser, not only this cogent formulation but also many well-formed examples. In the years since *Monogram*'s editorial, Elsaesser has never forgotten how culture and politics shape cinema, but he has also preserved his zest for the manifold ways in which the medium can be used artfully.

Monogram's contributions to our understanding of the Hollywood tradition were extensive and insightful. Perhaps the most celebrated piece in the magazine's history is Elsaesser's intricate, erudite essay on melodrama, which soon became a cornerstone in the study of that genre. Just as important, *Monogram*'s emphasis on 'actual films being made today' acknowledges that our knowledge of cinema's past can inform our understanding of our contemporaries. Thus in the journal's second issue, Elsaesser offered a wide-ranging reflection on the current state of European cinema. His insights into then-current films by Buñuel, Bergman and Godard proceeded from a detailed knowledge of the directors' cultural positions and an easy familiarity with their directorial signatures (see Elsaesser 1971: 2–9). Faithful to the *Monogram* premise, his approach was comparative, looking for ways in which the filmmakers had taken up or taken apart the conventions of classical cinema. This comparative approach informed many subsequent essays in the journal, notably the studies on the 'Cinema of Irony' (issue 5) and Elsaesser's fine 'Notes on the Unmotivated Hero' in then-current US cinema.² And Elsaesser's unflagging concern with understanding the present in terms of its past drives many of his writings over the years; to take only a few examples, his work on Wim Wenders (1996a), his essay on *Bram Stoker's Dracula* (1997) and his magisterial volume on Fassbinder (1996b).

The enduring influence of classical style, the fruitfulness of a comparative method, and the need to make sense of contemporary cinema – these precepts triangulate my efforts in what follows. If Hal Hartley had been making films in the 1970s, or if *Monogram* were still publishing, it seems likely that the two would have intersected, perhaps around concepts like the unmotivated hero or the perils of irony. What I hope to show by looking more closely at one Hartley film, *Simple Men* (1992), is that analysis sensitive to the avatars of tradition can still shed light on the formal changes and continuities on display in contemporary cinema.

Weighting the isolated image
Hartley belongs to the more formally adventurous wing of the US indie scene, a quality perhaps most evident in his storytelling strategies. He brings a low-key absurdity to romantic comedy (*The Unbelievable Truth*, 1989) and melodrama (*Trust*, 1990).³ He has experimented with plot structure as well, most notably in the three-episode repetitions of *Flirt* (1995). Hartley is also one of the most idiosyncratic visual stylists in contemporary US film. Yet every innovator draws upon some prior traditions, and Hartley is no exception. The actors' eccentrically flat readings of soul-bearing dialogue, for example, are evidently his reworking of the neutrality he finds in Bresson's players.

At the pictorial level, several broad trends seem to have provided models and schemas which Hartley has creatively recast. Perhaps least obvious is the group style dominating Hollywood since the 1960s, a style I've called elsewhere 'intensified continuity'. The label seeks to capture the fact that although American mainstream directors haven't rejected traditional continuity filmmaking (analytical cutting, 180-degree staging and shooting, shot/reverse-shot, matches on movement, etc), they have modified it by heightening certain features. They have made shot lengths, on average, shorter. They have amplified the differences between long-lens shots and wide-angle ones. They have increased the number of camera movements, particularly tracks in to and out from the players and circular movements around them. And they have employed more and tighter close-ups than were typical before the 1960s. Many of these options may be traceable to the fact that the television monitor is the ultimate venue for most films, but there are probably other causes at work as well.⁴

Most indie films adopt the idiom of intensified continuity, but Hartley's style assimilates it prudently. He does not favour fast cutting: compared to the 3–6 second average shot length which became dominant in Hollywood during the 1990s, his shots run, on average, twice or even three times as long.⁵ He does employ long lenses to pin figures onto landscapes, but for dialogue scenes, he seldom uses the extremes of lens lengths, favouring medium-range lenses like the 50mm. His camera seldom traces the arabesques of today's florid Steadicam images; apart from the digital experiment of *The Book of Life* (1998) his tracking shots tend to be reminiscent of the solid, heavy-camera style of the 1940s studios.

Where he is most akin to his mainstream contemporaries is his reliance on fairly close views. His two-shots frequently squeeze characters into almost cramping proximity, and his disjointed and cross-purposes dialogues are often played out in medium-shots and medium-close-ups, sometimes with only faces and hands visible. We shouldn't minimise the economic advantages of staging in this manner. Hartley has observed that, 'The less you show, the more pages you can shoot each day' (Fuller 1998: xxiii). Yet he has turned these cost-cutting manoeuvres to artistic advantage.

For one thing, he achieves effects quite different from those yielded by today's standard tight close-ups. The difference is partly traceable to his proclivity for certain tactics of depth staging. During the 1940s, directors like Welles and Wyler began to explore staging which not only set characters in considerable depth but also – almost as a consequence of depth staging – turned one or both away from each other (Fig. 1.1). This tactic wasn't unprecedented, of course – something like it can be found in 1910s cinema[6] – but Welles and Wyler gave it a looming force by placing one character quite close to the camera. Hartley's debt to this tradition seems evident. In many of his dialogue scenes, characters turn from each other as they talk: 'I've noticed a lot of times that we don't always look at each other, and sometimes it's much more interesting to detail the way people avoid contact than it is to detail the way people try to gain contact' (Fuller 1994: xxv). Quite often the characters' evasions lead them to

Fig. 1.1

Fig. 1.2

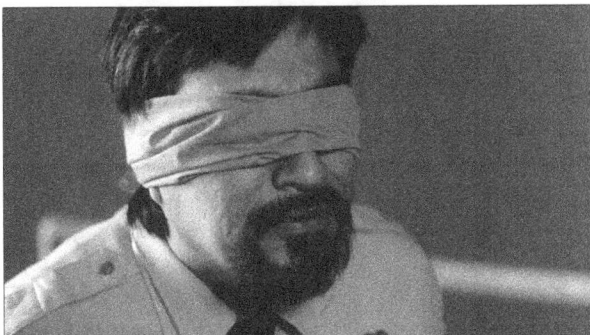

Fig. 1.3

Fig. 1.4

move to the extreme foreground, favouring us with a facial view not available to their counterparts. Occasionally, the composition yields a big foreground face with other planes tapering into depth, often not in focus (Fig. 1.2). This sort of staging is fairly rare in today's cinema, and one might be tempted to see it as an ex-film-student's self-conscious revival of the schemas which André Bazin celebrated.

Hartley's prolonged close-ups and his insistence on keeping significant background planes out of focus complement other stylistic tactics. When characters do face one another, Hartley often avoids establishing shots and relies on the Kuleshov effect to connect his isolated actors. He has remarked: 'Establishing shots tell us nothing except where we are. "Where we are" will be elucidated entirely by what the actors are doing and experiencing' (Fuller 1992: xiv). Moreover, Hartley's sharply defined pieces of space aren't linked smoothly. He seldom cuts on movement, pushing matches on action to the sides of the frame, and he likes slightly high angles that don't cut together fluidly (Figs. 1.3 & 1.4). His one-on-one cutting often produces ellipses, signaled chiefly by jumps in the soundtrack.

Hartley's emphasis on singles also yields oddly timed shot/reverse-shots. In such passages, most of today's directors cut on each significant line; this is one reason even dialogue-heavy films have a rapid editing rate. In Hartley's films, after one character speaks, we are likely to linger on him or her while the other character replies, often at length. Or we may cut away quickly from the speaker in order to dwell on the listener's reactions to a flow of offscreen lines. In *Simple Men*, when Bill (Robert John Burke) confronts Kate (Karen Sillas) near the end of a long night of partying in her

Fig. 1.5

tavern, Hartley presents the exchange in an irregularly paced string of shot/reverse-shots. In a medium-close-up Kate asks how long Bill will stay. In the answering shot, Bill announces that he will spend the rest of his life here. Hartley cuts back to Kate as she says, 'Really', and a muted solo guitar is heard.

But then Bill utters a key line: 'With you.' Since Bill has earlier announced that he intends to meet a beautiful woman whom he will seduce and abandon, it is crucial for us to see his expression as he declares his love, so that we may gauge his sincerity. Instead, Hartley holds on Kate, putting Bill's pledge offscreen and thus maintaining an indeterminacy about his motives (Fig. 1.5). Kate replies: 'You seem pretty confident about that', and again Hartley keeps Bill's important reply – 'I am' – offscreen. 'I hardly know you', replies Kate, still in her single shot. Not until midway through Bill's next line – 'Oh, you'll get to know me in time' – does Hartley give us a brief, and fairly uninformative, shot of Bill completing the sentence. His final line is heard over a repeated reverse-shot of Kate reacting to his remark.

In all, the enjambed cutting rhythm maintains mystery about Bill's motives and lets us scrutinise Kate's cautious uncertainty. Her response is weighted in another way. Of the five shots, Bill is allotted only two of them, totaling merely eight seconds; Kate gets twenty-nine seconds, and the prolonged shot mentioned above alone lasts eleven seconds. The device of dividing our attention between offscreen dialogue and onscreen response becomes especially vivid in the film's final shot, when Bill's reunion with Kate is presented as a tight shot of the couple and the unseen Sheriff's voice intones: 'Don't move' (see Fig. 1.34 below).

All these factors cooperate to give each image a modular, chunky weight seldom achieved by the rapidly refreshed close views of mainstream movies. 'Continuity bugged me,' Hartley says. 'It got in the way of the image' (Fuller 1994: xx). The artificiality of his dialogue and the slightly stilted, confessional performances are heightened by solid, even stolid, shots, joined by cuts which, by short-circuiting the rhythm of normal give-and-take editing, impede the flow which a great deal of mainstream cinema seeks to provide.

Godard meets Antonioni at the diner

In some respects, this cluster of options might seem to be a less rarefied version of Bresson's technique of impassive single shots. But I think that it bears an even stronger

Fig. 1.6

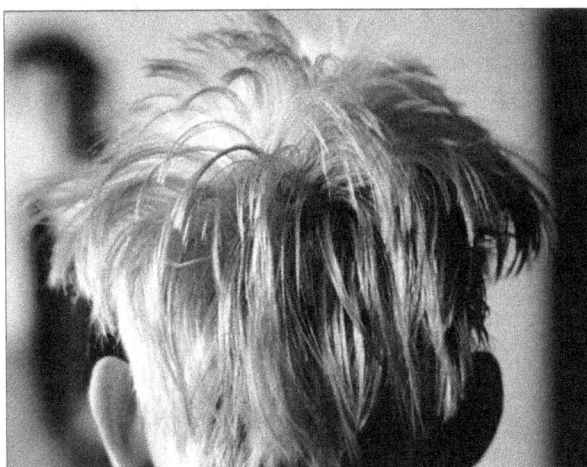

Fig. 1.7

resemblance to the style developed by Godard in films from *Sauve qui peut (la vie)* (1979) onward. It is as if Godard sought to dismantle the intensified continuity style exactly while Hollywood directors were elaborating it. He will stage whole scenes in extreme partial views, thereby refusing to specify all the characters who are present or offering clues only through offscreen voices. The angles often suppress information about locale, and significant planes of action are cast into blur (Figs. 1.6 & 1.7). And his reverse-shots, often cutting against the dramatic arc of the dialogue, may be one source of Hartley's off-the-beat image/sound rhythms.

Hartley has not been shy about acknowledging his debts: 'In the late '80s I became excited by the way [Godard] arranged shots in juxtaposition to sounds. That's how it began. It was graphic. I had no idea what actually occurred in *Hail Mary* [1985] in a concrete sense.'[7] Yet Hartley's films can't be reduced to a sum of influences: 'I find I'm having a kind of dialogue with Godard by trying to describe what's beautiful in his work. Of course, even if I try to imitate it, I get it wrong, because I fall into my own groove.'[8] His groove channels a more replete and causally-propelled narrative,

Fig. 1.8

more clear-cut character motivation, greater cohesion within and between scenes, and less self-consciously poetic digressions than we find in Godard. Hartley delays or syncopates his reaction shots; Godard deletes them. Hartley's space is gappy, Godard's is fractured. One is laconic, the other is sphinx-like.

Is this another way of saying that Hartley offers a domesticated version of Godard's disjunctions? While there is enough 1970s *Screen* sentiment still around to demand that we favour the more 'radical' style, I think that we ought to recognise – in the *Monogram* spirit – that artists who bend innovative techniques to accessible ends can also be highly valuable. (Prokofiev comes to mind.) Hartley's intelligent blend of the trends I've mentioned (and probably others I've missed) gives his films a credible originality within contemporary cinema.

Hartley's commitment to close views, depth compositions and partial revelation of a scene's space have led him toward a delicacy of staging which his contemporaries, mainstream or indie, seldom undertake. The first shot of *Simple Men*, a 51-second take showing a robbery, is arranged with a flagrant precision (Fig. 1.8). Another early scene affords us a chance to see how Hartley creatively revises some pictorial schemas circulating in both European and American cinema.

In a coffee shop, Bill meets his ex-wife Mary (Bethany Wright) after the holdup and gives her the money that Vera (Mary McKenzie) and her double-crossing paramour have tossed at him. In the course of the scene, Bill learns that his father has been arrested and that Mary has found a new lover. Hartley provides no establishing shot, and he packs his frame with close views of his players. Across its four shots, three of them quite long takes, the scene unfolds as a series of deflected glances, with Bill and Mary persistently looking away from one another. In addition, the tight framings allow Hartley to create a rhyming choreography of frame entrances and exits, along with some small spatial surprises.

At the outset Mary is seen in medium-shot; as she turns, Bill slides in behind her (Fig. 1.9). We are at a counter by a window. As in Godard's films, no long shot lays out the space, and Bill's arrival in the frame is not primed by a shot of him entering the coffee shop. The shot activates greater depth as a waitress's face appears in a new layer of space and Bill orders coffee (Fig. 1.10). Mary shows Bill the newspaper story about his father's capture, looking at him for the first time (Fig. 1.11), but Bill ignores her, and we hold on her as he walks out of the shot reading the paper (Fig. 1.12).

Fig. 1.9

Fig. 1.10

Fig. 1.11

Fig. 1.12

Bill had entered Mary's shot, but now she enters his, as he stands reading the paper near the (offscreen) front counter (Fig. 1.13). The frame placements are reversed from

Fig. 1.13

Fig. 1.14

Fig. 1.15

Fig. 1.16

the first shot; Bill in the foreground turns away from her insistently as Mary talks to the offscreen waitress, who praises 'William McCabe, the radical shortstop' (Figs.

Fig. 1.17

Fig. 1.18

Fig. 1.19

1.14 & 1.15). And as Bill had left Mary's shot, now she leaves his, giving him time to peel off the money he will give her for his child (Fig. 1.16). As in the intensified continuity style, hand movements and props must be brought up to the actor's face if we are to see them.

Track back with Bill to the window counter, where he rejoins Mary in a slightly more distant framing than the first shot had afforded. Throughout that earlier shot, a man had been sitting at the counter in the background out of focus, and the new framing makes him somewhat more prominent. At this point Mary refers to her new man, gesturing (Fig. 1.17); we are prepared to identify him as the man in the background. But Bill's look activates a quite different offscreen zone (Fig. 1.18). Using the Kuleshov effect, Hartley cuts to a glowering man in a bandanna at the pinball machine (Fig.1.19). Coming after prolonged shots of the couple, this single phlegmatic cutaway has an almost comic effect, as if a new piece of Mary's situation were striking Bill with a thud.

The fourth shot continues the setup of Bill and Mary at the counter, replaying the turned-away postures that have dominated the scene. Bill passes Mary the money, saying it should go to their boy (Fig. 1.20). After he glares at her for an instant, she throws his bad conscience back at him, and he grabs her (Fig. 1.21). Now, for significantly longer than just before, they are facing each other and exchanging direct looks. Then Mary tears herself away (Fig. 1.22) and the waitress brings Bill the doughnut Mary had ordered (Fig. 1.23). Where can the shot go now? One possibility is a dialogue with the now-curious man in the background, cued once more as Bill gestures vainly with the plate on which a doughnut sits (Fig. 1.24). Instead Hartley springs another quiet surprise.

Fig. 1.20

Fig. 1.21

Fig. 1.22

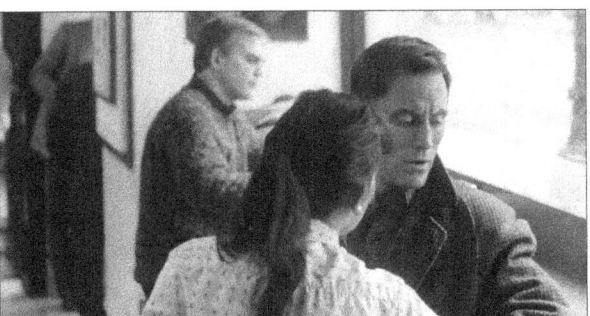

Fig. 1.23

Fig. 1.24

Fig. 1.25

As Bill ponders the doughnut, Mary and her boyfriend are visible outside the window, talking to a figure seen from the rear (Fig. 1.25). ('The back of someone's head,' Hartley wrote in a 1987 note, 'is part of that person too, worthy and necessary to be seen' (Fuller 1994: xi–xii)). Hartley calls our attention to this zone by having Bill turn (Fig. 1.26), then studiously ignore his brother Dennis at the window (Fig. 1.27). Eventually Dennis enters. In a compressed replay of the Bill/Mary exchange, Bill launches an oblique dialogue with Dennis, at first indifferent (Fig. 1.28) and then, when Dennis tells him that their father is in the hospital, facing him directly (Fig. 1.29). It is on this note that the shot ends.

The rhythmic entrances and exits of figures recall Antonioni's 1950s films, as does the avoidance of shared looks.[9] Beneath their indifference to one another, the characters guardedly probe each other's feelings, and these states of mind are expressed

Fig. 1.26

Fig. 1.27

Fig. 1.28

Fig. 1.29

through crisscrossing patterns of movement: 'I watch Antonioni more closely and with greater appreciation now than at the time I made *Simple Men* or when I was introduced to him at school. But I remember I was always struck by work of that kind of artfully constructed blocking, the interaction of the actors' movements with the camera movement.'¹⁰ Still, in this scene and others Hartley makes the technique his own.

For one thing, the proximity of the characters to the camera accords with the premises of intensified continuity; not for Hartley the distant, often opaque landscapes and interiors of Antonioni's work. Yet while mainstream US filmmakers use the close framings in order to show characters' eyes locking onto one another, Hartley shows us fleeting eye contacts. Each of these comes as a distinct beat, marking a moment in the drama. He could not punctuate his scenes this way if he were more 'radically' Godardian, for in Godard's uncommunicative découpage we are often not sure when anybody is looking at anybody else.

The choreography played out in the coffee shop finds one contrasting climax later when Bill, now on the run, becomes attracted to the café-keeper Kate. Slightly drunk, he vows to stay with her in the shot/reverse-shot sequence already mentioned. Now he sits down in a chair, angled slightly away from her (Fig. 1.30). At first she resolutely won't return his look. Then, for nearly 100 seconds, they stare mesmerically at each other as they talk about who's seducing whom (Fig. 1.31). Asked about this blocking, Hartley replies: 'The logic I used had to do with the flirting they were involved in, almost two animals circling each other.'¹¹ During this, perhaps the film's most erotically charged exchange, the camera winds around them in a subdued variant of an intensified-continuity spiral before moving in slightly as they kiss (Fig. 1.32). Immediately, however, Kate leaves the frame (Fig. 1.33).

Fig. 1.30

Fig. 1.31

Fig. 1.32

Fig. 1.33

Fig. 1.34

In a film where characters tell each other that there is only 'trouble and desire', we see a dance of attraction, hesitation and abrupt breakoff. It is played out in the way bodies and faces, often cast adrift from their wider surroundings, warily shift in and out of view. The figures may align but more often they split apart, with Hartley consigning them to backgrounds or to separate shots before the roundelay starts again. When the thrust-and-parry dialogue fades, eye contact helps mark the rare moments of emotional synchronisation. The dance of glances and bodies continues to the very end. Bill, one of the simple men, has returned to be arrested, but he throws off the deputies and advances toward Kate. A shot/reverse-shot sequence captures their shared look, but in their last shot, their eyes don't meet. Bill's face slides into the frame to nestle against Kate's chest (Fig. 1.34).

Hartley isn't the only indie filmmaker attracted to a mix of poker-faced absurdism and unabashed romanticism. His tone echoes Alan Rudolph's work, particularly *Choose Me* (1984) and *Trouble in Mind* (1985), and has parallels in Paul Thomas Anderson's *Punch-Drunk Love* (2002), which seems structurally a Hartley film. But Hartley's style in *Simple Men* remains idiosyncratic, selecting and reworking schemas ranging from Hollywood to Godard. Most filmmakers can be understood as tied to traditions in just such ways, as *Monogram* noted. Across three decades Thomas Elsaesser has reminded us, in pages which will inspire reflection for many years, that in order to understand the art of cinema we must nurture in ourselves an awareness of the varied and unpredictable forces of history.

Notes

1. The original version of this essay was published as 'Nah dran und unpersönlich: Hal Hartley und die Beharrlichkeit der Tradition' in Malte Hagener, Johann Schmidt and Michael Wedel (eds) (2004) *Die Spur durch den Spiegel: Der Film in der Kultur der Moderne*, Berlin: Bertz Verlag, 410–21. The piece appeared in the original English on the Danish film studies website *16:9* at http://www.16-9.dk/2005-06/side11_inenglish.htm. The current version is lightly revised from that.
2. See Elsaesser, 'Introduction: The Cinema of Irony', *Monogram*, 5 (n.d.),1–2; and Elsaesser, 'The Pathos of Failure: American Films in the 70's', *Monogram*, 6 (n.d.), 13–19.
3. Kent Jones sensitively invokes the tone of Hartley's work in 'Hal Hartley: The Book I Read Was in Your Eyes', *Film Comment*, 32, 4 (1996), 68–72.
4. For more on these features, see my *The Way Hollywood Tells It: Story and Style in Modern Movies* (Berkeley: University of California Press, 2006), 115–89.
5. *Surviving Desire* (1989) has an average shot length of 10.5 seconds; *Theory of Achievement* (1991), 17.9 seconds; *Amateur* (1994), 10 seconds; *Flirt* (1996), 18.7 seconds; *Henry Fool* (1997), 11.2 seconds. *No Such Thing* (2001) has a more rapid editing pace, yielding an average shot length of 7.9 seconds.
6. See my *On the History of Film Style* (Cambridge: Harvard University Press, 1997), chapter six; *Figures Traced in Light: On Cinematic Staging* (Berkeley: University of California Press, 2005), chapter two. A 1910s director displaying intriguing parallels with Hartley is Robert Reinert; see my essay, 'Taking Things to Extremes: Hallucinations Courtesy of Robert Reinert', in *Poetics of Cinema* (New York: Routledge, 2008), 263–80.
7. Author's correspondence with Hal Hartley, 14 May 2003.
8. See also the interview 'In Images We Trust: Hal Hartley Interviews Jean-Luc Godard', *Filmmaker*, 3, 1 (1994), 14–18, 55–6.
9. For a brief analysis of Antonioni's dynamic exchange of looks exchanged and deflected, see David Bordwell, Kristin Thompson and Jeff Smith, *Film Art: An Introduction*, eleventh edition (New York: McGraw-Hill, 2016), 141–2.
10. Author's correspondence with Hal Hartley, 14 May 2003.
11. Ibid.

CHAPTER TWO

'Young. Middle-Class. College-Educated. Unskilled.': Hal Hartley in 1991

Mark L. Berrettini

> All my films are a desperate attempt to make some philosophic sense out of my own experience. I want to know more. And what the characters go through are little exercises, little experiments; the most effective means with which to make the world and my own experiences understandable to myself.
> – Hal Hartley, 'Finding the Essential: Hal Hartley in Conversation with Graham Fuller' (2002: xxi)

In 1991, Hal Hartley's 'short feature' *Surviving Desire* and his short films *Ambition* and *Theory of Achievement* were produced and/or released by PBS outlets, and later, they were shown in retrospectives dedicated to Hartley's career and were released on home video formats. These films, along with the features released before 1991, *The Unbelievable Truth* (1989) and *Trust* (1990), occupy a significant place within Hartley's early career as he became a professional filmmaker in New York during the American independent film era of the late 1980s and early 1990s. Hartley's shorts and features fit well within this period as filmmakers and film viewers encouraged and embraced aesthetic and narrative challenges to cinematic convention. In many instances, these same filmmakers engaged in a low-budget approach to filmmaking that afforded them some freedom to experiment with a 'DIY' approach that incorporates low-budget economics into the creative process as a valuable way to challenge mainstream practices within film, art and music.

Viewed together, *Surviving Desire*, *Ambition* and *Theory of Achievement* signal the direction of Hartley's career development from its earliest points to the present as he 'attempt[s] to make some philosophic sense out of [his] own experience', and as his filmmaking moves toward a more unconventional style and narrative structure. As Caryn James writes, *Surviving Desire*, *Ambition* and *Theory of Achievement* 'crept a bit further away from realism [when viewed alongside some of Hartley's features and move] toward ... extreme stylization' as they push standard boundaries of cinematic narrative (1992: n.p.). These films display Hartley's burgeoning exploration of aesthetic and narrative cinematic strategies that have become notable features of his work, including: the jarring interplay of sound and image; the use of a generally flat acting style to compliment unusual dialogue; the rejection of basic cinematic standards, such as establishing shot; and a sustained coordination of precise cinematography and stilted, sometimes comedic character blocking that runs counter to 'naturalistic' forms of direction (see Berrettini 2011; Rawle 2011; Manley 2013). As in most of his films, *Surviving Desire*, *Ambition* and *Theory of Achievement* include some of Hartley's sparse musical compositions and his minimalist block letter white-font-on-black-background titles, consistent (and insistent) elements that designate a signature connection between the films in his oeuvre in a manner unlike most contemporary directors (Woody Allen's regular use of jazz and a standard title font comes to mind as a similar case). Finally, these three films include some of Hartley's earliest collaborations with cast and crew who continued to work with him for much of his career: the producers Jerome Brownstein and Ted Hope, who along with James Schamus founded Good Machine, one of the foremost American independent film companies of the 1990s; the cinematographer Michael Spiller, who shot many of Hartley's productions through to *No Such Thing* (2001); the production designer Steven Rosenzweig; and the actors Bill Sage, Martin Donovan, Elina Löwensohn, Matt Malloy, Rebecca Merritt Nelson, Mark Chandler Bailey, Gary Sauer and Jeffrey Howard.

Theory of Achievement
Set in Williamsburg, Brooklyn, a location announced in one of Hartley's standard intertitles, *Theory of Achievement* opens as Bob (Bob Gosse, Hartley's cousin), a prescient, bohemian writer-philosopher-realtor, talks with a black clad, beret-wearing 'artistic' couple (Jeffrey Howard, Jessica Sager) under a graffiti-covered overpass and attempts to sell them on moving into the area. Although he does not use the term gentrification, Bob describes the area in relation to artists moving into the neighbourhood, terming it 'the Paris of Brooklyn': it 'doesn't look like much, but plenty of people are moving [into it]. Writers, painters, filmmakers, rock and roll musicians ... it is just a matter of time before this neighbourhood becomes the art capital of the world' because people can afford to live in it. In a later scene, Bob describes such people as, 'Young. Middle-class. College-educated. Unskilled', a phrase that is recycled in the film and describes the characters in Hartley's films from 1991.

The film eventually depicts a gathering of about nine young, mainly white people in a stark white apartment where they drink and talk with and past each other about, as the film's title indicates, how to achieve success in their artistic pursuits and in relation to the material conditions of their lives. Much of the film is made up of tight close-ups and medium shots that are static, somewhat flat, and suggestive of a rigidity that compliments some of the characters' pronouncements, but runs counter to the 'hanging out' quality of the moments depicted in the film's locations – the streets of

Williamsburg, a diner and an apartment. The central narrative thread that ambles through these locations involves two couples, Bob and Ingrid (Ingrid Rudefors) and Bill (Bill Sage) and his unnamed girlfriend (Elina Löwensohn) as they negotiate their relationships and a housing scheme constructed by Bob (within this essay, I will refer to unnamed characters by the actors' names). Bob has sublet Ingrid's apartment while she is out of town for work to Bill and Elina without Ingrid's approval. Bill and Elina are engaged in a conflict as well, the source of which is not immediately clear to viewers.

The first scene in Ingrid's apartment, the film's main setting, depicts Elina and Bill in conflict via a series of quoted phrases and dance-like movements. In a medium shot, Elina is shown on the right side of the frame as she sits at a table in the kitchen with a window that looks out at an exterior wall that nearly matches the whiteness of the room. There is not much depth to this shot, and it is Elina's deep blue robe-like blouse that sets her apart from the white stove, refrigerator, walls and window-exterior wall as she sits at a table facing the left portion of the frame and reads aloud from a book: 'He who does his own work well will find that his first lesson is to know what he is and that which is proper to himself. And he who understands himself will never mistake another man's work as his own, but will recognise the value of his work as being the appropriate outcome of his temperament and his needs'. While Elina reads this text, the following actions occur within the static shot. Bill walks into the shot from offscreen left wearing a suit in a colour similar to Elina's shirt. He tries to caress Elina's face, she rebuffs him, and he moves around behind her and to her front, where he kneels down. Level with Elina's face, Bill leans in and looks at her, but Elina pushes his face away. He moves offscreen left and then returns to the frame, settling behind Elina, at which point he attempts a kiss, which Elina pulls away from. Bill walks offscreen left again and then suddenly pops back into the frame, slamming his hands onto the table as he stares at Elina. She stops speaking and looks up from her book, stares back at Bill, and shoves him out of the frame in a fluid movement, the kind of stilted and even slapstick comedic violence that Hartley regularly includes in his work.

From Elina's move, the film cuts to an overhead shot of Bill falling onto a black-and-white tiled floor before it cuts back to a close-up of Elina, who briefly casts her eyes down to look at Bill. In the close-up, Elina settles back to read her text: 'He will refuse superfluous employments and reject all unprofitable thoughts and propositions.' Offscreen, Bill says in a soft voice, 'Love is a form of knowledge', and Elina smiles and responds, 'I know that'. The film then cuts to Bill on the floor, where he shouts, 'To know we can die is to be dead already!', and the film cuts back to the close-up of Elina, whose smile fades to a look of slight concern. (On Hartley's staging and dialogue in scenes such as this one, see David Bordwell's contribution to this volume.)

The film next cuts to a brief scene in a diner in which three characters (Naledi Tshazibane, Nick Gomez and Mark Chandler Bailey, credited as M.C.) talk about how complex ideas might be communicated by writers and artists. Gomez plays a Godard look-alike and whispers a Godardian-Kuleshovian passage to Bailey, who then speaks for him: 'When two images or sounds are juxtaposed in a relationship that is not concrete or logical…' The film then returns to Bill and Elina in the apartment where a distraught Bill seems to pick up the thread of the diner conversation and yells, 'Meaning is differential!', before he and Elina silently move through the white rooms in the apartment in a three-shot scene that is part chase, part dance. The camera glides through the rooms of the small apartment as Bill follows Elina and again tries to engage her, while she rebuffs him and finally slaps him and walks into the background, leaving Bill with his head tilted in a prolonged response to the slap.

As an example of Hartley's stylised repetition, the blocking, choreography and cinematography in this scene are similar to scenes in the earlier *The Unbelievable Truth* and the later *Amateur* in which characters enact confined 'chase sequences' within the rooms of one house. Some of Bill and Elina's dialogue is repeated throughout the film by other characters to suggest that they have a shared language based upon their 'Young. Middle-class…' subjectivities. Clipped and repetitive conversations like those in the apartment and in the diner in *Theory of Achievement* exemplify the flat and circular dialogue style that Hartley uses over the course his career, and the 'quoted' quality of the lines is made explicit late in the film. Elina, Naledi and Gomez's Godard are shown in a three-shot as Elina reads three lines off of strips of paper, vaguely explains their sources, and hands them to Gomez's Godard: '"To know we can die is to be dead already." I read that in a book somewhere. "Meaning is differential." I heard that in a course I took at college. "Love is a form of knowledge." I copied that out of my notebook. I can't remember where I found it, but I believe it.' Here, the quoted-tone of these statements corresponds to Hartley's consistent use of such phrasing and flat delivery of poetic-philosophic lines in other films: 'A family is like a gun. You point it in the wrong direction, you're gonna kill somebody' (*Trust*); 'There's nothing but trouble and desire' (*Simple Men* [1992]); 'An honest man is always in trouble' (*Henry Fool* [1997] and *Fay Grim* [2006]).

From Bill and Elina's conflict, the film returns to the diner where Ingrid confronts Bob about his sublet scheme, and Bob first states the phrase 'Young. Middle-class…' to explain who Bill and Elina are and why they are living in the apartment. Ingrid tells Bob that he must find them another place to live, which in turn sends Bob to the apartment to talk with Bill, where Elina has locked herself in the bathroom and threatens to stay until Bill quits his job. Inexplicably, the inhabitants of the diner and the artistic couple from the film's opening join Bob and Ingrid in the apartment, where Bill expands upon his conflict with Elina: she wants him to quit his job so that he can follow his passion, to write 'really beautiful, timeless love songs [even though he] can't sing and [he] doesn't know music'. He only works to pay the rent, and like the others in the film, making money interferes with his artistic goal, even if he admittedly is unprepared to achieve this goal, a joke that Hartley pokes at those unformed artists who do not work to advance their art.

Once the entire cast is in the apartment, drinking takes over and the conversations meander through snippets of dialogue centring on how the characters define themselves in relation to work – the kind of work they must do to pay the rent and the kind of work they want to pursue, intercut with Jeffrey playing his accordion during three musical interludes interspersed through these conversations. Bob repeats a version of his Paris description of Williamsburg before we see Bill and M.C. Bailey's character seated at the kitchen table. The framing differs from the earlier shot of Elina and is more cramped as a two-shot, but it maintains the earlier shot's flatness by again setting the characters apart from the space through their clothing – Bill's dark suit and M.C.'s blue shirt, which matches the colour of Elina's blouse. Beer cans, cigarettes and a wine bottle populate the table as the men write out a diagram of their subjectivities based upon Bob's assessment of his crowd:

M.C.: Young. Middle-class. College-educated. Broke.
Bill: Young. Middle-class. White. College-educated. Unskilled. Broke.
M.C.: Young. Middle-class. White. College-educated. Unskilled. Broke. Drunk.
Bill: That's it.
M.C. Yeah, I think we got it now.

Following this moment, the film cuts to a high-angle close-up of Jeffrey in the kitchen playing his accordion and singing his catchy polka, 'Let Me Win Lotto', which fits into the spirit of the film's focus on labour: 'Quit my job/Take a vacation/Of 64 nations/Let me win Lotto tonight.' Bob is slumped over the sink behind Jeffrey in the left portion of the frame, and this shot persists throughout the runtime of the song, at which point the film cuts to a medium shot of Elina in the bathroom and then a medium shot of Bill outside the bathroom door. A doubled voiceover with lines spoken by Bill and then by Ingrid is audible as Hartley's minimalist score (music he wrote and produced, under the pseudonym Ned Rifle) plays over these shots as an abstracted bridge to the film's conclusion: perhaps inspired by the conversations and the diagram as well as being troubled by Elina's ultimatum, Bill quits his job, which he reports to Elina through the bathroom door. She emerges, they reconcile and kiss; soon after in the kitchen, they peruse a newspaper for real estate listings and Elina repeats her phrases to him (fig. 2.1). Bob joins them in the kitchen to offer his apart-

Fig. 2.1: Bill (Bill Sage) and Elina (Elina Löwensohn) reconcile through words and phrases in *Theory of Achievement*

ment since he will move in with Ingrid, and M.C. then joins in, stating, 'Love is a form of knowledge'. Accordion music acts as a sound bridge out of this scene into a close-up of Elina as she walks into frame and slowly turns her head around to look off screen right. She speaks, but her speech is not included on the soundtrack, an unusual moment in this otherwise wordy film, and we are left to wonder what she has said when the film cuts to the white-on-black concluding title.

Theory of Achievement's tone is comedic, and while Hartley mocks the aimlessness-yet-grand visions of the characters, the mockery seems to be good-natured and sourced in an appreciation of New York's 'hustle'. In Hartley's 2012 interview with Scott Indrisek in *Modern Painter*, his comments about living in New York versus living in Berlin offer an instructive frame for *Theory of Achievement*'s perspective on labour, artistic pursuits and professionalisation: 'The hustle of New York, I like the hustle you feel in New York. It's true that it's inexpensive to live in Berlin. I like the European lifestyle … But I met a lot of people in Berlin who were just lazy, not doing much work. The film business is unbelievable. They don't really make good films there. There are so many people who are just talking and talking – and not doing anything. And that extended to painting and sculpture. It was refreshing to come back to New York and meet some 23-year-old who absolutely believes he or she is going to change the entire world in the next six months. I love that hustle' (2012: 21). (Hartley and his wife, Miho Nikaido, lived in Berlin from 2004, when he was awarded a fellowship by the American Academy, to 2009.) While Bill's talk about making music resembles the inhabitants of Berlin, Bob is a consummate Hartley hustler in the vein of Bill McCabe (Robert John Burke) in *Simple Men*, Henry Fool (Thomas Jay Ryan) or Satan (Thomas Jay Ryan again) in *The Book of Life* (1998). Through such characters, their dialogue and their actions, viewers can appreciate variations of Hartley's sense of hustle, work and follow-through throughout his oeuvre, and in *Ambition* we see a radicalised version that is inspired by, or perhaps necessitated by, living in New York.

Ambition

As a film produced in the early days of Good Machine, *Ambition* was shot as a companion film to *Theory of Achievement* so the films could be broadcast together on PBS's 'Alive from Off Center' and meet the program's runtime. The films share a look in terms of cinematography, mise-en-scène and a comedic tone in their approach to artistic creation and work, and again, this film includes quite a few tight close-ups and medium shots that are static and flat. Hartley continues to make use of repetitive phrasing and flat delivery of poetic-philosophic dialogue, and in this case, the dialogue seems even more nonsensical. *Ambition* is more abstract, concise and overtly experimental in terms of cinematic convention when compared with *Theory of Achievement*, and its characters are less developed and function more as general types who are unnamed and are not contextualised or connected to each other through explicit relationships.

Ambition opens in another sparse kitchen in a New York apartment where George Feaster's character shoves dishes off of a table and outlines his ambitions to a man who has entered the scene. He wants to 'be awed by his own accomplishments …

be compared to great men ... set trends [and] be loved by beautiful women'. We next see a wide shot in which George walks on a New York City street and fends off several attackers, including a woman with a machine gun, with over-the-top and stagy fight choreography; on the soundtrack, we hear a woman's low voiceover, and at the film's conclusion, this voiceover is revealed to be the words that Patricia Sullivan's character whispers to George after another series of physical confrontations. George's altercations continue inside an unidentified building before he is shown in a shallow, staggered two shot with a woman who tells him that, 'the world is a dangerous and uncertain place. A few odd moments of respect and affection here and there are about as good as life gets.' They kiss, and he says, 'I'm good at what I do', as they walk off screen in opposite directions.

What George does and why he is good at it is unclear throughout the film, but it seems that his work is related to the art world, and *Ambition* might be seen as a representation of a condensed version of his rise-and-fall career arc. The building where most of the action takes place is revealed to be a gallery of sorts, with bright blue walls, odd, heavily-shadowed lighting and well-known classical paintings in gilded frames. He is welcomed and praised for his work by the denizens of the gallery, and then he sits down for a quick shot/reverse-shot conversation with a woman (Patricia Sullivan), perhaps the gallery owner. Patricia wears black and sits in a red leather chair that stands out against the blue wall, while George wears a black motorcycle jacket, a teal shirt and sits in a matching chair:

> Patricia: This must be an exciting time in your life.
> George: I feel lucky to have the opportunity to prove myself.
> Patricia: You're being modest.
> George: The world is a dangerous and uncertain place.
> Patricia: Why do you work?
> George: Because I can.
> Patricia: Do you work a lot?
> George: As much as I can.
> Patricia: Why do you work as much as you do?
> George: To escape the emptiness of my own life.
> Patricia: What are you afraid of?
> George: Of not being able to work.
> Patricia: What are the obstacles to work?
> George: Indecision. Indifference. Fear.

An unnamed man enters the scene and, shown in a medium wide shot, as he waits for an elevator, he begins an animated monologue to Patricia and George:

> You know, you work and you work, and you make sacrifices. You try to get up on your own two feet by yourself so no one can hold that against you. And when you make it, when you accomplish it, they take it away. Or worse, they prevent you from working. They don't let you do what it is that you're good

at. They don't want to hear about you when you took a subway to work. Now you take a cab and you pay for it with your own money, and now they want to make you feel guilty for trying to work yourself to death!

He leaves via the elevator, and Patricia moves over to sit next to George, at which point the two light cigarettes as their conversation takes a dark turn:

Patricia: Do you think he'll try and kill himself?
George: I don't know.
Patricia: The world is a dangerous and uncertain place, isn't it?

George's dialogue continues as he makes explicit the 'quoted' tone of his dialogue when he claims that he once saw a film where a character outlined differences between men and women in terms of suicide and purpose, which leads him to conclude in his own voice, 'life is dull, a good fight keeps it interesting'. A man off screen yells 'Next', and the film briefly cuts to black as a boxing bell rings. George is next seen in a medium wide shot sitting at a conference room table as a man in a suit paces behind him and berates him in a one-sided conversation that is somewhat comprehensible to viewers – the man (George's superior?) gestures and screams, but no sound comes from his mouth, while George responds to the silent questions and accusations posed by the man (George: 'What? Me? No one told me! How should I know?'). Gradually, a chant of what seems to be 'power to the people', along with a helicopter, fades up on the soundtrack to connote a protest on the streets.

The conference room argument marks the start of George's downfall, and the film thus progresses into a peculiar, stagy fight sequence that enacts what we might consider to be a conflict with his critics, positioned here more as his work supervisors. Two men (one who silently berated him) chase George out of the conference room into the same area where we saw the man at the elevator, and we see George run into the space and the two men follow, all in slow motion, falling over each other before

Fig. 2.2: A whispered voiceover in *Ambition*

they can grab him. Hartley repeats the shot again before cutting to a close-up in which the two men, now in regular speed, pin George to a table and make him repeat their philosophy of work. When he does not follow their directions, they pin him to a wall and repeatedly slap him as he spouts of his quasi-nationalistic cultural passions:

> I love England, not because of Churchill, but because of rock and roll and Virginia Woolf.
> *Slap.*
> I love the French because of Victor Hugo.
> *Slap.*

Like so many of Hartley's characters, George ends up on the floor when the film finally rests on a shot of him pressed to the hallway floor desperately repeating 'I'm good at what I do'. Patricia crouches over him and whispers in his ear, the soundtrack that served as a voiceover earlier in the film (fig. 2.2). Much like Ned (Jeffrey Howard) in *Simple Men* – 'There's nothing but trouble and desire' – George repeats his mantra as he becomes locked into a near catatonic state, perhaps by his realisation that being good at what he does is not enough to achieve or maintain success. The use of exaggerated fight choreography in *Ambition* externalises George's struggle, and this technique extends to Hartley's use of dance and gesture as a way to convey characters' internal states in other films, such as *Surviving Desire*. In an interview in *Cineaste*, Hartley plots out this development: 'I started with fight choreography in *Ambition*, one of my shorts. Once that was finished, I went straight into *Surviving Desire* and we developed the dance' (Fried 1993: 38). With this in mind, I want to conclude my discussion of Hartley's work in this time period with a consideration of *Surviving Desire*.

Surviving Desire
Produced for PBS's American Playhouse, *Surviving Desire* offers a glimpse at literature professor Jude's (Martin Donovan) short, doomed romance with a student named Sofie (Mary B. Ward). The film again engages with explicit experimental techniques as Hartley deploys an unconventional style more explicitly for comedic effect. *Surviving Desire* opens with Hartley's usual credit sequence intercut with images of Jude's literature class in full revolt: Jude reads from *The Brothers Karamazov* while students throw things at him, leave the class and shout (onscreen and offscreen): 'Teach us something useful'; 'This is ridiculous'; 'We're paying for this'; 'You're a disgrace'. Jude aims his attention at Sofie, emphasising Dostoyevsky's phrase, 'active love is labour and perseverance', and when he concludes the passage, a student (Gary Sauer) accuses him of being stuck on the same paragraph for a month and a half. When Jude does not answer the student's questions about the passage, their conflict devolves into a physical altercation as the remaining students leave the classroom.

Jude then meets, in a campus café, his friend Henry (Matt Malloy), a Ph.D. student in theology who has been thrown out of school, and admits that he is falling in love with Sofie. Henry walks Jude through a philosophical conversation about active love, faith and infatuation to test Jude's interest in Sofie, while Sofie and her roommate Jill (Julie Sukman) sit nearby and discuss the merits of Sofie getting involved with Jude. The action then shifts to New York City where Jude drops off Henry and meets a possibly deranged, possibly homeless woman named Katie (Rebecca Merritt Nelson) who asks Jude to marry her. Jude turns her down, and the film moves onto a bookstore where he browses and Sofie works (or to be more accurate, stands and asks, 'Anybody need any help?' as customers walk past her; Hartley includes a version of Sofie's bookstore scene three times in the film). Jude and Sofie have a sustained conversation about his class and the importance of literature, and after a transitional scene with Jude and Katie, Jude and Sofie continue their conversation in a bar where she kisses him and suggests that they will sleep together eventually.

Sofie's actions prompt *Surviving Desire*'s much-discussed set piece, a one-minute, five-shot dance sequence. A lone guitar plays clipped, heavy notes on the soundtrack as the bar sequence cuts to a wide shot that contains multiple actions. Jude enters the frame from the right and jumps onto a tall gate that hangs between two buildings and separates the street from a back courtyard/parking area. With Jude's action, the gate swings open towards the camera, and he rides it as he dramatically arches himself backward, and then the camera moves in toward Jude and reframes into a medium shot of him as he walks offscreen left. This shot dissolves into a wide shot of Jude in the parking area as he dances back-and-forth to the camera before he is joined by two unnamed men, each entering from opposite sides of the frame to join him in a synchronised dance. The guitar concludes on the soundtrack, and the men dance in a line with no accompaniment as the camera reframes to capture their actions. At first, their movements are reminiscent of conventional, classical Broadway choreography and staging, and their execution of the dance looks like a rehearsal walk-through; the street setting, some of their gestures and the costuming of one man directly recall *West Side Story* (1961). This rehearsal-quality is made more explicit when the men, lined up across the frame with Jude out front, next count out their movements as they swing their legs and arms right-and-left in a chorus line pattern. From this action, the film jump cuts into another moment with the men positioned diagonally, background to foreground, as their dance takes a contemporary turn with a crotch grab/pelvic thrust, perhaps reminiscent of Michael Jackson in the 1980s, before the film cuts on action to show Jude 'shovelling' as the men shuffle alongside him. They move from background to foreground as a lone keyboard comes in on the soundtrack, at which point their dance concludes with the two men kneeling in a prayer on either side of Jude as he comes to rest in a crucifixion pose. The film then cuts to Sofie and her roommate in their apartment.

In an interview with Graham Fuller, Hartley describes the development of this striking dance in *Surviving Desire*; it is worth quoting at length:

> I don't like rock videos, but I like to see dance. I like to hear music and play it. I like that live recording, that documentation, that authenticity. That has a lot to do with the dance sequence as well – the documentation of the work and concentration that goes into the execution of a simple spectacle. Here, it's men dancing. It kind of started when I was rehearsing some scenes for

> *Theory of Achievement*; Jeff Howard ... came over one day with his accordion and played the song for that film. I remember thinking, 'That's how easy it is to make honest cinema'. Just turn the camera on and point it at somebody doing something, and they'll do all the work. They'll feel it – they won't be pretending anything. I find that very pure and fascinating. When I was writing the script for *Surviving Desire*, I devised this joke of Sofie kissing Jude and then leaving him there, hanging. The script then goes on to say, 'He stumbles out of the bar, falls off the curb, but kind of saves himself by doing this little shuffling dance'. And then, very unrealistically, this other man happens by and does the same sort of funny dance step, and then they go their separate ways. Somewhere we began talking about it and it became more and more elaborate. It introduces archetypal gestures that we were very conscious of: the grabbing of the crotch (where we were deliberately quoting Madonna, who was already quoting an existing cultural gesture herself), the crucifixion, *West Side Story*, etc. The dance is not disturbing particularly, but it is very emotionally confusing. By the time they get to the end, I feel that what started out as a lighthearted dance of joy, because he's been kissed, is turning into a complex expression of vague doom. (1992: xvii–xviii)

Hartley's characterisation of the dance in terms of authenticity and honest cinema is compelling in what it tells us about his testing of the boundaries of fictional narrative cinema, the film's diegesis, and the knot of signification that he presents to viewers of this 'emotionally confusing' dance sequence. The conventional use of song and dance in standard realist musicals communicates emotion, which might signify authenticity and honesty to an audience about *the character's* emotional state – Jude is elated and must dance to express his feelings. As I have written elsewhere, in *Surviving Desire*, primarily a non-musical film, the dance does not fit conventionally within the narrative, but it does convey Jude's emotional response to Sofie's kiss (2011: 27–8). Hartley's allusion to musical convention in effect characterises Jude's state, which viewers recognise as a musical convention even in this non-musical film. However, Hartley's other terms for the dance sequence – documentation, work, concentration – give authenticity and honest cinema a different cast with an emphasis on *the performers'* actions. Hartley documents the authenticity and honesty of Martin Donovan and the two men as they work to concentrate on their performance of the dance (elements that distort the diegesis), which in turn expresses Jude's emotions. The performers will 'feel it – they won't be pretending', and the 'fact' of their work as performers is announced by the rehearsal aspects of their performance – walking through the choreography and counting out beats.

Some of the confusion of the dance sequence and its genre-blurring extends into a sequence a few minutes later in the film when a band (Hub Moore and the Great Outdoors) plays with full amplification in the middle of a New York street and serenades a woman in a window above the street. Several people dance while Jude and Henry walk through the scene and speak to each other. This musical interlude does not connect up with Jude's dance, nor does it advance his narrative with Sofie, but

Fig. 2.3: Jude (Martin Donovan) and Sofie (Mary B. Ward) contemplate literature in *Surviving Desire*

instead again displays Hartley's layered approach to the documentation of nonfictional performance within the fictional. The film's diegetic continuity is maintained by the interaction of Henry and Jude while the band's appearance complicates it.

The remaining portions of the film meander a bit as Jude and Sofie debate their coupling, sleep together, and then break up because Sofie does not want to be involved with anyone. (Additional scenes intercut with their interactions include Sofie talking about Jude with her roommate, Jude talking with Henry about his love of Sofie, and Henry and Katie meeting and immediately becoming engaged.) Jude implodes and acts out very much like we would expect Donovan's characters Matthew in *Trust* and Martin in *Simple Men* to act – turning over tables and yelling out of car windows – before he comes to rest back in the classroom at a chalkboard. In a medium shot that mirrors the film's opening, Jude sketches out Dostoyevsky's biography and writes on the chalkboard, but the camera angle does not allow viewers to see what he has written. When he concludes, the camera pans right to follow Jude as he casually moves to sit amongst his students just in front of Sofie with the rest of the students in the background (a medium shot with Jude and Sofie flattened into the foreground; fig. 2.3). He looks offscreen right and says, 'I have nothing else to say. I can't teach you anything. Class dismissed.' The film dissolves into the same medium shot in which only Jude and Sofie remain; he looks offscreen left, and she looks offscreen right before another dissolve quickly removes Sofie from the shot. At this point, the film cuts to a shot of the chalkboard from Jude's perspective, where viewers see Jude's final lecture notes, 'KNOWING IS NOT ENOUGH', written in block letters that resemble Hartley's regular title font. A brief shot of Jude walking on a city street leads to an overhead shot of Jude stretched out over a sewer grate in a gutter. An offscreen male passerby asks if he is alright, and Jude assures him that he will be OK if he can rest his head in the gutter for 'five or ten minutes' (fig. 2.4). The passerby then asks for directions, and Jude stands up out of frame to assist him in his last action shown within the film. (Jason Wood has noted that the image of Donovan in *Surviving Desire*'s conclusion virtually leads into the image of Donovan stretched out on a cobblestone street in *Amateur*'s opening; see 2003: 6.) Hartley cuts to Sofie's

Fig. 2.4: Jude learns that knowing is not enough in *Surviving Desire*

third scene in the bookstore, and the camera moves into a close up as she repeats, 'Can I help someone', before the film cuts to the closing credits.

In relation to the themes that run throughout these three films and the epigraph of this essay, Jude's final chalkboard message exhibits with an emphatic flourish a (pleasant) tension that weaves throughout Hartley's work. Vis-à-vis his characters, the 'little exercises, little experiments' that make up the situations in his films, and his investigation into the alteration of cinematic style and narrative convention, Hartley attempts to know more about his own experiences of and with love, labour, desire, aesthetics, productivity, youth/age and creativity. In so doing, he attempts to engage his viewers with these concepts and questions as well, but does not present easy answers. As one film proposes 'love is a form of knowledge', another answers that 'knowing is not enough'.

Acknowledgements
Thanks to Steven Rybin for his development of this project and his editorial work on it, and to Marcelle Heath for her comments on this essay.

CHAPTER THREE

'Some Things Shouldn't Be Fixed': Frameworks of Critical Reception and the Early Career of Hal Hartley

Jason Davids Scott

Key narrative elements from two of Hal Hartley's films seem notably resonant from a current cultural and historical perspective, functioning as a kind of mediated prophecy about where culture is headed, and framed and stylised in Hartley's bold, distinct and well-honed expressiveness as a filmmaker.

The first instance: *Henry Fool*, made in 1997, partially facilitates its plot by connecting the success of Simon Grim with the growth of internet communication: he 'goes viral', and his success eclipses the possibilities offered to him by the traditional print media that does not seem to understand his value. From a metatheatrical perspective, one can see this as an expression of Hartley's internal conflict with traditional filmmaking practices, whether aesthetic, industrial or technological. Henry Fool, the well-read, and in a sense 'classically trained' auteur, gives way to the more instinctive and effective presence of Simon, just as Hartley himself begins to turn more towards experimental short filmmaking, digital technology, other performing arts and further away from the mainstream of American commercial filmmaking culture.

The use of the internet communications technology to reflect this, however, becomes even more significant when one remembers that in 1997, the internet was far from a ubiquitous presence in American life or independent film. For example, by the end of 1996, there were only 100,000 websites (there were over a billion as of September 2014; see Anon. 2008); and the Pew Research Center indicates that in 1997, only about 25% of adults in the US used the internet 'at least occasionally' (the rate in 2014 approached 90%; see Anon. 2014). In an even more emphatic way, then, *Henry Fool* suggests the impact the internet might have on our culture: the presence of portable technology (the bulky personal laptop used by Fay Grim circa 1997 was something of a luxury – only ten million laptops were sold worldwide in 1995), the ability for individual agents to work around tightly regulated modes of mediated communication, and the phenomenon of becoming an overnight sensation. These plot elements make *Henry Fool* notably prescient about the role of modern technology in everyday life, hewing much closer to present-day reality than what was predicted or imagined by blockbusters like *The Lost World: Jurassic Park, Starship Troopers, The Fifth Element* and *Men in Black*, each of which came out in 1997.

The second example echoes this. Hartley's monster movie *No Such Thing*, which premiered in May 2001 (though it was not released in the United States theatrically until early 2002), resonates even more from a contemporary perspective. In its anticipation of a post-9/11 world where entertainment seems dominated by various forms of fantasy that incorporate an ironic, self-reflexive criticism of media-saturated culture, as well as its portrayal of the troubling tendency of hegemonic narratives to both represent absolute evil in a single body and exploit the bodies of its subjects to public humiliation and destruction, *No Such Thing* anticipates many current cultural trends reflected in the complex and addictive mythology of *Game of Thrones* and the various Marvel/DC comic universes that dominate movie screens. Consider this description of the plot of *No Such Thing*: an unlikely heroine (an aspiring television news producer) embarks on a quest for her lost lover, survives death, is rebuilt by medical technology, and is able to confront and ultimately facilitate the defeat of a terrorising, monstrous, humanoid enemy who lives in a desolate netherworld. (And, if you care about such things, Helen Mirren in a scene-stealing supporting role, and the guy from *RoboCop 3* [Fred Dekker, 1993] as the monster.) That kind of plot summary sounds like the stuff of a cinematic culture that embraces superheroes as reflections of our own seemingly endless need to justify violence towards an imagined 'other' – a slightly more fantastic and romantic version of *Zero Dark Thirty* (Kathryn Bigelow, 2012).

Needless to say, it is unlikely that you will find much reference to either of these Hartley films in mainstream discussions of culturally relevant films about technology, history and the contemporary human condition. And, admittedly, there's not going to be more discussion of them here: this is not an investigation of how critics at the time missed or failed to understand these films (particularly for *No Such Thing*, which was pilloried by most mainstream film critics who seemed completely blind to any cultural relevance, even post-9/11; see Ebert 2002, Mitchell 2002). This is an investigation as to why, perhaps, critics might have failed to see the value in these and many of Hartley's later films because they misread or misunderstood the value of his early films, specifically the features through *Simple Men* (1992).

What fascinates me is why such profoundly effective and powerful articulations of cultural identity found in Hartley's body of work are so invisible to most film audiences. He's no longer mentioned aside the notable and lasting filmmakers of 'his generation', and his early films, once lumped in with the early work of Linklater, Soderbergh, *et al.*, are (comparatively speaking) less well distributed and remembered than films such as *sex, lies, and videotape* (Soderbergh, 1989), *Slacker* (Linklater, 1991) and *Dazed and Confused* (Linklater, 1993).

One of the principal challenges of a scholar, historian or critic engaged in a project that is, for the most part, biographical – that is, focused on the life and/or work of a single individual – is how to construct a history that has resonance and relevance to the present day. When considering an individual director's film career, for example, it is natural to look at the director's films in historical sequence, attempting to document, infer or somehow measure the filmmaker's 'growth' or 'development' as professional. But what is often left out of that examination is the examination itself. For filmmakers, artists and others who live in the 'public eye' for extended periods of time, that personal history is always being written and rewritten as the person ages and creates (or does not create) new work. The frameworks of that 'living biography' are constantly evolving as history is simultaneously written and re-written.

This essay looks at those critical frameworks as they are expressed and articulated in the critical reaction to and extended discourse surrounding Hal Hartley's early films. From the beginning, critics and film industry professionals who marketed and distributed his films (and thus were seminal in establishing the terms of this critical discourse) staked out ground in defining both Hartley and his films in their immediate historical, cultural and biographical context. Some of these frameworks, from the perspective of the present day, seem problematic, simplistic or reductive: others, particularly ones that place Hartley's films in comparison to each other as evidence of his growth as a director, suggest a more complex understanding of the developments in Hartley's career that cannot be measured by evaluation of the films alone. This is not, then, an attempt to trace Hartley's actual artistic development through these films, but rather to analyse the discourse surrounding those films in order to document Hartley's perceived relevance and cultural value during this point in his career.

* * *

> I came to this conclusion that we no longer have a culture as we would have defined it in the past – a manner of living together as a community that has matured organically, so to speak, through common experience. Now, our manner of living together is dictated immediately through publicity and advertising. That is the thing we actually share. We don't, in fact, live together and experience things together that much anymore. It is mediated. In fact, not all of this worries me. A lot of it's fascinating, even. (Hartley and Kaleta 2008: 139–40)

The impetus for this examination of the critical reception of Hartley's early films is also, admittedly, one motivated and informed by my own personal history. In the early 1990s, shortly after graduating from New York University with an undergraduate degree in Cinema Studies, I worked for several years for the publicity firm Clein + White, one of the more successful 'boutique' entertainment PR agencies, with offices in both New York and Los Angeles. Our firm represented the projects and clients that now seem like a 'Who's Who' of independent film history, though at the time we viewed those clients (and they often viewed themselves) as struggling newcomers. From the perspective of an industry professional, working with these young filmmakers meant connecting them with influential critics and magazine editors who would offer favourable word-of-mouth for their projects. These critics and magazine editors were obligated – in both professional and corporate terms – to cover mainstream, 'Hollywood' events, projects and figures. With limited space dedicated to independent projects, the value of these reviews and profiles was in many ways immeasurable. Even a negative review or mixed review, if printed alongside a review of a major feature film, gave the independent project a credibility and measure of achievement. There was a payoff for the journalist and outlet as well: in an era when the value of 'new filmmakers' who made their first film(s) outside of the system was arguably as high as it has ever been in Hollywood history, there was great cachet in 'finding' and promoting the next generation of film artists.

The film publicist – whether an independent firm or an in-house staff working for the distributor – is the focal point of this exchange between artist, text and critic. Publicists must create and distribute information about the film to the working press, and these materials – in the form of production notes, press photos, trailers, electronic press kits (behind-the-scenes material, interviews, etc) – must be considered alongside the reviews, interviews and profiles that were eventually published by newspaper and magazine outlets.

A brief example of one of my duties in regards to Hartley's career will illustrate this. I was asked to create the 'About the Production' section of the printed press kit for Hartley's third feature release, *Simple Men*. A typical press kit also included cast and crew credits, production stills and other materials that are supplied to critics and editors in order to facilitate publication of reviews (in the pre-digital age, the stills sent in the press kit were often the ones used to create the images published in the newspapers).

The section I wrote – with guidance and approval from the film's producers and distributors (and presumably Hartley himself) – emphasises key critical frameworks that we felt were collectively important to communicate about understanding Hartley's work. Even though this was only Hartley's third film, the production notes emphasise the 'familial' nature of Hartley's production process, both in terms of production and behind-the-camera personnel, as well as working with actors on multiple projects. Second, the notes frame Hartley as a 'regional' filmmaker making movies about the place he grew up in and examined previously in *The Unbelievable Truth* (1989) and *Trust* (1990) (suburban Long Island). This was a deliberate obfuscation of the fact that Hartley actually shot *Simple Men* in Texas – union regulations would have made producing the film on location financially impossible – as well as an attempt to create an affinity between Hartley's previous films and his current one. These production notes (rewritten slightly and edited down for space) continue to service the film, as they are reprinted on the inside cover of its DVD release. They all suggest that Hartley is a filmmaker of continuity – that what you understand from one film translates to the next.

Considering over a hundred different reviews and other published pieces related to Hartley's early films, it is clear that those various points of focus as articulated in the production notes for *Simple Men* were the dominant frameworks through which critics discussed his early work. Indeed, these are the frameworks by which critics and the extended critical industry/community 'fixed' their idea of Hal Hartley. The word 'fixed' here should be read with both meanings: as 'repair', in the sense that Matthew means in *Trust* when he shouts at his boss about a faulty computer, 'Some things shouldn't be fixed!'; and as in 'affixed', or bound to a place, time or identity that is expected to remain. In 'fixing' Hartley – translating his unusual technique and individual creative identity so that an audience would better understand his first two films – critical discourse also attempted to 'nail down' Hartley's career and identity in a way that would allow him to become a more stable commodity in both the industrial and cultural marketplace. The first section looks at how critics of *The Unbelievable Truth* identified Hartley's position as both an industrial and creative force – a potential 'auteur' (using the term very informally) – and how his style was understood as actively unconventional. Second, the definition of Hartley as a filmmaker associated with a 'region' will be explored as reviews of *Trust* – retrospectively including assessments of *Truth* – associate regional or location-specific identity with narrative themes and the film's/Hartley's position towards mainstream culture. Finally, the cumulative effect of these various frameworks will be seen in the reviews of *Simple Men*, a film that seemed to frustrate critics as well as represent a professional crossroads in terms of the 'end' of Hartley's early career. After working so hard to understand, appreciate and explain Hartley's films, the release of *Simple Men* also represents Hartley fans and critics throwing their hands up in the air, seemingly resigned to only measure Hartley through the memory of his first two films. The Hal Hartley that the critics fixed early on in his career, the Hal Hartley they talked about, the Hal Hartley they compared to the great directors of his and every other generation, is ultimately not the Hal Hartley that eventually emerged as a major international media artist and experimental filmmaker, the one who should be better recognised for producing work that is culturally relevant and not just stylistically distinct.[1]

Hartley-esque: Defining the Formal Properties of Hartley's Films
As a way of further clarifying the industrial/professional context of Hartley's early films, examination of the critical response helps tell the story of how these films – and Hartley himself – shifted in importance and value over the first few years of his career. *The Unbelievable Truth*, a very small film, was seen by a few people; *Trust* was seen by a few more, who then went back and watched *The Unbelievable Truth*; and the process repeated itself to some extent with *Simple Men* and *Amateur* (1994), each of which essentially represented a step 'upward' in respectability, control and connection to the independent film industry, roughly at the pace of one film per year.

As might be expected from a community that is engaged with a variety of filmmaking practices and critical traditions, many, if not most, popular film critics tend to associate a film's meaning with the film's director. This is particularly the case in independent film, where a director is also more likely to be the screenwriter and/or producer on the film. While this is not, strictly speaking, a rigorous application of the auteur theory on the part of these critics, the informal understanding of the term 'auteur' is the key operating function in many of these reviews. For many critics, 'auteur-ness' is signified by formal elements that make the individual artist distinct from other artists and/or can be seen from film to film as evidence of a stylistic 'signature'.

Often part and parcel with this definition is the understanding that this authorship function has a value in the film community that is defined in terms of the filmmakers' professional status and the professional quality of the film. In the early 1990s, being a young auteur meant not only expressing one's self as a unique cinematic artist, but also being able to do so on a limited budget, and 'against' broader cultural and industrial forces assumed to have less artistic (but higher commercial) value. Auteurism was not just description of a style, or a process for understanding the meaning of a film, but was a 'brand' signifying quality and importance.

Thus, taking a chronological perspective at how Hartley is 'fixed' as both a viable and noteworthy independent filmmaking commodity, as well as an artistically-motivated auteur, is helpful in examining how his critical identity gestated and evolved over time. The point is not to define Hartley's reputation entirely in terms of consensus – Hartley has never been universally loved, and critics' interpretations of his work are varied – but rather to see how so many critical responses are framed through these perspectives.

For example, the comparative scarcity of reviews for *The Unbelievable Truth*, which received minimal theatrical release, and the packaging of those reviews with reviews of other films in 'notebook'-style newspaper columns, is reflective of Hartley's status as a 'new' filmmaker. These reviews are little more than extended mentions, often less than a paragraph, but notably contain some qualitative reflection or assessment of the film. Here is one such listing in its entirety, minus screening times: 'Provocative black comedy supposedly made for about $300,000 by US producers Bruce Weiss and Hal Hartley and director Hartley. One of the hits at the Sydney Film Festival. Catchlines tell it all: "teenage sex, nuclear winter and the mechanics of emotional capitalism"' (Bourke 1990; see also Hutchinson 1990).[2] In some columns, Hartley is discussed alongside other 'new' filmmakers such as Whit Stillman (Kelly 1990) or Charles Lane (Giulliat 1990), a process that will continue through his successive films as more independent filmmakers begin to attract attention from distributors, audiences, and critics.

New York Times writer Caryn James, in two separate columns, reflects the 'story' of Hartley as he emerged as a new talent. Her first mention of *The Unbelievable Truth* comes from her 'Critic's Notebook' column of 5 February 1990 (1990a). The 1,370-word article discusses how a number of independently financed projects (including such disparate films as *Chameleon Street* [1989], *Blue Steel* [1989], *House Party* [1990], *Metropolitan* [1990] and *To Sleep with Anger* [1990]) found success and distribution deals, following the path of *sex, lies, and videotape* from the previous year. She uses 81 of those words to very briefly mention Hartley's debut in the context of the film's ultimate distributor, Miramax:

'Prizes help, but popularity in terms of audience buzz is more important', said Harvey Weinstein, co-chairman of Miramax Films. Miramax's film 'The

Unbelievable Truth' won no prizes, though it is precisely the kind of original film the festival can help. A first feature by Hal Hartley, it is a low-budget, surprisingly upbeat takeoff on film noir in which a young woman, convinced that the apocalypse is around the corner, falls for a handsome murderer who returns to his Long Island hometown. (1990a)

Then, in July of 1990, James and the *Times* published a full review to coincide with the release of the film in Manhattan. The critical value of the film is bracketed by comments about the film's budget, notably in the third paragraph (the first two describe the film's plot and characters):

This is the kind of small-scale independent movie with a familiar story behind it. The film was written, directed, edited and co-produced by Mr. Hartley, whose relatives took out bank loans and let him use their suburban houses on Long Island as sets during the 11 1/2 days it took to shoot most of the movie. (1990b)

Notably, James's strongest point of negative criticism suggests that Hartley is not culturally very sensitive: she criticises the attempt at a 'topical' tone, and says the film is 'behind the curve' in representing the influence of Wall Street culture, and the director 'pushes the theme of crass commerce too hard'. The 'timeliness' and relevance of Hartley's work is a framework that will persist throughout his career. Ultimately, however, James praises Hartley and Michael Spiller with the compliment that 'they have made a film that is visually and verbally much richer than their budget'.

Other extended reviews of the film, such as both those published by *The Washington Post* when the film opened in Washington, DC in August, immediately cite the film's borderline amateur status. 'A bent comic cogitation on sex, lies and the cost of living, this engaging first feature was shot in 11 1/2 days in director Hal Hartley's back yard for a piddling $200,000. Now Hartley is this year's low-budget Wunderkind, and "Truth" one of its ragged art house pleasures', writes Rita Kempley (1990), making not-so-oblique reference to the Soderbergh film. Kempley's *Washington Post* colleague Joe Brown uses the same point of reference to make both an industrial and a critical point: 'Casual, clearly inexpensive (Hartley got his $6,000 seed money when his local bank offered a special on low-interest computer loans) but good-looking, it shares some of the moral gamesmanship of "sex, lies, and videotape" and the small-town eccentricities of "Twin Peaks"' (1990).

Alongside the documentation and reporting of Hartley's budgets – one might consider the different implications inferred whether or not one emphasises that the film was made because of a $6,000 'seed' or 'a piddling' $200,000 – the reviews tend to take on the job of describing Hartley's distinct filmmaking style. Here, while the specific words differ, most of the adjectives used to describe Hartley's tone can be categorised as synonymous with 'unconventional' – that is, resisting typical or 'standard' models of filmmaking practices. Performances, themes, camera angles, patterns of editing, use of music and other elements of film language – whether or not they are described in detail or simply mentioned – are consistently framed as actively (and provocatively) eccentric. This is articulated directly in the review from the *Herald Sun* (Australia). The film 'stands out from the bigger budgeted mainstream simply because it doesn't conform to expected, well-trod paths', writes the uncredited reviewer, who subsequently describes the characters as 'slightly off-kilter and unpredictable' (Anon. 1990). The review also warns that 'its very style ensures that audiences will be distanced to a degree from becoming too involved', though the overall quality 'does keep the film from being just a technical exercise'.

Most critics are likewise inclined to describe Hartley's brand of eccentricity as one that is more cerebral than emotional, but the language used steadfastly assures that there is nothing conventional about the film. 'Turning the potentially stale into the surprisingly fresh, in taking narrative clichés and standing them right on their trite head' (Groen 1990); 'biting, dark comedy about love in an emotionally scarred landscape' (Kelly 1990); 'odd and funny … overtones of a David Lynch concept, but it clearly remains Hartley's film' (Baker 1990); 'delightfully skewed … a tantalizing, other-worldly quality … off-kilter comedy' (Mietkiewicz 1990); 'droll, lucid black comedy … with an archness and shrewd pessimism that seem to reinvent 1950s cool in the face of contemporary culture' (James 1990b).

Crucially, even the rare negative review investigates Hartley's auteurship as the primary framework for understanding why *The Unbelievable Truth* is distinctive. In a notebook-style piece, an uncredited columnist writes:

> Director, writer and editor Hal Hartley dresses this material in some fancy stylistic devices, an all-too-transparent fable of modern morality, slick photography and some infectiously attractive but sterile characters. Threatening to give 'art-house' cinema a bad name, the first-time feature film-maker is reluctant to deal with anything too risque, preferring to pay lip service, albeit comically, to his characters' dilemmas and plights, and reverting to reassuring and traditional outcomes that are best viewed through rose-coloured glasses. (Anon. 1990)

Ultimately, both the positive and negative reviews of *The Unbelievable Truth* seem to suggest various ways in which critics took it upon themselves to 'measure' Hartley as an aspiring filmmaker, not just the person who happened to direct the film they were reviewing. The suggestion is that they expected to see more from him, that they were beginning the process of fixing Hartley to a style or a biography that would transfer from film to film. These discussions about his status as a creative force, as well as how that creativity was consistently framed as unconventional, will continue through the critical reception of Hartley's subsequent films. But with the release of *Trust* and *Simple Men*, two other elements of Hartley's work will emerge as equally prevalent frameworks: his identity as connected to a specific region, and comparisons to his earlier films that prove complex and contradictory.

Trust: Putting things in 'Place'

'Trust,' a love story about losers as well as a satire on suburbia, written and directed by Hal Hartley, has started a minor buzz. 'I call Hartley America's Harold Pinter', said Mr. [Ira] Deutchman, the president of Fine Line Features, a division of New Line cinema, who had just picked up distribution rights to the film. 'And like Pinter, he's an acquired taste. We'll market "Trust" by trying to build a consensus over time. We'll take it to lots of festivals. When you don't have stars to sell and you don't have sex to sell and you don't have a recognizable genre to sell, all that's left is critical response and audience response'. (Harmetz 1991)

Like many – but not all – of his independent film peers in the 'Generation X' school of the late 1980s and early 1990s, Hartley's early critical identity was focused on the location in which is films were set, particularly since Hartley's personal biography indicated that he had grown up in Lindenhurst, New York, where both *The Unbelievable Truth* and *Trust* were shot. As will be reflected in the reviews, how one understands 'Lindenhurst' – or, more precisely, how each critic understands Hartley's attitude towards the place of his films – varies greatly.

One of the more nuanced discussions of Hartley's use of Lindenhurst is offered by Hal Hinson of *The Washington Post*, who wrote an extended (1,000+ word) review entitled 'Trust: The Cry of Suburbia'. On the basis of the two Hartley films he had seen, Hinson offers a definition of Hartley framed entirely by a sense of place. Both films, he writes, are 'cool, strikingly original case studies of middle-class anomie. Not many filmmakers have run their fingers along the scrubbed-down Formica countertops of suburbia and found their inspiration, but this is the territory Hartley knows best … the backdrop for both movies is Long Island, where Hartley grew up, and in each the environment is a cruelly impersonal one' (1990). *Trust* is described as 'a cross between Beaver Cleaver's home town and a minimum-security prison … a sort of suburban gulag', and the writer notes how 'the high school hallways here look familiar from countless John Hughes films, but Hartley pounces on precisely what Hughes leaves out' (ibid.). The location or setting is foregrounded in the title, first sentence, or paragraph of many reviews: 'absorbing suburban-angst nightmare' (Howe 1991); 'Surreal gem brings lost suburban souls to life' (Aird 1992a); 'Cool, deadpan comedy charts teen angst in suburbia', 'hermetic Long Island town' (Griffin 1991); 'a peculiarly un-photogenic part of Long Island' (S. French 1991); 'the backdrop is the suburban hinterland of America, a characterless area of Long Island' (Perry 1991b); 'domestic saga about the hellish burden imposed on two troubled young people … in the seemingly placid environment of Lindenhurst' (Knelman 1991).

Beyond the mere identification and description of suburbia, the critics are eager to both identify the contrast between the assumed promises and virtue of American suburban life and Hartley's attitude towards it. For his part, Hartley describes in his conversations with Kenneth Kaleta how he was reading a lot of Molière and Victor Hugo when working on his early films, so it's likely his perspective on contemporary

American culture was influenced by sources a bit broader than John Hughes films or television sitcoms, offered up at various points in time as points of contrast by critics (see Hartley and Kaleta 2008: 44).[3] Regardless of where the inspiration came from, the suburbia of Hal Hartley for critics becomes conflated with a kind of cynicism and lack of forward movement that came to more generally represent the so-called 'slacker' generation.

This generic suburban 'regionality' is then further abstracted to represent locations much more disparate and encompassing than Lindenhurst, particularly by critics who live outside the United States. One Australian critic clearly was not looking at a map when he observed of *Trust*, 'This is suburban, middle America, flat, stark, and apparently empty' (Crayford 1991). Other critics were not as geographically off the mark, but still tended to extrapolate beyond the actual location of the film. *Trust*, writes one British reviewer, is 'about what boils away underneath the skin of your average suburban American', hailing Hartley as 'the kind of filmmaker you get in America only once or twice in a generation' (Malcolm 1991b). 'Though the characters and their families are extreme examples', writes one Canadian reviewer, 'they are people who could come from any town or suburb' (Saxburg 1991). Another Canadian reviewer writes:

> Hartley's style is such a jumble that at one moment his psychological insights seem embarrassingly amateurish, and at the next you feel you're catching a completely fresh glimpse of the soul of Middle America. The film has the look of a completely predictable TV series unfolding in suburban living rooms and kitchens of stupefying banality, yet it has the excitement of complete unpredictability. (Knelman 1991)

Reviewers of *Trust* repeatedly locate Hartley's strength as a director with his ability to guide his eccentric characters who are 'drifting in the abyss of anomie' that is associated with 'the suburban shuffle' (Aird 1992b), as one critic wrote.

There is one other location that is frequently associated with Hartley's first two films: over a dozen separate reviews out of fifty found for *The Unbelievable Truth* and *Trust* mention either the television series *Twin Peaks* or the show's co-creator, filmmaker David Lynch. Although the series only aired for two seasons (a total of thirty episodes), it was a cultural phenomenon for several months after its debut on CBS in April 1990. With *Truth* receiving its commercial release three months later, and *Trust* debuting at the Toronto Film Festival that fall, Hartley's films, set in an eccentric and oppressive 'small town' populated by highly stylised characters with unexpectedly complex and darkly comic ways of thinking and speaking, became one of many easy points of comparison that caused a *Twin Peaks*-effect on contemporary criticism for a time. 'Quirkiness' of some sort – particularly the kind that had sympathy for misfit characters trying to get by in a somewhat crazy world exemplified by a small town or community – also found expression in highly successful (but now curiously invisible) television series such as *Northern Exposure* and *Picket Fences*, the Coen Brothers' *Raising Arizona* (1987), and later in early films by Wes Anderson,

Alexander Payne, Spike Jonze and others. At the time, it seemed, Hartley was in tune with this particular cultural perspective, which may have indicated that he was, by some measure, a 'commercial' filmmaker, or at least one with commercial potential.

'A Genre to Himself': Simple Men and Hartley vs. 'Hartley'

> My work has changed as my circumstances have changed. I don't live in the suburbs anymore, I'm in my thirties and I'm not a struggling, hungry filmmaker. The kinds of hopes and fears I have are different. That seems to be the cornerstone on which my creativity exists – trying to maintain freshness. To avoid presumption. Not taking for granted the experiences and the mysteries. You have to keep searching out and trying to pinpoint and be awake to the mystery that is life. (McKay 1993)

> 'I seem to have become the emblem for successful independent films in the United States,' he said during what he promised was the last interview for *Simple Men* in North America before doing many *Simple Men* interviews in Europe. 'For some reason, I represent more than what I am, more than what the films are. There are pressures, but they have shifted recently ... Now there's a little bit more money and visibility, so the pressures go to other things. Like accounting and publicizing.' (Griffin 1992)

It's important to keep in mind that for Hartley, at least at the time of the interview quoted above, being 'the emblem for successful independent films' was likely something he recognised as problematic, and indicative of an ambivalence about 'success' (often coded as 'Hollywood'). More problematic, perhaps, is the recognition that anyone who considered Hartley 'successful' was using a very low standard. *The Unbelievable Truth* had managed to earn a little more than $500,000 at the US box office; *Trust*, with a budget ten times that of the first film, earned less, officially just over $356,000.[4] *Simple Men*, with an estimated budget of $3 million, would make less than half of what *Trust* made. Hartley's 'success' was purely critical, and in public discourse he was thus playing to a very limited audience of film experts with shifting critical standards.[5]

Previous critical frameworks remain in place, but focus often has shifted. For example, connections to David Lynch and other articulations of the place of Hartley's films continued in the reviews of *Simple Men*. Typical is this extended interview/analysis of Hartley's films (which runs to nearly 1,300 words) from an Australian outlet:

> Unlike certain other would-be-auteurs, though, he didn't try to out-weird David Lynch in highlighting the hallucinatory nature of everyday America.
>
> His town wasn't an obvious clone of Lumberton and *Twin Peaks*, or even their self-consciously quirky offspring, *Northern Exposure*'s Cicely, Alaska. It was Hartleyville and nowhere else and we, too, were at home there.
>
> Long Island once again provides the setting for the new Hartley film,

> *Simple Men*, which has all the ingredients followers of his work have come to expect and enjoy. (Cremen 1993)

However, for some critics – notably some of the same critics who had offered praise of Hartley's earlier work – the setting and tone of *Simple Men* represented a step backwards. Rita Kempley of the *Washington Post* opens her review with:

> Like the populations of TV towns Twin Peaks and Cicely, Alaska, the inhabitants of filmmaker Hal Hartley's Long Island are more apt to be Proust-conversant felons than the average Joe. So it comes as no surprise that the 'Simple Men' of Hartley's third film are, at least to his way of thinking, supposed to be deep and mysterious. The truth is they really are as simple as sheep, tiresomely quirky relics of '80s alienation and its spawn, northern Gothic film noir. (1992)

By the time of *Simple Men*'s US release in October 1992, *Twin Peaks* had been off the air for nearly a year, having worn out its novelty and ultimately losing viewers and critical cachet following the May 1992 release of *Twin Peaks: Fire Walk with Me*, a critical and box-office failure. It is thus possible that Hartley's 'quirky' tone, previously so connected in critical discourse to the influence of the Lynch series, now grated critics, who seemed to expect more from Hartley on his third effort, a film that had a bigger budget and secured distribution through Fine Line Features, a high-profile distributor of independent films and a division of a much larger (and rapidly expanding) indie distributor, New Line Cinema.

The discussion of the production value and expectations about the film are also reflected in the continuing association with the setting of the previous films. *Simple Men*, of course, was not actually shot on Long Island, so the location did not literally 'provide the setting' for the movie. The film was shot in Texas, which, in the early 1990s under Governor Ann Richards, was particularly friendly to independent filmmakers and a 'right-to-work' state. Both Hartley and the film's producers, all of whom had offices in New York and understandably did not want to cause much of a stir with professional union colleagues, asked that the film's production location not be discussed (and it is not relevant to the content of the film itself).

Hartley is on the record in many interviews about his concern about union regulations that were changing in the early 1990s as the 'indie' film scene became a bit more professional (and Hartley was able to command larger budgets, modest though they may have been compared to a studio film). 'I felt the added costs of making union films would itself prevent me from being able to finance the kinds of films that were, in fact, successful', he said to Kenneth Kaleta. Significantly, the lesson Hartley draws from this is one that seems to indicate his ultimate path as an independent filmmaker. 'I felt like I was being penalized for making the mistake of becoming marginally popular. It was as if the world were telling me I should have been totally popular or totally unpopular' (2008: 49). This is echoed throughout the many interviews Hartley gave at the time of the release of *Simple Men* (by which point he was already preparing *Amateur*, announced with an international movie star, Isabelle Huppert, as part of the cast): 'A Firm No Thanks to Hollywood' (Cremen 1993); 'This Director's Wish List Doesn't Include Hollywood' (Pall 1992); 'Despite the post-*Truth* nibbles from Hollywood, Hartley doesn't expect to be working for the majors anytime soon' (Wilner 1992).

But the overwhelming majority of the reviews of *Simple Men* mostly evaluated the film as if it were an extension of Hartley's previous two features.[6] Of the twenty-eight reviews and articles about *Simple Men* examined in detail for this chapter that were written at the time of the film's release, all but one – an extremely negative review less than a paragraph long – make qualitative mention of and comparison to the earlier films (see McQueen 1993). At times, this comparison was a positive one, indicating that Hartley's style had grown, progressed, developed or shown some sign of 'maturity'. 'Both at one with his previous work and a significant step beyond it, Hal Hartley's "Simple Men" is a beautifully realized American art film', enthused Todd McCarthy of *Variety*, the industry trade publication that considers film reviews as a means of assessing a film's commercial viability as well as artistic merit. 'Pic is too rarified to break out commercially', McCarthy acknowledges, 'but it is a natural for fests and specialized venues' (1992). Chris Peachment of the *Independent* (UK) noted that '*Trust* had a lot of damaged people in it ... his new film is called *Simple Men*, and there is a lot less damage in it ... it is not hard to see a healing process at work, thanks to the agency of the good women in it' (1992).[7] Caryn James continued to express her delight with Hartley's work, as her opening paragraph indicates:

> In 'Simple Men,' Hal Hartley's hilariously droll third feature, deadpan dialogue becomes a philosophy of life. The 32-year-old writer-director has been heading there all along, with 'The Unbelievable Truth' and 'Trust' both critical hits on their way to gaining cultish followings. But his new film offers the purest, funniest view yet of the Hartley world, a place where dialogue is everything though disaster is imminent, where characters speak with utter conviction but drop-dead cool. There isn't much space for naturalism as the actors dance on some imaginary line between the banal and the deep. (1992)

Other critics merely use similarities between plots, characters and performers to demonstrate their understanding of *Simple Men* by reiterating their understanding of *Trust* and *The Unbelievable Truth*. 'Like his two previous movies, *Simple Men* is rooted in a family that has already been bent beyond the breaking point' (Harris 1992); 'Like Hartley's other two movies ... *Simple Men* has a rhythm all its own. Like that. Or this. Drives some people crazy' (Dunphy 1992); 'The key to Hartley's appeal may lie in his reassuringly familiar touches: the asynchrounous conversations, the bits of physical business ... and recurring characters ... Hartley uses these devices in every film to present wholly new material' (Wilner 1992).

A seemingly equal number of critics, however, used the same framework to discredit *Simple Men*. *New York Times* critic Vincent Canby, then the 'senior' critic at the paper who had not reviewed either of Hartley's previous two films, was particularly dismissive. The film 'is even less about real life than was his amusingly diffident "Trust"... "Simple Men" is mannered in the terrifically knowing way of someone who has looked too long at the movies of others' (1992). Most of Canby's review then reads *Simple Men* in comparison to Jean-Luc Godard's *A Woman is a Woman* (1961), finding the Hartley effort pale in comparison, even claiming that Michael Spiller's cinematography 'appear[s] to have learned a lot from Raoul Coutard, Mr. Godard's favorite cameraman for years' (ibid.). *USA Today*'s Mike Clark gave the film two out of four stars, calling Hartley 'the most self-consciously monotonous U.S. filmmaker since the late Jack Webb', noting that Martin Donovan, '*Trust*'s testy hero, has only a cameo here', and that the other characters 'are likewise on simmer, and at time the film threatens to vanish from the screen' (1992). Desson Howe of the *Washington Post*, like his colleague Rita Kempley (quoted above), sounds like a disappointed fan. 'This time around, in "Simple Men", nothing works anymore. Everything that was funny is dull and tiresome. The earlier movies worked in offbeat counterpoint to meandering storylines. This movie is all zestless cacophony' (Howe 1992).

Remarkably, in the same body of reviews, nearly half of them contain a critical disclaimer to the reader that communicates something along the lines of 'getting' how Hartley works – as if describing Hartley's newest film was simply a matter of liking or disliking the previous ones. This disclaimer is in both positive and negative reviews of the film. 'Hartley's anti-realist film-making style, deadpan line delivery, cyclical dialogue, stylised gestures and text-book theories on love and romance, will not woo everyone' (Gillespie 1994); 'If all of the above sounds too fey by half, this film may not be for you' (Hutchinson 1993); 'With a Hartley film, you know what you'll get – paradoxically that means unpredictable characters musing in unpredictable ways' (Lowing 1993); 'It will make Hartley fans happy, but it's certainly not for everyone' (Aird 1992b); 'Unpredictable and unaccountably charming – and exactly what we've come to expect from Hartley' (Dunphy 1992); 'If you're on Hartley's wavelength ... you'll relish *Simple Men*. Otherwise, you'll probably feel like you're on a journey to nowhere' (Harris 1992). Caryn James, even noting what she considers growth and a realisation of Hartley's potential in *Simple Men*, actually concludes her review with 'More than with most filmmakers, you get him or you don't' (1992).

One critic seemed to cut the baby in half when he observed, of a film that he accused of drifting 'into tedium': 'Hartley's third feature ... should appeal to people who like highly stylized and apparently innovative comedy – and who have not seen the previous films by this young American writer-director' (Jillett 1993). Hartley's work reached a critical paradox: when you see it, if you get it, you'll like it, but then when you see it again, you might not. Hal Hartley films are not films – they are novelties, one like the other, and an acquired taste at that.

Hartley had indeed, then, become to this critical community – the only community that seemed to have any interest in watching and talking about his films – a 'genre unto himself', as he described in an Australian interview. It's fascinating how Hartley uses a critical term – appropriated as a 'publicity' angle – to identify himself not as an auteur, but as a genre, something bound by convention:

Hartley's real trademark, however, is his dialogue. Terse, elliptical, at times brutally honest, it is so unmistakably his own that he occasionally runs the danger of self-parody:

> I actually coined the term 'genre of myself' in the publicity for *The Unbelievable Truth*. But to me that's a commonplace in the history of art. I mean, hell, Michelangelo was a genre of himself. So was John Ford.
>
> To me, the important thing is to follow the integrity of your vision, whatever it may be, the particular inquisitiveness that you have, rather than simply turning out product that simply fits the existing market.
>
> When I got out of film school, I'd ask whatever industry professional happened to be around for advice – as you tend to do when you're starting out – and most of them told me I'd never get anywhere. Because my work did things that they saw as preclusive to acceptance by audiences. Things like idiosyncrasy, a lack of immediate understanding with the text, deliberate obscurity.
>
> And I said, 'No, I'm not getting rid of them. Those are the things I'm going to base my work on.' (Danielsen 1993)

The mixed-to-negative reviews and poor public reaction to *Simple Men* were not the end of Hartley's career, obviously: *Amateur* would earn better returns, but vex critics who no longer had the familiar Long Island setting to cling to, as well as the presence of Isabelle Huppert alongside the Hartley 'regulars'. *Flirt* (1995) was a formal experiment, and ultimately *Henry Fool* would be the only Hartley film to earn more than a million dollars at the box-office. But it is clear that by the time of the release of *Simple Men*, Hartley himself could sense that he would not be forging a path alongside his peers in the independent filmmaking community, most of whom have maintained much closer ties to the mainstream film industry. However, like Hartley, many of these directors also have been widely misunderstood, had disappointing films, and openly expressed hostility towards the industry – and yet they remain much more culturally viable and visible. Few people remember Steven Soderbergh's second, third and fourth films (*Kafka* [1991], *King of the Hill* [1993], *The Underneath* [1995]) which cumulatively earned less than $3 million at the box office. Linklater's *Dazed and Confused* is well-remembered, but barely made back its budget, and his subsequent 'studio' films culminated in the big-budget *The Newton Boys* (1998), which only earned $10 million of its reported $30 million budget. But Linklater, Soderbergh and other 'indie' phenoms of Hartley's era who have maintained active careers, still have their work discussed, rereleased on video to much fanfare, and occasionally nominated for a big award. Like Hartley, both of those directors also embraced new technology early: *Dazed and Confused* was one of the first features edited with a non-linear editing system, while *Waking Life* (2001) and *A Scanner Darkly* (2006) use new digital animation techniques; Soderbergh was one of the first 'Hollywood' directors to embrace digital cameras with smaller projects such as *Full Frontal* (2002) and *The Girlfriend Experience* (2009); and both have also created materials directly for streaming and digital distribution.

But reflecting on the sameness of Hartley's early films – or at least how the critics and industry understood that sameness – it's easy to see how misguided were the attempts to define Hartley as an auteur, as a style, as a genre; to fix him as if he were as static, flat and cerebrally 'rooted' as his films and characters seemed to be. As he moves away from Long Island, as his 'ensemble' of actors becomes a bit more flexible (the 'type' of the leading man becomes more important than whether or not the part is played by Martin Donovan), as his creativity and reflection turns more towards nuanced and emotional human behaviour, the 'quirkiness' of the early films, so connected to a particular cultural framework of the era, make it look like Hal Hartley was going to become a Woody Allen-type director – always making these kinds of films about these kinds of people. While there's no question that Hartley has remained very true to his aesthetic, it has not contained him or fixed him in the way we all expected, which makes his later, and his less seen work, perhaps all the more remarkable.

Kenneth Kaleta states:

> Hartley has tried to observe his time and place so as to portray accurately their qualities in a way that will continue to resonate after that time and place have been outlived or replaced by other trends. This often sets him at odds with the popular culture, while at times allowing him to exist comfortably within it. Thus, neither critical nor audience acceptance of his films is necessarily germane to his process. (Hartley and Kaleta 2008: 11)

From the perspective of Hartley's later career, Kaleta seems spot-on, but I do want to argue that the critical discourse surrounding his films (the only 'audience' that Hartley seemed to have) was at least partially responsible for Hartley's attitude towards how he made the films he made, and why he made them. In defining himself, in fixing himself through his films, Hartley actually broke his connection to mainstream film culture, the business of critics, audiences and expectations. As he found his way towards a higher international profile, short filmmaking, new technologies, and a broader pallet as a creative artist, Hartley ultimately found a much more interesting and fascinating version of success. That break towards the truly 'independent' filmmaker route (rather than the 'co-dependent' career strategies of some of his peers) would not have happened without Hartley's strident commitment to his style in the face of ongoing and shifting critical resistance.

Notes

1 A longer version of this study would include an extended discussion on readings of these films as products of an ensemble of talent, as reviews consistently connect the actors and crew from one Hartley film to another. Actors also frequently gave interviews promoting the films, further framing Hartley's creative process and contributing to the discourse and identity of Hartley as a distinctive, auteurist talent.
2 Similarly, three major London outlets included a one-paragraph review of *Truth* at the end of a much longer review of another film: see Perry, *Sunday Times*,

January 1991; Malcolm, *Guardian Weekly*, January 1991; French, *Observer*, January 1991.
3   Hartley acknowledged this to Kaleta: 'Cynicism often seems to be the greatest argument for not acting', he agrees, when Kaleta characterises the cynicism of characters in Hartley's early films as 'the inability to act' (2008: 44).
4   By way of comparison, Richard Linklater's *Slacker* earned over $1.2 million in 1991; *sex, lies and videotape* had set the standard, earning over $24 million.
5   Publically available budget and box-office revenue, in this case courtesy of boxofficemojo.com, is only a partial measure of a film's 'bottom line' value. In many cases in the early 1990s (not just with Hartley), films had their budgets covered through pre-arranged home video and foreign distribution sales. The numbers here only intended to reflect general public reaction. Additionally, Hartley's films were only released in a few major cities, never on more than a few dozen screens: even in such a case, the per-screen average would have been considered disappointing.
6   A few reviews also mention *Surviving Desire*, which had aired on PBS's 'American Playhouse,' but the most qualitative comments and points of comparison were *The Unbelievable Truth* and *Trust*.
7   This is one of the few mentions of the film that indicates a more complex reading of gender than was offered by Hartley's first two films.

CHAPTER FOUR

The Locality of Hal Hartley: The Aesthetics and Business of Smallness

Steven Rawle

From the Lindenhurst settings of Hal Hartley's early Long Island films, 'the local' has been a key concern in his work. Even though his later work flirts with international locations, in films such as *Amateur* (1994), *No Such Thing* (2001), *The Girl from Monday* (2005) and especially *Fay Grim* (2006, with Berlin standing in for parts of Queens), the aesthetic of Hartley's work has, for the most part, remained singularly defined and local. This essay will explore the aspect of 'being local' (to use Hartley's words) in some of Hartley's later work, especially the second *Possible Films* collection of short films (2010, comprising *The Apologies, Implied Harmonies, Adventure, Accomplice* and *A/Muse*) and *Meanwhile* (2012), a short feature intended only for the small screen. I will argue that Hartley's local approach to locations (including shooting in his own apartment and offices), space and theme is one that spans this collection of experimental work, even though the productions are separated by Hartley's time in Berlin and New York.

In many regards, the local is defined as obsessively small or limited, which allows Hartley to explore themes relating to personal interaction (*Meanwhile*), obsession (*A/Muse*) and artistic production (a theme that runs throughout Hartley's oeuvre, from *Flirt* [1995] onwards). Hartley's locality speaks to his industrial situation as a filmmaker on the margins of the independent sector, as well as to his approach to space and place in his work (the locales of Berlin and New York), and the creative production methodology employed in the films made between 2009 and 2012. Despite being made on either side of the Atlantic, the films embrace the same basic creative strategy of being specifically local or small, and this approach has a strong impact on the films' themes and aesthetic. While the short films are rough, the longer *Meanwhile* is bright in high definition (shot on a prosumer DSLR), although none of the films employ moving cameras – they are statically shot, yet dynamically performed. This period in his career sees a further move toward the low- and micro-budget end of the independent sector, a relatively small business practice in relation to his career in the 1990s and early 2000s when his work was distributed by the specialty wings of Disney, Sony and MGM.

Consequently, this essay will explore Hartley's development as a guardedly (perhaps obsessively) independent filmmaker, his move away from the Indiewood sector and growing reliance on crowdfunding to fund new work, as he has done for the DVD release of *Meanwhile* and the production of *Ned Rifle* (2014). The local is a defining feature of Hartley's approach to both the aesthetic and business of filmmaking. Crowdfunding situates Hartley in close proximity to his audience, and extends the locality of the content into the production of his recent work and its distribution. This methodology and aesthetic positions Hartley in a particular place in relation to the development of independent cinema – even as the studios have gobbled up indie production and distribution – and shows how more marginal and artistic voices outside the mainstream continue to remain relevant with their audiences and how digital technology is connecting them to streams of funding and distribution. Perhaps paradoxically, the local is here also being enabled by the transnational.

* * *

In his book *The Cinema of Hal Hartley*, Sebastian Manley discusses the thematic and visual situation of Hartley's work within the regional terrain of Long Island and parts of New York City. In the 'Long Island trilogy' comprising *The Unbelievable Truth* (1989), *Trust* (1990) and *Simple Men* (1992), Manley contends, the 'setting of Long Island offers a secure and distinct regional identity that serves to ground the films in the familiar, connecting the worlds of the films to the "real" world' (2013: 25). The focus on regional identity, place and cultural sensibility is extended throughout Hartley's career, even into the films that range beyond the regional specificity of Long Island:

> A sense of regional particularity is combined in many of Hartley's mid-career and later films with a sense of the mobile, globalized character of modern life. In emphasizing travel, internationalism and broad social issues, films such as *Amateur*, *No Such Thing*, *Accomplice* and particularly *Fay Grim* position themselves at a distance from Hartley's critically admired Long Island-set features, which frequently emphasize small communities and family drama. They also position themselves at a distance from the majority of European or foreign-themed indie films, in which identifiably international elements are balanced, or outweighed, by identifiably American elements. (2013: 192)

Manley's description of Hartley's blending of regional identities and elements (one might use Koichi Iwabuchi's [2002] term 'cultural odors') with global sensibilities demonstrates the continuing pull towards the 'local' in his work. The 'regional particularity' is often apparent in Hartley's distinctive style of writing, evident from his debut feature but also present in those films that move away from the small town milieu praised in those early films (particularly outside the US). In many cases this would sit with Deborah Shaw's definition of transnational cinemas that feature 'films with multiple locations' but that don't necessarily engage with politics of globalisation (2013: 55). *Fay Grim* is Hartley's most transnational film in this regard, with multiple locations across France, Germany and Turkey, with some pick-up shots in New York (the majority of the Queens-set sequences were shot in Berlin). The regional features of Hartley's work, for Manley, are part of their defining aspects, something that strongly connects his work with place and theme, even where their internationalising aspects pull them away from the more traditional centres of his work. Rather than the regionalist aspects of Hartley's work explored by Manley, my analysis suggests that the later works of Hartley are more micro in their turn toward a locality. This turn to the 'micro' is a factor in Hartley's recent production methodologies, as well as his shift away from more traditional centres of independent film finance and distribution (enabled by digital video shooting and editing) but also in newer methods of e-commerce, such as crowdfunding, with which Hartley has experimented, alongside traditional methods of distributing work though established independent companies.

The Business of Smallness

Hartley's work from the late 1980s to the mid-2000s relied on global networks of financing (from the UK to Germany and Japan, as well as the US) and the power of independent distributors such as Miramax, Sony Pictures Classics and United Artists. His more recent work has drawn on alternative means of finance, such as the digital aggregator New Media (see Harris 2012), as well as Kickstarter to crowdfund the DVD release of *Meanwhile* and the subsequent production of *Ned Rifle*. While *Ned Rifle* was also partly subsidised by a more traditional sale of international rights to Fortissimo at the Cannes film festival in May 2013 (see Brzeski 2013),[1] Hartley largely rejected theatrical exhibition – after premiering at the Toronto film festival in 2014, it opened day-and-date on 1 April 2015 with a roadshow launch (led by screenings at the IFC Center in New York), and simultaneously on Vimeo On Demand (see McNary 2014):[2]

> 'Following an exclusive 60-day window through the HalHartley.com/Vimeo portal, an aggregator like Cinedigm can get it on to Netflix and Fandor and all these platforms,' explained Hartley [to *Indiewire*]. 'So the whole paradigm has shifted and it makes a lot more sense for a producer right now.' (Bernstein 2014)

The paradigm Hartley mentions has been characterised by Geoff King as 'Indie 2.0'. In his book of same name, King argues that while independent American cinema is seeing a number of continuities with previous incarnations of independent film, the discursive formation of that independence is changing. Indie 2.0 sees 'a tightening and simplification of the film-value chain, a reduction in the number of stages and intermediaries that exist between the initial and subsequent windows through which any particular production might move during its release' (2014: 86). King also mentions Hartley within this tightening, as a 'well-established indie filmmaker … whose work has remained more commercially marginal' (2014: 115), and also discusses his earlier establishment of the Possible Films website to sell and promote his work. As Hartley mentions in an interview with *Variety*, this website is part of an attempt to remain independent: 'One can never be independent enough' (McNary 2014). This implicates traditional discursive notions of independent cinema, opposed to mainstream sensibilities and commercial interests, although as Hartley has mentioned, there is positive commercial value in the filmmaker pursuing these methods, as there is less risk for the producer in assuming the burden of debt (see Bernstein 2014).

Hartley's retention of his independence is core to the adoption of Indie 2.0 methods in 'hybrid distribution' and in funding. As he has commented:

> It's … doing the business of being an artist that changes. Being an artist doesn't change. Probably the significant thing is, you know, I think of myself as an artist rather than an entertainment professional really. When I call myself an entertainment professional I'm admitting something obvious, but it feels less to the point I learn more about how to cultivate my audience and keep them alert from my artist friends, people who are painters, choreographers, small theatre companies, people who are much more obviously outside the commercial industry. (2011)

The situation of his artistic creativity is here defined in local terms ('my artist friends'), at the margins of contemporary commercial art. What is also critical here is the discussion of 'cultivating' the audience. While Hartley has a significant audience base from his prominent indie authorship in the 1990s – something exploited in his crowdfunding efforts (alongside industry connections in the list of backers for his projects) – audience development that sustains the 'alertness' of the audience to respond to developments in his work is largely carried out on the substantially global platforms of Facebook and Twitter, in trade publications like *Variety* and *Indiewire*, and through traditional press outlets in the form of reviews from limited exposure at festivals. Where hybrid distribution methods are employed this might involve a combination of methods (reviews and interviews shared on social media, for instance). While this might happen on global platforms, the address is often local, particularly to audiences in cities in which limited runs might be happening, as with the *Ned Rifle* release.

What emerges here is the sense of a scale of business that positions Hartley much closer to the micro- and low-budget end of the independent cinema scale. This is just one end of a scale described by Yannis Tzioumakis as 'heterogeneous and polyphonic', a description that sees contemporary American independent cinema in 'another transitional period' (2013: 39) (although we might argue with Tzioumakis here that independent cinema has always been in a period of transition, despite his attempt to situate it on a spectrum of 'Independent', 'Indie' and 'Indiewood' as defined steps along the way to a mature independent sector of distributors and production companies, many of whom are associated with Hollywood majors). Hartley's career is defined largely by his association with the 'Indie' period of the 1990s, following the crossover success of Soderbergh's *sex, lies and videotape* (1989), a period defined by its plurality of voices drawn from 'the margins of the industry' (2013: 35), and by key distributors such as Fine Line and Sony Pictures Classics, both of whom distributed Hartley's work (including what Tzioumakis describes as the 'now-celebrated canonical "indie"' *Trust*) (2013: 33). There is a scene in *Meanwhile* in which the protagonist Joe (DJ Mendel) meets a formerly renowned author (Stephen Ellis) in a bar in Midtown Manhattan. Joe expresses his admiration for the author's work, and asks when he had his first success (32, the author says), and how he is still living off it. Hartley comments that:

> The conversation with the author in the bar, which is the film's centre – actually geographically the centre of the movie too – that really came out of conversations I had with DJ. We'd often talk about early times in my career: he'd say, 'You had what we want. You had your day in the sun. Everybody wants that. I've never had that.' (2011)

While Hartley has denied that the film is in any way autobiographical (ibid.), there is a clear analogy between the successes of the young author and the film's writer-director (Hartley was 32 around the time of *Simple Men*'s release, his third feature), especially when we consider Hartley's location at the margins of the independent sector. While he has achieved significant critical success (especially outside the US, in France and Poland particularly), his voice never developed significant commercial appeal. Because Hartley identifies himself as an artist, there is an appeal to outsiderhood, to a marginal community of artists, choreographers and theatre practitioners (from which he has drawn a number of collaborators, including Mendel and David Neumann, a choreographer with whom Hartley has worked a number of times). This fits with Michael Z. Newman's image of independent cinema's appeal to autonomous alternatives: 'In independent music and movies, the ideal of separation is most often figured as autonomy, as the power artists retain to control their creative process. Autonomy, in turn, is seen as a guarantee of authenticity' (2009: 19). This separation, which is both geographical (although Hartley still remains close to the New York centres of independent cinema) and ideological, positions Hartley away from the mainstream. The proximity of his films to his audience (just a click away, as a participant and consumer) protects this 'guarantee of authenticity', as Hartley's voice retains its independence, free from the perceived taint of commercial pressure. The smallness of Hartley's business practice is a source of autonomy (his comments about remaining free of debt through crowdfunding) as well as direct interface with his audience. Hartley indeed might share similarities with the author in *Meanwhile*, in drawing on the successes of his past (and thereby sharing in independent cinema's more conventional 'deployment of authorship' [Tzioumakis 2012: 8]), and the access it grants him to an established audience base, locally and globally.

As Ethan R. Mollick has shown, there is a local dynamic to crowdfunding in the US, in that, as he and others argue, 'the underlying success of creative endeavors is dependent on the characteristics of the location of the founders' (2014: 10). Geographic studies of successful and unsuccessful projects show that a 'proportionally greater creative population was associated with a greater chance of success for founders' (ibid.). Mollick's mapping of Kickstarter projects demonstrates that the chance of success for such projects is increased depending on the location of the originator. He charts projects by media type (art, comics, dance, design, fashion, film, games, music and so on) and their proportion by location, as well as the proportion of successful and unsuccessful projects by location. Projects tend to group by city and in accordance with the already established creative industries in those cities. Hence, there is a higher proportion of music projects in Nashville (over 75% of all Nashville-based projects are in music), of games and design in San Francisco (over 50% combined), of design projects in Portland (approximately 40%), whereas New York and Los Angeles show the highest proportion of film projects (approximately 40% and over 50% respectively). Mollick therefore demonstrates that crowdfunding is highly location specific, despite the tendency to see crowdfunding in more transnational terms. The traffic for Kickstarter's site (according to Quantcast [2013] statistics for December 2013)[3] reports around twelve and a half million unique hits during the month, with around half of those coming from inside the US, approximately two million from Canada, Australia, Germany and the UK (who Quantcast separate from the rest of the world), and another four million global unique hits. While it has not been possible to map donations to Hartley's campaigns, there is a suggestion that the project is highly reliant both on local factors (Hartley's membership of a New York-based independent cinema community) and on transnational factors (his global fan base, as well as contacts in the world cinema industry). However, this is also reliant, as Mollick states, on the strength of social networks that determine the likelihood or failure of a crowdfunding campaign on Kickstarter:

> social network size predict[s] success, though they use a restricted sample, since not all founders had linked Facebook accounts. For the sake of interpretation of [these] results, consider an average project holding all other variables at their mean, and considering only projects that have linked Facebook accounts with non-zero numbers of friends (about 1/3 of all projects) in order to include all covariates. To take an average project in the Film category, a founder with 10 Facebook friends would have a 9% chance of succeeding, one with 100 friends would have a 20% chance of success, and one with 1000 friends would have a 40% chance of success. (2014: 8)

At time of writing, Hartley's Facebook network numbers well over 10,000, with 4,925 'friends' on one account, and another 5,935 'followers' on a Possible Films page (we have to assume a high degree of overlap between the two accounts).[4] There are also another 3,000 followers for the @possiblefilms account on Twitter (again we have to assume a degree of overlap with the Facebook audience). These numbers tally with Mollick's conclusions regarding the chances of success in relation to the size of social networks. While the numbers are relatively low for social connectivity for a major filmmaker (Spike Lee, who has also crowdfunded a feature, has an official page with over 408,000 followers, although more recent indie filmmakers such as Joe Swanberg and Andrew Bujalski number well under 1,000), the numbers demonstrate the cultivation of an audience online, as Hartley has mentioned. This is an important factor in the development of his authenticity and the connection with other artistic communities, rather than the connection with bigger entertainment industries.

The Do-It-With-Others (DIWO) (King 2014: 89) approach to funding and audience cultivation adopted by Hartley (although there are strong elements of the Do-It-Yourself [DIY] approach in the use of the Possible Films website to self-distribute work) developed from prior attempts to self-distribute *The Unbelievable Truth* on home video, which was languishing in the Disney catalogue due to its prior ownership by Miramax (despite a 2001 Anchor Bay DVD release):

> When I started thinking about Kickstarter was because I bought the rights to *The Unbelievable Truth* back from the Disney organisation, who had the home video rights for North America. They had three more years of a license, and told me that they had no intention of doing anything with the film in those three years. So I said, 'let's talk and I'll buy back the rights, because I think I can make money with it.' So, I asked myself, 'is that true?' How much are they going to charge me, and can I make my money back? So, Kyle Gilman asked me to put it on the newsletter: 'we've got several thousand people on the newsletter, subscribers to this site, put a question up there: how many of you would spend $40 for a brand new redone *Unbelievable Truth* DVD?' And thousands of people got back to us, and said 'yeah, I'd spend $40 for that. Is it going to have new artwork, new pictures?' Yes. And we went 'yeah, we'll make it as cool as we possible can, cool and new.' And, then, based on that, you just do that math, and we said 'alright, if I could get the rights for a certain amount of money … you stand a good chance of doing good business with this. And then, so we went through that, and said 'I think this is what Kickstarter is about'. (Hartley 2011)

This strategy fits strongly with the notion of separation discussed by Newman as a signifier of autonomy. Although $40 was a high price point for a DVD, the offer of added value in the form of remastered print, new artwork, additional extras like making-of and retrospective documentaries, as well the direct route to the filmmaker (a form of what Dana Polan [2001] has termed 'auteur desire', the need for the cinephile to get close to the origins of a work – here that desire is more about consumption than about the desire to *know* the work), are attractive features. Also notable is Hartley's ability to bypass the traditional layers and filters of the indie sector to connect with audiences more directly (and thereby to benefit more from the work without the intermediary):

> All my career I've had distributors and the whole three tier system of publicists, distributors, sales agents, everyone telling me who my audience was, and depending on how good or bad their business was from my film, it would always change. ... Now I feel like I have a real, direct line to these people. (2011)

Despite Hartley's comment in another interview that the Kickstarter method 'has a lot in common with the way I used to finance my films in the '90s' (Marvar 2011),[5] the DIY (facilitated, he says, 'when fulfilment got a lot cheaper' [Hartley 2011]) and DIWO methods allow the filmmaker to skip the previous filters of independent (and Indiewood) distribution. Returning to Newman's conception, this acts to confirm Hartley's autonomy, as well as to act as a marker of authenticity and 'true indieness' (Brandon Harris uses the term 'Truly DIY') so prized in independent cultures.

During the crowdfunding campaign for *Ned Rifle*, Hartley made an unusual offer to bypass theatrical distribution altogether, citing that the majority of his films' income comes from video on demand and home video. As rewards, he offered the theatrical distribution rights to a number of international territories (this was after the sale to Fortissimo had already been announced). Hartley again used the offer to position himself in relation to the margins of the independent film industry. In a message to backers, he stated:

> I'm drawn to crowd-funding exactly because of how sensible it is for certain types of effort. (I'm still not certain my *Ned Rifle* effort is exactly right, but I'm willing to risk it.) I'm not trying to 'buck the system' or throw a wrench into the works of the established film distribution business. I've had great experiences with companies in that business. I just have come to think (as I thought at the start of my career) that there are exciting marginal streams that exist on the boundaries of the mainstream and they almost constitute different businesses. By temperament, I've always felt more in tune with those marginal streams. (2013a)

Deliberately positioning himself at the margins, Hartley's practice parallels that of other artists, including small theatre companies. This a classification reminiscent of Michael Newman's description of the independent scene as 'Off-Hollywood' (2011: 13), in the margins of the dominant indie scene. It appeals to the smallness of scale in much of Hartley's recent business practice, and functions also as an admission that his films' niche appeal no longer has a place theatrically (like that of many independent filmmakers in the lower-budget sector).

The offer of distribution rights through the Kickstarter campaign for *Ned Rifle* was controversial. For $9,000 ('600 tickets sold at $15:00 each' [Hartley 2013a]) the backer could

> Become the theatrical distributor (only in movie theaters and other public venues) of *Ned Rifle* in the United States of America for 7 years. Make money

with it or not, it's up to you. All income you receive from theatrical exhibition during that term in your territory will be yours. Other licenses, such as Home Video and Electronic Distribution, can be negotiated after the film is completed and premiered. Once you pledge, I'll email you the script and deal memo immediately. (Hartley 2013b)[6]

Kickstarter quickly ruled that Hartley could not offer distribution rights as a form of reward (see Saperstein 2013). The offer of distribution rights was considered to be a form of investment, which is against the terms and conditions of Kickstarter. Although some rights had been purchased, Kickstarter and Amazon (who process Kickstarter's credit card payments) reported they would not be processing payments. This is a reminder of crowdfunding's status as a form of consumption (and hence its attractiveness for producers such as Hartley, since there are no investors or creditors to pay once the project is in profit, which is from its first sale, since the products have been pre-sold and costs covered). Although the US JOBS (Jumpstart Our Business Startups) Act of 2012 made equity crowdfunding more attractive, as well as exempt from taxation up to $2,000 for small investors via internet portals, the offer of distribution rights (although a traditional means of funding production for independent producers) was deemed to be a breach of Kickstarter's rules, and the rewards were very swiftly removed. However, the incident demonstrates again Hartley's shift to a 'smaller', more marginal place in the independent sector, with the admission that his films have no place on the big screen; they're now targeted at the 'small' screen, something returned to later in this essay, when I look at Hartley's 'small' production methodology.

As a filmmaker who combines the DIY and DIWO methods of production, funding and distribution, Hartley is thus squarely at the margins of the independent sector. While his reputation often precedes him, the positioning of his work at the margins is perhaps at odds with the perceived importance of his films in discourse surrounding independent cinema, and he still garners substantial coverage in trade publications like *Variety* or online sources such as *Indiewire*. (It is possible to argue his work has always been at the margins of the sector; despite his work being picked up by prominent specialty wings of Disney, Sony and MGM, it has never gained popular commercial or crossover success.) Despite his marginality, he remains in demand with actors, with his recent work growing beyond his regular ensemble of players. Indeed, in some respects, *Ned Rifle* is a Hal Hartley reunion; it his first film with Martin Donovan in fifteen years, alongside Robert John Burke, Karen Sillas and Bill Sage, as well as the returning cast of *Henry Fool* (1997), and includes Aubrey Plaza (a new doyen of independent cinema, best known for her role in *Parks and Recreation* [NBC, 2009–2015]) as well as Jeff Goldblum and Saffron Burrows (both in *Fay Grim*). By contrast, smaller works such as the self-distributed *The Girl from Monday* (2005) and *Meanwhile* have drawn more on Hartley's local ensemble of players. It's to these films that I now wish to turn to consider the small-scale production methodology employed by Hartley in his more recent work.

'It's local': The Production and Aesthetics of Smallness

While Hartley has turned to funding and distribution options associated with low or micro-budget filmmaking, and a combination of DIY and DIWO methods, his production methodology has also strayed towards the small scale, particularly for more experimental works such as the *Possible Films 2* (*PF2*) collection of shorts and *Meanwhile*. Larger scale works such as *Fay Grim* and *Ned Rifle* stray much closer in production scale toward the higher budget range of indie features (still $1 million and under). This is particularly true of *Fay Grim*, with its multiple international locations and its greater reliance on film stars (the idea of the films as part of a trilogy or franchise also means they are closer to the Hollywood model). However, it is the economy of scale with which I'm concerned in this part of this essay.

Hartley's methods in *Meanwhile*, he points out, are an extension of those he employs in the *PF2* films, made across 2008 and 2009 during his time in Berlin: 'it's local … *Meanwhile* stems naturally from these short films that I made in Berlin where I was exercising this approach, being extremely local; you know, what happens day to day in local life, and not to have an idea [they're] abnormal events' (2011). In the documentary that accompanies the DVD of *Meanwhile* (entitled *The Everyday*), Hartley (interviewed at the same desk his assistant sits at in the film) described the films he made in Berlin and *Meanwhile* as 'little fictions, made from everyday stuff'. Situating the films in the everyday is a conscious creative strategy, not necessarily to be autobiographical, but to make a series of films that extend what it means to be part of this universe:

> What is it to be someone who reads as much as I do? Thinks about pictures all day; who has an assistant; who travels, and so that the approach in Berlin I was exercising was local to me. And when I moved back to the United States, I said, 'what's the first thing I want do?' The next film needs to be the same creative strategy but the scope of the whole city. (Ibid.)

As Manley (2013: 9) argues, Hartley's work is infused with a regional identity, here made very specific in its 'scope of the whole city', from Brooklyn to Uptown Manhattan. The approach is specifically local in its scale of reference to Hartley's milieu.

Meanwhile concerns Joe (Mendel) and his efforts to traverse Lower Manhattan up to Hal Hartley's apartment to pick up the keys to Miho Nikaido's (Hartley's wife's) apartment that overlooks the Brooklyn Bridge. Joe is a jack-of-all-trades, a designer, an importer of European windows, a drummer, plumber, filmmaker and author whose natural habit is to help everyone with whom he comes into contact. Structured in fourteen segments, each part of *Meanwhile* documents a different part of New York and an encounter with a different person: a woman Joe meets walking across the Brooklyn Bridge who he thinks has committed suicide; a young actress he hasn't paid for a photoshoot; a once-famous author who just wants his typewriter fixed; an ex-girlfriend who is a semi-recurring character on a major TV show; and Hartley's Hispanic cleaner with a bad back. Joe's selflessness causes him to defer his own goals (his bank account has been frozen for unpaid taxes – despite this, he still helps out others financially). Hartley describes the film as strongly influenced by Joyce's *Ulysses* (1922), Joe's journey across New York inspired by both Leopold Bloom's day in Dublin and the specificity of Joyce's description of the city. Hartley attributes the thematic background to the film to a comment from the poet Richard Wilbur: 'whatever the Self is, any proper definition of it is going to have to include the idea that the Self is constituted of other people' (Butts 1990: 23). The film was intended to be 'a portrait of this guy who's this cue ball hitting all these different people … that elicit from him different aspects of his personality and his ambition' (Hartley 2011). This humanist approach is explored in the film as Joe's selflessness allows him to express (and Mendel to perform) the different faces of his own Self; Joe's nature is not singular, but multiple, emphasised by his numerous interactions across this day (the structure of the film also makes this clear in the overt use of the chapter structure to show us the different sides of Joe's nature, that his Self is 'constituted of other people').

Part of this universe, however, is Hartley himself. The film takes place in the world of Hartley's everyday. Again, it is important to note that the film is not autobiographical, despite the interaction with the author having elements of his relationship with Mendel embedded in it. The approach to the story is defined by Hartley's production methodology: keep it local. The locations in the film are 'real' places – they are Nikaido's and Hartley's apartments. The film draws a line from Brooklyn (where Mendel lives and performs) to the two apartments, and back down to Lower Manhattan. Joe navigates the city; the Citibank is on the intersection of William Street and John Street; Joe helps the young man in need of assistance moving across Nassau Street; Joe is knocked down on Stone Street in Lower Manhattan. The local details are specific and linear enough so that the inquisitive viewer could construct a map of the film through the use of Google Maps' Street View, just as a reader might reconstruct Joyce's Dublin. The city provides a very specific local background to the film's humanist theme – locations are treated as they were when the crew arrived. Little set dressing was done, and there is an attempt at 'an aesthetic about finding the actual' (ibid.). The strong, vibrant, colourful images in the film respond to the locations. The woman on the bridge wears a red coat, which merges with the colour scheme of parts of the city; and the street signs and cabs of New York, as well as painting by Philippe Richard in Hartley's apartment, give a clear indicator of the film's colour scheme. This is part of a conscious production design and shooting methodology on Hartley's part (along with Richard Sylvarnes, his production designer) to find local details and respond to them rather than to attempt to manufacture an artificial aesthetic in those spaces (this is perhaps surprising given the strongly artificial, abstract sense of dialogue and performance in Hartley's work – there is a clear sense of realism about the settings in *Meanwhile*, as there often has been in his work, from the Long Island films onwards).

The approach to the everyday in *Meanwhile* has strong affinities with the work of Yasujiro Ozu (there are also affinities with *Flirt* in this regard, with its more explicit reference to the Japanese director through the inclusion of a character named Ozu; see Rawle 2011: 196–209 for a more detailed discussion of *Flirt*). Sharing what J. M.

Hammond describes as a 'concern for the modest, the everyday, and the accidental,' (2015: 83) *Meanwhile*, even with a 55-minute running time, is in keeping with the more relaxed, character-driven narratives of independent cinema, the segments structured around the fourteen encounters, mostly accidental (the meeting with the woman on the bridge), some more planned (such as Joe's audition). The local approach to methodology is modest, albeit with the inherent production values of shooting in New York City (particularly the view across the Brooklyn Bridge from Nikaido's apartment). The narrative is woven around Hartley's everyday, however: although we never see the filmmaker, it is clear he is a feature in the film, with Joe striving to get uptown to pick up the keys from Hartley's assistant, Tuesday (played by actress Penelope Lagos). The scenes with Tuesday in Hartley's apartment/office (and on the subway) are the only ones in the film that don't feature Joe – we see her engrossed in reading Joe's unpublished novel, self-reflexively named *Meanwhile* (like many important texts in Hartley's films, such as Simon's poem in *Henry Fool*, we never see a word of the book). Understandably, Hartley's office is daubed with references to his films, and to his commerce as a filmmaker: Tuesday's desk is located beneath a poster for *Fay Grim*, and next to a line of DVDs, the most prominent of which is *Surviving Desire*, while we can also see a poster for *Trust* (with its French title, *Trust Me*) in the background in the bedroom. The comedy derived from the vacuum cleaner's plug is a reference to Hartley's time living in Europe, something embedded in the everyday (and of course these references to Hartley's earlier films also function as a kind of fan service, a reflexive nod to Hartley fans, more notable given the film's status as a kind of offer to his established audience, since the film wasn't released theatrically or even submitted to festivals, although it showed at a number of them by invitation).

Meanwhile is a local film (specific to the geography and cultural odours of New York), set on a major canvas. In addition to the smallness of the story and the commitment to the accidental everyday, the film is also micro on the level of its aesthetic. Like many recent Hartley films, *Meanwhile* features no moving shots. All shots are static, locked-off; throughout the film, the camera frames rather than reframes the action. Characters tend to walk in, out and across shots without being reframed (Hartley has been vocal as well about his lack of establishing shots as a way of representing space and place, as in *The Everyday* documentary, as well as in my interview with him), while this also captures Hartley's distinctive approach to performance: Mendel brings to Joe a sense of continual movement within the locked-off frame. The scene where he sits in the park is a strong example here of the kind of business developed by Mendel (something Hartley explained was developed on location, with Mendel working out the movement and the rhythm in around fifteen minutes), as is his play with the chair in his brother's office. In the park, Mendel is always on the move, even though he's mainly sitting down: he tries three times to light a cigarette, stands up, checks his pockets, takes out and checks his wallet, picks up and opens his briefcase. The performance is strongly physical and fluid within the locked-off frame, rather than embellished through camera movement or editing. Whereas earlier films like *Simple Men* were marked by a greater use of camera movement, Hartley's later films have used

Fig. 4.1: D.J. Mendel, and 'the little fictions and everyday stuff' in *Meanwhile*

more static cameras and more canted angles to frame performances. As previously argued, performance is a key way of understanding Hartley's approach to cinema, and this has been reinforced in later works that (following the blurred-pixel digital experiments of *The Book of Life* [1998] and *The Girl from Monday*) return to a strong focus on the performer – as a vehicle for Mendel, *Meanwhile* continues this tradition. The minimalism of the aesthetic (not to be confused with a minimalism of action) is emblematic of this. Shot on a Canon 5D DSLR camera, it is also an emblem of the small-scale practice of independent cinema, with the use of a prosumer camera (now common, particularly in short filmmaking) rather than a more professional one (an Arri Alexa for instance). In many regards, this helps understand both the positioning of Hartley as a filmmaker in tune with low- or micro-budget production methods, as well as his own distinctive minimal aesthetic.

The other locality in this dynamic is Berlin, where Hartley's experimental shorts originated the production methodology employed in *Meanwhile*. The short film medium has been one to which Hartley has returned throughout his career (and perhaps unlike many feature filmmakers, his shorts have often been a key part of his oeuvre, rather than an oddity, as so many filmmakers use shorts as a calling card into the industry before leaving the medium behind), just as he has also made shorter features for television (*Surviving Desire* offers an important parallel with *Meanwhile*, which twenty years prior might have been produced for PBS rather than as a crowdfunded, self-distributed DVD/download).[7] The shorts produced by Hartley earlier in his career have been available on VHS (the UK Tartan release *Three Shorts by Hal Hartley* [1994] packaged the shorts *Theory of Achievement* and *Ambition* with *Surviving Desire* [all 1991]) and later on DVD (the three shorts have regularly been packaged together, subsequently under the banner of *Surviving Desire*, with the other two films accompanying as extras [Wellspring's 2002 edition, along with Microcinema's 2010 release])[8]. A later collection, *Possible Films: Short Works by Hal Hartley 1994–2004* anthologised a series of films, from the gallery installation *The Other Also* (1997), to a film assembled from outtakes of a Breeders video, *The Sisters of Mercy* (2004), and notable early shorts like *Opera No. 1* (1994), produced for Comedy Central and starring Adrienne Shelly, Parker Posey and James Urbaniak. The DVD also features excerpts from Hartley's play *Soon* (2001), inspired by the Branch Davidian standoff with the FBI in Waco, Texas. The shorts are regularly analysed alongside Hartley's features (as they are in Manley's book, and my own), in keeping with the ways in which the internet has expanded the canon of films from just features to include shorts, as both transmedia extensions and oddities. Patricia Zimmerman argues that digital filmmaking and distribution both reinforce mainstream media industries, but the technology also offers filmmakers, both professional and amateur, new avenues: 'digitalization solidifies older transnational media formations but also offers new public media possibilities' (2005: 250). From the remove of a decade, the landscape of independent cinema has seen both 'change and continuity' (to reflect the title of King's *Indie 2.0*) in the ways that Zimmerman speculates. She also imagines the potential opening up of the indie sphere as new technologies become more widely adopted:

> Flash and streaming, as two digital modalities unique to digital networked media of the internet, are important because they help to chart the imagined broadening of the indie scene from features to shorts... [A] new horizontally networked universe that sprawls between the analog world of theaters and the digital domains of online festivals, Flash and streaming presents an overwhelmingly vast landscape that is simultaneously global, regional, local, individual. (2005: 246)

This essay has already discussed the ways in which new methods for distribution and funding have been implemented by Hartley, but this 'broadening' that Zimmerman imagines from features to shorts is particularly interesting in that it offers an image of the breadth of the independent sector, from the professional to the amateur, encompassing viral films, online film festivals and short and feature work by established, higher-profile filmmakers, like Hartley. His short work, originally available as a download (and on DVD via Microcinema) but now as a rentable or purchasable stream through Vimeo, emphasises the ways in which the global, regional, local and individual are wrapped up in these works, as a production methodology, but also as a business practice.

Three of the *PF2* films (*A/Muse*, *Accomplice* and *The Apologies*) strongly overlap with the creative strategy later employed in *Meanwhile*, while the other two (*Implied Harmonies* and *Adventure*) share more in common with aspects of the documentary and are more autobiographical. They are local in the sense that each is shot by Hartley himself, often in his own apartment in Berlin (on view are some of the same books and the *Trust Me* poster that are in Hartley's apartment in New York in *Meanwhile*). As Manley (2013: 159) notes, the value generated by the production and release of these films is generally an extension of the artist's need to demonstrate their identity as an active producer. Despite releasing the films through the Possible Films website, there is little possibility of these films developing significant return, even on such a low investment. Returning to Zimmerman's comments, the films connect with the networking of filmmaking online, in the realms of the regional/local (Hartley's immediate milieu), the individual (a localised production methodology of self-shooting and editing), and the global (the American artist abroad, as well as the globalised distribution of the films). They also represent a comingling of the amateur and professional: Hartley sees himself not just as an artist, but also as a participant in the global entertainment industry (a contradiction implicit in some of the *PF2* films), functioning as both the amateur (or artist-as-thief theme in *Accomplice*) and the professional producer. The films are also quite rough (especially on the level of sound, something that marks them out as different from his features stylistically), and exhibit the qualities of the short that Hartley once described as being 'essentially sketchy', suggesting that the films can 'collapse, explode or disintegrate' (1992: 223).

A/Muse tells the story of an aspiring actress (Christina Flick) trying to make contact with an American director in exile in Berlin (another connection to Hartley's own reality). She attempts to track him down to a number of places, including his apartment and a theatre where, she hears, he has been directing a play. In the end, she discovers he has returned to the States. He writes a letter to her, in which he explains that he gave up producing films to become an importer of European windows, just as Joe aspires to do in *Meanwhile*. *The Apologies* is also about an artist, this time a writer (Nikolai Kinski), working on a musical version of *The Odyssey*, about which he's highly conflicted commercially and artistically. He allows a friend, an actress (Bettina Zimmerman), to rehearse in his apartment (the film was shot in Hartley's apartment). We watch her rehearsing, revising and reinterpreting, until the writer's girlfriend (Ireen Kirsch) arrives to deliver a perfect monologue of her own, full of platitudes, to which the actress listens locked in the bathroom. The film questions the authenticity of performances, both social and artistic, in their process of becoming. The writer (a common character in Hartley's work) seems to represent Hartley's own dilemma, between the commercial demands of popular cinema and the artistic need to create. Once more, this local, minimal creative strategy examines Hartley's immediate milieu. Finally, *Accomplice*, also shot in Hartley's apartment, returns to earlier concerns in his work: the influence from Godard (a poster for *Made in USA* [1966] is also visible in *The Apologies*), and the drive to make small films, like those in the *PF2* collection. The smuggled tapes in the film are from an interview with Godard by David Bordwell – the young woman in the film (Jordana Maurer) has received them with instructions to duplicate and erase them before the authorities get to her. Although the tapes are of the Bordwell interview, Godard's reply (a key one thematically) is in fact from an interview between Godard and Hartley:

> After all, I say I am, innocently representing a certain belief in motion pictures. We will always be able to do a small movie with friends and to show to someone. Ok, you won't get the Oscar for this, but, after all, why are you writing? And why are you…? So, it will be possible… I have always said that … to make movies, to make images and sound is possible one way or another.[9]

Fig. 4.2: Jean-Luc Godard lingers in the background of Hartley's short film *Accomplice*

The 'small movie with friends ... to show to someone' is the most localised strategy possible in both amateur and professional filmmaking. The need to express *something*, however limited the audience, is at the root of the film's positioning of creative identity, something at the heart of the *PF2* films, including the autobiographical pseudo-documentaries. Hartley's creative strategy in the films, a method he also later employs in *Meanwhile*, is highly local in space, place and theme: they embrace the everyday milieu of Hartley's artistic 'exile' in Berlin, whereas *Meanwhile* does so with New York as its locale after his return. In this, there is a continuity between these periods of his career.

Conclusion
For Hartley, the period of his career from 2008 onwards has seen him embrace a range of different production and business strategies associated with the smaller, lower-budget end of the independent scale. While the Indiewood sector has been scaled back by Hollywood from its mid-2000s peak, Hartley has explored more local strategies creatively and industrially. Earlier films like *The Book of Life* and *The Girl from Monday* represent experimental aesthetic strategies with digital video cameras, and *Fay Grim* adopts the day and date strategy that distributor Magnolia had introduced with Soderbergh's *Bubble* (2005). Hartley, therefore, had previously explored the possibilities offered in terms of digital production and distribution, albeit on a different scale. The approach taken toward his filmmaking since 2009 has been noticeably smaller, a more guarded approach because, as he has said, 'one can never be independent enough'. The adoption of crowdfunding and the shift away from

anything besides very limited theatrical runs is a business strategy that allows Hartley to avoid assuming the risk of debt for production capital (with the ability to parlay his connection with his audience into quantifiable value), and to locally manage the distribution of his work via the halhartley.com website and partners such as Vimeo. As a filmmaker who occupies a space in the margins of the independent sector (despite his prominence in discourses surrounding indie cinema), the small-scale DIY and DIWO approaches to funding and distribution offer a more direct avenue to his fanbase, and therefore to the (limited) revenues from his filmmaking. Hartley has matched this scale of the business of filmmaking with his creative strategies of exploiting his immediate milieu for subject matter and locations. Employing DV and DSLR prosumer cameras allows Hartley to take more control of the production process, and his local approach to location and the everyday occurrences in his environment matches a naturalism of place with the distanced performances and cadences of his dialogue. *Ned Rifle* partly opens up this scale again with a return to feature-making (his first in nearly a decade), but there remains in Hartley's work a strain of practice that appeals to the margins of the independent sector and to the smallness of scale associated with low- and micro-budget filmmaking, in the aesthetic of the films and in Hartley's business of being an artist.

Notes

1. Fortissimo also handles international sales for a number of films in Hartley's back catalogue.
2. The film opened on 1 April at IFC Center, then moved onto Los Angeles, Chicago, San Francisco, Columbus and Toronto for 3 April, before Seattle, Portland, Boston and Huntington, New York on 10 April and San Diego on 17 April.
3. Quantcast have ceased quantifying traffic for Kickstarter since then.
4. This is in comparison with just 807 followers of the Possible Films page when I was writing *Performance in the Cinema of Hal Hartley* (Cambria Press, 2011) in 2010, potentially a consequence of Hartley's audience discovering him during that time as more individuals (specifically older ones) have taken to using Facebook.
5. Here, Hartley likens crowdfunding to a Medieval barter economy, in which buyers and sellers with mutual needs meet without the need for an intermediary.
6. Rights to distribute in Greece and Hungary were available for $3,000, while Israel, France, Spain, Russia and Spanish-speaking Latin America were also available for $9,000. The US rights had sold prior to Kickstarter's removal of the offer.
7. Given the explosion in quality television over the past decade, many directors who have formerly worked in indie features in the 1990s and 2000s are now directing in television, such as Allison Anders or Jay and Mark Duplass, while some, such as Rian Johnson, move back and forth between television and features.
8. *Surviving Desire* is now available on Vimeo VOD, with *Theory of Achievement* available for free as a 'bonus feature', while *Ambition* is a separate download.
9. The transcription appears slightly differently in the published version of the interview (see Hartley 1994: 18).

CHAPTER FIVE

Hal Hartley's Romantic Comedy
Sebastian Manley

One of Hal Hartley's gifts to the world of independent film is a form of romantic comedy that opens Hollywood representation and engages us through a vivified, densely meaningful vision of romantic love and the relationship between men and women. In film after film in the late 1980s and early 1990s, Hartley worked determinedly to bring fresh images and textures to the screen, in the process greatly enlarging our sense of film's positive potential to speak about reality's everyday mysteries – not through literal exposition or the emotional 'codes' familiar to all cinema-goers, but through a kind of poetic design that stimulates the imagination.

Those who are familiar with the early films discussed here – the features *The Unbelievable Truth* (1989), *Trust* (1990) and *Simple Men* (1992), as well as the TV featurette *Surviving Desire* (1991) – will not have to think long to conjure some of their remarkable binding features. Many of these have a distinctly 'European' flavour, registering Hartley's affinity with film artists such as Robert Bresson and Jean-Luc Godard. The articulate, philosophical characters, smoking cigarettes with the unself-conscious poise of another era; the laconic, elliptical editing style; the emphasis on the absurdity at the heart of everyday life; the bitten-back acting style, sometimes so minimalistic as to provoke laughter; the swerves into a form of dreamlike hyper-choreography, most famously represented in the dance sequences that surprise us in the otherwise non-musical *Simple Men* and *Surviving Desire*: all these features are in kinship with the traditions of European art cinema of the 1950s and later decades, though of course in their particularities they remain unique to Hartley. The relishable art-film magic that forms one of the dimensions of Hartley's cinema is held in balance with another, less often celebrated, dimension that in many ways distinguishes the films from the work of Godard, Bresson and others. We might describe this as a kind of emotional glow, an evident affection for the characters at the centre of the narrative combined with a lightness of touch that speaks of optimism and of a belief in the comic (rather than the tragic) as the prevailing force in human existence. More simply, we might call this 'charm'. A familiar if under-examined quality in film and the other arts, particularly in their more commercial forms, charm at its worst can conceal and obscure, oxygenate old clichés, gloss over disturbing ideologies, allow us to close our eyes to the fullness of reality. But charm can also serve a more wholesome function. In the right circumstances, charm can become a powerful ally in the making of fresh meaning, allowing viewers to enter into a process of pleasurable engagement with complex ideas and feelings. Hartley's considerable achievement in these early works is to bring into fruitful contact a 'charm' aesthetic and an 'art' aesthetic in the service of developing his own form of narrative film, one capable of exploring with great subtlety and originality the themes of romantic love and the possibility of connection between the sexes.

In all of the four films, romance dominates. It rouses the main characters and inspires the films' most poetic and moving imagery. In *Trust* and *The Unbelievable Truth*, perhaps Hartley's most respected and loved features, romance hangs in the air as a possibility even before the two leads meet, the future bond between the characters being evoked by Hartley's skilful use of narrative convention. Both films lead us on a journey through the knotty realities of romance in which narrative and gender conventions are at once playfully and profoundly questioned, asking us to open ourselves to the more unfamiliar currents that animate male/female relations. *Simple Men* takes us into darker territory. Here romance almost fails to develop, owing to the toxic fantasy of the male principal, Bill, and the retreatist fantasy of the female principal, Kate. But in this deeply moving and complex romance, Hartley shows us that, miraculously, it is possible to draw fresh water from a poisoned well. The story of Bill and Kate's unusual romance and eventual coming together as a couple offers a strange mixture of disturbing and delightful moments that makes *Simple Men*, of these four films, the most likely to be misunderstood, especially if we are not attuned to Hartley's abiding concerns and vision of intimacy and romance, so I will save discussion of it for this essay's final section. The first three sections will be dedicated to *The Unbelievable Truth*, *Trust* and finally *Surviving Desire*, which incorporates some of the same themes of *Simple Men* in a witty and entertaining tale of characters less in love than blinded by desire and their own dreams of love – a narrative situation that held promise for Hartley but that in its filmed form suffers in comparison to his earlier, more richly realised romantic narratives.

The Unbelievable Truth

The opening seconds of Hartley's first feature-length film tantalise us with images of charismatic masculinity. When Josh (Robert John Burke) appears, he is on his own, attempting to thumb a ride on the side of a desolate-looking highway. The qualities of male self-sufficiency, independence and rugged endurance associated with the figure of the hitch-hiker seem etched onto his face: brownish complexion, short hair kept well clear of his features, solid, angular nose and jaw, closed mouth, a vaguely contemptuous look in his eyes. Covering his lean frame is a faded all-black outfit that suggests an affinity with the villainous gunfighter of western iconography. Is this a modern-day Jack Wilson come to shake up some unfortunate New York township?

Any notion we might have that the film will trade in traditional conceptions of masculinity is soon severely tested, though, by the nature of Josh's interactions in the next scenes. Having finally managed to get a ride in a car, Josh, sitting alone in the back seat while the family ride up front, is asked by the driver where he is going. He answers simply, 'Prison' – at which point he is unceremoniously ejected on the side of the road, where he 'looks around and waits patiently', as the screenplay puts it (Hartley 2002: 4). The aura of contained machismo that Josh initially seems to give off starts to dissipate further when it is revealed that despite being a mechanic, he doesn't drive, and furthermore doesn't drink (this is an incongruity that inspires confusion and amusingly stubborn disbelief in one character and that contributes to Josh's characterisation on several occasions as a priest). When we finally cut from Josh to Audry (Adrienne Shelly), another figure of wonderfully complex tonalities, and similarly good-looking, though in a different way, we know immediately that they will converge and develop some sort of relationship. From her very first moments on screen, Audry emanates a complicated energy that moves her beyond the stereotype of the pretty, romantic young girl. Above her floral-patterned duvet hang black-and-white photos, one of which features a nuclear blast, and as she sits up in bed and starts to yawn, she unexpectedly makes an explosion noise – heard as a real explosion on the soundtrack: *bwooooom* – with her mouth, bringing her arms up to form a cloud shape. We might detect in this mysterious gesture an echo of Josh's oddball version of youthful angst; her plain dark bedclothes and serious expression align her with him further. At the same time, though, Adrienne Shelly's features form a contrast between Audry and Josh, the actor's full lips, large eyes and long hair registering Audry's relative youth and suggesting a sensuousness that counterpoints Josh's austere quality.

Although Audry is much younger than Josh (she is seventeen; he is around thirty), this is not a tale of youthful female enthrallment to older male wisdom, even if on occasion it might seem to be. Both the texture and the plotting of Audry and Josh's romantic narrative function to give us a vivid sense of a relationship filled by a spirit of fluidity and equality. Audry and Josh share a connection that remains untouched by the (sexist) power dynamic familiar from more conservative romantic comedies in which an older, more powerful man 'rescues' a younger woman from a life of hardship and yearning. If in the contemporaneous *Pretty Woman* (1990), the rich male protagonist, Edward (Richard Gere), takes it upon himself to teach his poor female love interest, Vivian (Julia Roberts), how to live life, while Vivian administers emotional care to Edward – a gender dynamic resulting in an old-hat fairy-tale narrative (albeit one enlivened by Roberts's genuinely charming and subversive energy in the early parts of the film) – in Hartley's film the two leads assume roles that are both unorthodox and unsentimental in nature. Audry and Josh each surprise us in their approach to romance. Josh displays an openness and honesty that short-circuits expectations about the action-oriented, tunnel-vision character of male desire. In one entertaining scene he talks with Mike, a fellow mechanic at the garage where he works, about how being in an intimate relationship compels one to pay more attention to the cleanliness of body parts that usually nobody sees, such as one's back – a goofy and touching conversation completely emptied of the clichéd macho posturing familiar from commercial (and less commercial) narratives, particular those featuring working-class men. Audry, though she initially seems seduced by Josh's rugged, 'older man' qualities, easily holds her own in their exchanges, demonstrating a sensitivity and eruditeness that complement his sexy asceticism and impressive auto skills. Indeed, it is Audry who takes the initiative in the early part of their romance. Soon after their first chance meeting, she contrives to see Josh again, cycling to the garage to give him a biography of George Washington – a figure who in their earlier interaction provided the main topic of conversation. Their ensuing flirtation carries an authentic charge of potential because the two characters are not compelled to read from the cultural script by which the female speaker is in some way subordinated to the male. When talk turns from Washington to Molière's *The Misanthrope*, Audry readily and without embarrassment demonstrates her literary knowledge, defining the word 'misanthrope' for Josh and talking about the play's characters. Josh responds with the fluid confidence of a man totally at ease with his female conversation partner's intelligence. The easy flow of erotic energy between them in this exchange, captured by Hartley in a single shot and accompanied by only a few seconds of music during the final lines of dialogue, provides the viewer with a precious moment of raw (if somewhat melancholic) romantic intensity, unconstrained by either cultural prescriptions or the pesky demands of everyday life (the spell is broken when Audry's father, out of frame, demands to know what she's doing on the garage repair floor).

The potential of Audry and Josh's relationship is underlined by the nature of the relationships that exist in the world around them. Outside of the film's main romantic pairing, real connection and intimacy seem to be at best a dim hope, and at worst a flat-out impossibility. Many of the male characters play out a kind of manhood by numbers, a conception of masculinity in thrall to cultural clichés that flatter them in their patriarchal dominance but foreclose the possibility of deeper, more meaningful satisfaction. The continually frustrated Todd (David Healy), a character that the screenplay describes as a 'sleazy, good-looking, young hustler' (Hartley 2002: 17), adopts a language of flirtation refracted through the rhetorics of commerce and commodification that were particularly foundational to 1980s clichés of the masculine (his you-could-be-a-model come-ons don't cut much ice with the women in the film). Audry's boyfriend, Emmet (Gary Sauer), whom she dumps in an early scene, is a lumpen careerist, completely uninterested in Audry as anything other than a symbol of his success (and later as a sexual prize he must win back). Only Mike's (Mark Bailey) relationship with Pearl (Julia McNeal), his girlfriend, contains a modicum of tenderness – yet Mike clearly doesn't fully get Pearl, whose mysterious sadness seems beyond the comprehension of everyone except Audry.

Audry and Josh run up against obstacles in their own relationship, of course, although their potential as two people sharing a real and enduring connection remains a vivid reality at all times. In keeping with Hartley's understanding of film as an art form whose power is released when plot is de-emphasised and character experience is allowed to become the narrative's essential focus – an artistic philosophy Hartley associates in particular with Bresson and Carl Dreyer (see Hartley 2002: viii, ix) – external obstacles are attributed far less importance than our experience as viewers might lead us to expect. Although Vic (Chris Cooke) tries to separate Audry and Josh on account of Josh's criminal past, it is not Vic's actions that drive them apart, but their own. Both characters falter just at the point when love seems about to bloom. When Audry visits Josh at his home and declares her desire for him, Josh reacts badly, thrown by her forwardness and, we must assume, by some significant feelings of guilt brought on by the situation (the last time Josh was close to becoming intimate with a seventeen-year-old girl, after all, he ended up causing her death, crashing the car they were in while under the influence of alcohol). Audry is crushed. It is at this point that she flees to New York City to work as a model, succumbing to her pessimism and embracing a cynical belief in deals as the only thing worth a damn in a cruel world of commercialisation and self-interest. 'People are only as good as the deals they make and keep', she angrily tells Josh, unable at this point to open herself to the love that holds the potential to redeem reality – Audry's reality, and Josh's too.

Josh and Audry's path back to togetherness, though conventional in the abstract, is rendered by Hartley with a complexity of tone and texture that transcends clichés and engages our imagination. In some respects the film's conclusion exploits our desire to see these attractive, charming and interesting people reunited in some kind of passionate union. But it is also in these last sequences that Hartley takes the greatest risks in departing from conventional storytelling – just at the point when we expect a satisfying romantic payoff – to create a poetic moment of mutual commitment capable of moving us in mysterious and unexpected ways. Having found Audry living with Todd in the city, Josh returns home in a fog of anger, only to find Pearl waiting to talk to him about something important. At his house she tells him that he wasn't responsible for her father's death – the crime for which he went to prison for fifteen years was not a crime, after all. As Josh tries to take this in, one by one other characters also arrive at his house: Vic has come to check whether his plan to bring together Audry and Josh has worked; Mike is looking for Pearl, who he is worried might have got together with Josh; and Audry is looking to reconnect with Josh, having followed him back from the city. If such a convergence of characters in a more conventional film might presage a series of drawn-out cathartic dialogues, though, in Hartley's film dialogue is unexpectedly supplanted by a highly choreographed form of hide and seek, as characters tiptoe through rooms and peek round doors in Josh's almost empty house. When confrontation does erupt, dialogue is balanced by rhythmically timed pushes and shoves that imbue proceedings with a kind of silent-film poetry.

The eccentric energy of these sequences carries over into the final moments of the film, in which Audry and Josh at last commit themselves to each other. Both characters experience the connection they have shared since the early parts of the film as an intense source of inspiration and consolation. Narratively, their deep bond has enabled the happy conclusion of Audry's character arc, which moves from depression to a bitter cynicism to, finally, a new optimism once she finds the courage to accept Josh's love for her, and hers for him. At the same time, though, the complicated

Fig. 5.1: An expansive gesture of trust – Adrienne Shelly and Robert John Burke in *The Unbelievable Truth*

resonances of the final sequence call on us to see this as something other than, something more mysterious than, a traditional happy ending of the kind associated with mainstream romantic comedy. When Josh asks Audry how he knows that she isn't involved with Todd, Audry says that he has to trust her, and Josh, after a moment's consideration, embraces Audry, lifting her high in the air in an expansive gesture that seems to signify that he does (Fig. 5.1). What he actually says, though, is 'I don't trust anybody' – an explicit expression of uncertainty but one delivered by Josh in exactly the tone of an affirmation. A delicate ambivalence also defines the film's final shot, in which Audry and Josh look up at the sky, the wind blowing gently through their hair. 'Listen', says Audry. He listens, and appears to hear nothing, but we suspect that Audry is hearing the sounds of bombs, as she seems to have done several times throughout the film. As we cut to the black credit screen, we are left with a vivid sense of Audry and Josh's fully real romantic bond – perhaps Hartley's most touching and inspiring representation of an authentic love free of the distorting forces of cultural cliché – but also a sense of the indeterminacy at the heart of all intimate relationships. This is assuredly not the kind of affirmation we know from the *Pretty Woman*s of the film world. But it is an affirmation that honours our complicated feelings about love and desire and points us in the direction of a fuller and richer understanding of how we live our romantic lives.

Trust

The making of *Trust*, released just a year after *The Unbelievable Truth*, gave Hartley the chance to resume his exploration of romantic love and romantic narrative with perhaps an even greater freedom and originality. For Hartley *The Unbelievable Truth* started something that *Trust* finished – or at least gave shape to in a fuller, more deeply resonant way. In particular, Hartley saw the later film as a response to the 'kind of ironic dichotomy' he perceived in the conclusion to *The Unbelievable Truth*: the sense of enigmatic ambivalence flowing specifically from Josh's intimation that he both loves and does not trust Audry (Hartley 2002: xii–xiii). The story of Maria (Adrienne Shelly) and Matthew (Martin Donovan) in *Trust* both amplifies this ambivalence and speaks consolingly of its potential reconciliation, building a complex picture of love in its heterogeneous reality.

The opening moments of the film convey to us just how reduced a role the comforting stability that characterises much romantic and comic film will play in what we are about to watch. In the first shot, we see Maria, the female protagonist, and her mother, Jean, their faces filling the entire frame. While Maria puts on her lipstick she argues with her father and mother about her life choices: she has just dropped out of school and has plans to marry her boyfriend – also, she reveals coolly, she is pregnant. Hartley films all this in a single frontal shot, the father offscreen throughout the entire conversation. At this point we finally cut to a title and then another shot, but rather than providing us with a wider view of the room, this next shot confronts us with another close-up view, this time of Maria's mother, as Maria and her father stand behind her arguing. When Maria's father calls her a slut, Maria, shocked, responds by slapping him sharply on the face. We cut during this action to a close-up of the father's face, then back to Maria, looking slightly unsure. Maria leaves, and a moment after she slams the door we see what she doesn't: her father falling dead to the kitchen floor – the life mysteriously forced from his body by his daughter's act of defiance.

In both its presentation and its scripting this passage casts us into profound uncertainty. The reassuring conventions of 'realist' editing – by which we expect to gain a sense of the whole space of a scene and a clear understanding of the characters' positioning in relation to one another – here give way to a disorientating presentational logic that hides the reactions of a key character, renders spatial relations indeterminate, pushes the dramatic crux of the scene to the background plane, and generally requests that we let go of any nice ideas we might have that we will be allowed to experience the world of the film from a privileged position of comfort and stability. The sequence of events itself only reinforces the feeling of disorientation: if Maria's mall-rat look and comically bored tone seem to provide a note of generic familiarity, the sudden and absurd death of Maria's father – turning our puckish heroine into a killer before even the warmth has left our popcorn – locates the film somewhere far beyond the realms of the commercial teen comedy.

Instability quickly becomes the defining aspect of Maria's life, and initially it seems that she will be overcome by the disruptive forces that seem to spring, in some mysterious way, from within her. After accidentally killing her father, she is evicted from her home by her mother and is forced to wander around town alone; when she tries to buy beer at a convenience store, the man at the till harasses and then attempts to sexually assault her. Her boyfriend, Anthony (Gary Sauer), rejects her on learning she is pregnant – she simply is no longer the kind of person or body he wishes to commit himself to. Her plans for life coming down around her ears, she schedules an abortion. Maria's tumbling towards what Hartley calls her 'zero point' does not make for easy watching, and we fear she will be unable to cope with all that life is throwing at her (Hartley quoted in Berrettini 2011: 21). But Maria's narrative is not a fable about the dreadfulness of modern complexity; Hartley has no interest in telling this kind of story. For him, complexity is a deep feature of human reality, not a localised development, and it is not to be lamented – it is part of what keeps life and love interesting. Though the crisis Maria undergoes is real and harrowing, it is in fact, as we will see in the later parts of the film, the painful early stages of a transformation that sees her move towards a greater understanding of herself, and of the complexity and indeterminacy that are the conditions of existence. This is a transformation that takes hold only when she steps away from her old life, lets go of the fantasies that she has allowed to rule her, and, particularly, meets Matthew.

Matthew too is living a life defined by instability. When he and Maria meet he is locked into a pattern of violence, seemingly the result of a bad relationship with his controlling father, that has reduced his life to a succession of personal disappointments and angry encounters with co-workers, portrayed by Hartley in both their disturbing and their comic aspects (in one scene of high cartoonish energy Matthew puts his boss's head in a vice). The connection that develops between them represents a new hope for them both. The ways in which Maria and Matthew's lives are paralleled in the early sequences, as well as their equally remarkable good looks, allow us to know before they do that they will form a relationship, but both Adrienne Shelly and Martin Donovan's charming performances and Hartley's direction invest that relationship with a poetic magic that far surpasses the mechanically engineered effects of narrative convention. In the scenes they share together, Maria and Matthew talk and move their bodies in unexpected ways, displaying a poignant sensitivity to each other and the energy flowing between them. Often their dialogue exchanges feature the kind of easy shifts in tone and attitude that we intuitively associate with genuine rapport but that are rarely seen on the cinema screen, as when Matthew impulsively asks Maria to marry him and raise her baby with him; Maria tells him not unkindly that he's delirious, Matthew immediately says 'Sorry' and Maria, also without taking a pause, says 'It's OK.' That theirs is a connection that goes beyond an emotional rapport and somehow links them at a more primal, physical level is suggested in the memorable scene in which Maria, to demonstrate her trust in Matthew, climbs to the top of a concrete wall and calmly falls backwards off it, Matthew running forward and in one perfectly fluid movement diving to his knees and catching her just as she is about to hit the ground.

The complicated but clearly meaningful relationship Maria has with Matthew gives her strength in difficult and uncertain times. But it is not rescue that Matthew offers Maria but a sense of real connection, based in equality, that lends impetus to her own quest for enlightenment. Through engaging in a painful process of self-development that starts (as Mark L. Berrettini perceptively notes) just before she meets Matthew, in a shattering scene in which she confesses her internalised feelings of worthlessness to an abortion nurse,[1] Maria comes to possess the power to move past cultural and personal limits, exploding clichéd conceptions of heterosexual romance in which the man takes action and the woman just 'is'.[2] She starts to read widely and makes a conscious effort to improve her vocabulary. She loses the elaborate make-up, a protective shell of glamour that had kept her at a distance from reality. At the same time, she becomes more in touch with her own desires, realising that she does not want to get married to Matthew or have her baby with him. When Matthew reacts badly to Maria's news that she has had an abortion and attempts to kill himself via hand grenade in the computer factory where he works, Maria walks without hesitation into extreme uncertainty and danger to disarm him – a gesture of selflessness that enables a last moment of intimate connection, as, thrown to the floor by the nearby explosion, they lie gazing into each other's eyes in a highly stylised, almost geometrical configuration of balance and equality. In the film's last moments – completely silent except for the melancholy but somehow reassuring mid-tempo music – Matthew is led wordlessly away to a police car while Maria looks on, holding his gaze intensely as he disappears over the horizon. This complex, greatly moving ending doesn't tell us in any rational way what Maria and Matthew are thinking but instead harnesses the power of image and sound to allow us to feel the complexity of their relationship as a vivid reality. In some ways it functions as an answer to the film's opening scene, richly conveying to us the sense of possibility that Hartley believes is the flip-side to instability and indeterminacy.

Although at the end the film we feel that there is hope for both Matthew and Maria, and their relationship, *Trust*'s narrative has not pulled its punches in depicting the difficulties of navigating the treacherous waters of our own being and desire. In its central couple the film presents us with two different people who react very differently to pervasive complexity. Matthew, though he is sincere in his feelings for Maria, cannot ultimately turn away from the violence and anger that offer a fleeting sense of control but that prevent him from awakening fully to the true nature of reality. He is a character who gives memorable expression to our human tendency to cling to what we know, happiness be damned – even when filled with feelings of what seems to be real love, Matthew proves unable to transcend the limits he has set for himself. Rather, it is Maria who finds the courage to let go of her old life and embrace, in a rather Buddhist spirit, the instability of the world. In the film's last shot she is pictured against a blue sky as she stares off after Matthew, the camera angle creating the impression of her being suspended mid-air – an image that forsakes the stability of the standard Hollywood romantic comedy ending but one that in its ambiguous possibility strikes a powerful note of hope.[3]

Surviving Desire
Surviving Desire too closes on an image of its female protagonist isolated in the frame, staring ahead as the closing music plays, but it is an image that clinches a new narrative feeling of sorrow for Hartley, concluding a romantic story with a very different focus to that of both *Trust* and *The Unbelievable Truth*. An hour-long featurette made for PBS, the film chronicles an affair between Jude (Martin Donovan), a college literature professor, and Sofie (Mary B. Ward), one of his students. Jude obsesses over Sofie, waxing lyrical – in that slightly cool, analytical way that Hartley characters have of doing these sorts of things – about her eyes, her smile, her voice and her 'white, slender neck' to his friend Henry, with whom he also has intense and often very

comical conversations about the nature of love and desire. Sofie meanwhile nurses her own obsession: she digs Jude's tragic, literary quality ('His name is Jude, like in *Jude the Obscure*', she tells her friend) and wants to write a short story about him. After Jude confesses his feelings for her, they embark on an intense affair, spending a night together in Jude's apartment. Jude is elated, but Sofie has second thoughts. Worried that word will get out of their sleeping together, Sofie denies even knowing Jude to Henry, and soon after breaks things off with him. Her rejection sends Jude into a tailspin of anger and despair. In the film's last scenes we see him resting his head in a gutter and her standing in the bookshop where she works, surrounded by customers who ignore her repeated offers of help.

In *Surviving Desire*'s core premise of an ill-conceived relationship that burns up just as quickly as it catches light, Hartley saw the opportunity to explore the nature of a desire quite distinct from that portrayed in his first two features: one sustained not by connection but by fantasy. Neither Jude nor Sofie is truly alive to the person who excites their passion. Sofie for Jude represents a vividly sensual alternative to his intellectualism, a vision of loveliness with the power to dissolve his existential anxieties and inspire a new appetite for life. Jude for Sofie is a kind of fantasy figure sent to satisfy her youthful yearnings for grand and possibly tragic romance. When Sofie and Jude are about to sleep together for the first time, she unexpectedly brings a halt to proceedings in order to speculate on how Jude will react if he never sees her again – 'will you be … tortured by the memory of having been with me? […] Will you carry your disappointment around with you forever? Will you be maudlin and antisocial? […] Will you expect other women to be somehow more like me?' – a comically elaborate monologue that also has a disturbing aspect, because she is speaking as though she and Jude were characters in a clichéd novel, not real people with real feelings. Sofie's excessive idealisation of her lover suggests an essential difference between her and Hartley's more positive protagonists. If Maria, Matthew, Audry and Josh (to different extents) display a feel for the complexity of real relationships that is informed by a questioning spirit, or at least a quality of openness or receptivity, Sofie seems walled in by her own fantasies. Her series of questions in this scene betokens not a questioning spirit but a closedness to the reality in front of her that for Hartley invites only trouble and pain.[4]

Jude asks a lot of questions over the course of the film, particularly in his conversations with Henry, but in his affair with Sofie his instinct for reality fails him and desire takes over. He has only the weakest sense of Sofie as a real person; he hardly knows her, as Sofie herself puts it. Obviously enough for the spectator, Jude's reality problem – his confusion of desire for a real person with desire for experience, for ecstasy (to use a term from an Anatole France passage quoted by Jude) – points to trouble ahead, but Jude cannot see or accept this.[5] In the dance sequence initiated by Jude's first kiss with Sofie, Jude articulates with his body what he can't consciously grasp, performing a series of dance moves that comprise a complex expression of joy, machismo, desire and finally suffering.

In its broad aspects *Surviving Desire* constitutes an effective, unsentimental romance that casts a light on the difficult and disturbing realities of human desire.

But by Hartley's standards it is a flawed film, its potential for illumination too often compromised by a tendency towards conventional storytelling, and particularly an uncharacteristic (for Hartley) over-reliance on dialogue as a source of meaning for the spectator. Much of the dialogue hums with an undeniable wit and vitality. It is funny to hear Jude rattle off the elements constituting his fantasy of intimacy with Sofie, without hesitation or embarrassment (the full list: 'Kissing. Caressing. Holding. Slapping. Shouting. Talking. Waiting. Sleeping. Crying. Listening. Hoping. Encouraging. Forgiving. Laughing. Relenting.'); or a barman nail the nature of Jude's interest in Sofie ('you're impressed with her charming combination of unassuming conscientiousness and girlish naïveté?'); or Sofie nail Jude's argumentative strategies ('Whenever you're losing an argument, you always depict yourself as hopelessly incompetent – as if humbly admitting your shortcomings somehow places you above the argument in hand, therefore negating the other person's point of view entirely') – the characters seem to have more insight and articulacy than they have any right to. Dialogue of this kind gives the film a distinct, heightened quality that marks its eccentricity to mainstream romantic comedy. But more deeply mysterious deviations from naturalist convention – of the kind that release us from traditional, rational understandings of human relationships through a bold counterposing of image and sound – are limited to a small number of sequences, most notably the justly celebrated dance routine.[6] If sequences such as this one delight and confuse us with their complex, disruptive energy, they offer only a momentary surge of Hartleyan possibility in a narrative whose central relationship remains too conventionally drawn, too tinged by gender clichés about naïve young women who don't know the consequences of their actions and brilliant men who are violently floored by desire, to truly engage the imagination. However, Hartley has more to say about the darker side of desire. In *Simple Men*, also made in 1992, Hartley offers us another tale of romance imperilled by fantasy, in which the richly expressive quality of his two earlier features is developed in thrilling new directions.[7]

Simple Men
Simple Men shifts narrative focus in order to give us a sustained, up-close look at male desire – and it isn't always pretty. Our two male protagonists, brothers Bill (Robert John Burke) and Dennis (Bill Sage), both have a shaky grip on the realities of love and intimate connection. Their confusions are sometimes a source of humour, but often they inspire our unease and discomfort, especially in the case of Bill, whose explicit sexism disconnects him from reality and threatens to block the development of the film's central romance. As various commentators have noted, the film's male characters are defined partly in distinction to its female characters, Kate (Karen Sillas) in particular. Kate's characterisation as an 'earth mother' figure by some writers captures something of her transcendent strength of character, a kind of saintly integrity that seems to be the exact opposite of Bill's rage-fuelled mania.[8] But in fact Kate's integrity also bespeaks an anxious desire for simplicity and certainty in a complex world – a desire that in Hartley is always self-limiting, at best.[9] As we will see, Kate as much as Bill will have to learn to give up fantasies of control and accept the inherent difficulty

of human relationships in order to achieve the higher satisfactions of love and real connection.

Simple Men's initial scenes sketch a complex relationship between two brothers who for different reasons need to leave town, their situation and characterisation evocative more of the crime film or road movie than of the romantic comedy. After Bill is betrayed by his girlfriend during a robbery and cheated out of most of his cut, he returns to his hometown in New York City, where he runs into his younger brother, Dennis. Dennis is in search of their father – a complicated figure who may or may not be a terrorist and who is on the run after recently having been arrested. Looking for somewhere to hide from the law for a while, Bill joins Dennis in his search, which takes them via Lindenhurst (the setting of Hartley's first two features) to eastern Long Island, where they meet Kate and her friend Elina (Elina Löwensohn). At this point it becomes clear that the focus of the narrative will be on Kate and Bill's developing romance, rather than the two brothers' relationship or Bill's struggle to evade the police – although Hartley skilfully interleaves both these elements with the main romantic plotline, creating strange resonances and absurdist situations in which the familiar coordinates of both romance and crime narratives are dramatically disordered.

Kate and Bill's first meeting – a series of intense looks as Kate stands against a blue sky, her light dress blowing in the wind – effectively expresses their potential for romantic connection. But viewer expectation here is likely to be laced with anxiety, owing to Bill's earlier declaration to Dennis that he intends to make the first good-looking blonde woman he meets fall in love with him before using her as 'a little toy, a little plaything' and discarding her. These words, obviously, are not the words of a man with any great understanding of possibility or reality. Like Jude in *Surviving Desire*, Bill has stepped away from the complexities of reality into the sublime convictions of fantasy – and worse, his delusions have inspired in him a conscious desire to do harm to women (or a woman, more specifically). The conflict between Bill's shadow desire to hurt women and his romantic desire for Kate individually is at the heart of *Simple Men*'s innovative reworking of the romantic comedy narrative, but, crucially, for much of the film Bill's true feeling or intent remains unclear. As David Bordwell notes, Hartley's unconventional editing functions to withhold crucial visual information that might clue us in to Bill's motives. In a scene where Kate and Bill slow-dance together and talk about the future, Bill's pledge to make a life with Kate is kept offscreen, the camera holding on Kate, and when Bill confirms his intentions, the line again comes from offscreen, denying us the opportunity to look him in the eyes and judge his sincerity.[10]

The depiction of Bill in *Simple Men* expresses in an extreme form Hartley's belief in the instability or ambiguity that is at the core of all things and that continually frustrates our attempts to establish certainties and to order the world around us (though not necessarily our attempts to attain happiness, as we have seen). At first glance, the character of Kate would seem to suggest a different, much more conventional, vision of reality. Kate projects a reassuring image of straightforwardness and control. Her interest in tree-planting aligns her with the eternal cycles of the natural world, an association strengthened by the plain textures and blue and green tones of her clothing (Bill, in contrast, wears a brick-red shirt for most of the film). There is a moral dimension, too, to Kate's down-to-earth personality – she doesn't tell lies, apparently having realised at some point in the past that lying just makes things harder. These are all qualities likely to be seen by viewers as virtuous, and they suggest Kate as a positive (and possibly progressive) model of strong femininity, a corrective to the troubling model of masculinity represented by Bill and other male characters.[11] But for Hartley, devotion to strength and stability cannot provide the foundation for a happy life, for men or women. To truly appreciate the deepest lessons of *Simple Men*, we will have to adopt a fresh perspective and see Kate's good qualities as both artificial and self-limiting.

That the forms of stability in which Kate places her faith in fact function to keep her at arm's-length from reality and thus from real possibility is suggested at various points throughout the film, though not explicitly. In various ways, Karen Sillas's wonderfully sensitive performance as Kate speaks of an anxiety or sadness not acknowledged at the level of the script – indeed, Hartley recalls that Sillas brought a loneliness and a 'weak spot' to the character that he hadn't originally articulated in his writing (Hartley, wisely, capitalised on Sillas's interpretation).[12] Sillas uses her considerable skills as a performer to create moments when Kate's confidence suddenly and affectingly slips, as when, after talking matter-of-factly to Elina about a violent episode involving her ex, she finishes her story by saying 'I can't remember', her face assuming an intense expression of pained melancholy. Sillas's performance allows us to start to see Kate's most prominent character traits for the emotional props they really are. Once we let go of the idea of Kate as a near-saintly paragon of strength and virtue and embrace the idea of her as a complicated person whose being is coloured by fear and sadness – at least partly the result, the script makes clear, of her poor treatment at the hands of her violent ex-husband and possibly other men – her devotion to nature begins to seem less like an expression of some inner peace and more like a desperate retreat from the troublesome realities of social and romantic life into a fantasy space of soothing stability. Indeed, Kate says as much to Bill when she tells him directly that planting trees is for her really only a hobby. 'It keeps me busy, and I like that', she says, suggesting its importance for her as an emotional support rather than an authentic source of meaning. Her principle of never telling a lie is rooted in a similar desire for simplicity. Like many rigid principles, its true value is not as a guarantor of moral behaviour but as a means of denying the knotty nature of human reality. Its ultimate emptiness is signalled in a scene near the end of the film when Kate wants to hide Bill from the police. Talking to the sheriff, she resorts to various forms of evasion and deflection to both not tell a lie and not give Bill away, desperately clinging to a principle almost entirely irrelevant to the complex emotional and ethical problems of human desire (Kate's wilfulness here often generates an air of absurd comedy; when the sheriff asks her whether she can be more specific in response to one of his questions, she answers simply 'Yes').

It is her faith in an illusory stability that Kate must surrender in order to realise the potential of her relationship with Bill. Kate's decision to lie to cover for Bill is in fact the first step towards genuine connection, although at this point we're not sure how to feel about it, because we don't know whether Bill is manipulating Kate in order to escape the clutches of the law. It is only when Bill finally gives up his self-interested attempts to control his situation and chooses to make himself vulnerable, signalling his wish to start a relationship on an equal footing with Kate, that love becomes a real possibility. This possibility is richly evoked by the film's final sequence, an ending that in its complex interweaving of visual and aural elements surpasses even the remarkable conclusions of *The Unbelievable Truth* and *Trust*. Bill, having turned down the opportunity to escape on his estranged father's boat, drives back to Kate's house, where he knows the police will be waiting for him. As Bill approaches, Hartley cuts between Kate, her view of Bill's car coming down the road towards her, and the sheriff – whose semi-comical jeremiad on the essential futility of love is layered on the soundtrack with plaintive guitar music. 'Falling in love is like sticking an ice pick in your forehead … but we keep doing it', says the sheriff to no one in particular. Bill stops the car near Kate. Everything goes quiet. Bill gets out of the car and shakes off two police officers to get to Kate. We cut to a close-up of Kate, then a close-up of Bill, then Kate, then Bill, then finally a high shot of Kate that feels slightly wrong, because this isn't the wider shot that we might expect at this point, a shot that could give us a good view of the two principals leaning in for a final kiss. Bill doesn't initiate a kiss but instead slowly lowers his head onto Kate's shoulder – a gesture that captures the true significance of this moment as one in which Bill moves past self-imposed limits and opens himself to a real closeness free of the distorting fantasies of wilful male dominance. Neither character speaks, but offscreen the sheriff says 'Don't move', just after the guitar music starts up again. This line is the last in the film, and like Audry's final line in *The Unbelievable Truth* ('Listen') it colours the romantic moment with a complex ambiguity. Most obviously, the sheriff's voice here is the voice of the social world, his words reminding us that even those in love cannot transcend circumstance; Bill must soon be led away, like Matthew in *Trust*, to answer for his crimes. But perhaps the sheriff's words also express Bill's or Kate's (or our?) desire, a desire for things to stay this way, for the two of them to stay just where they are, how they are, at this moment, even though they cannot, because reality is instability and everything changes. Hartley sees this kind of desire as ultimately destructive, because it involves a denial of reality. But if these final words create the feeling that Bill and Kate are not completely free of those human fantasies that seem to be a source of affirmation but in fact are a source of pain, they also, in evoking the film's beginning, remind us that even someone as wilfully deluded as Bill can come to a more enlightened understanding of life. At the start of the film, when the line 'Don't move' was first spoken (by Bill's girlfriend, Vera [Mary McKenzie]), Bill was constrained by a hyper-masculine perception of the world according to which being in love and 'thinking with your prick' (as Dennis puts it) are one and the same thing; now, in this moment of connection with Kate, he is free, finally receptive to the possibility of love in its fullness. People really can change. Real connection is possible.

The possibility that Kate and Bill embrace in the last part of the film suggests itself in a number of earlier exciting moments of connection, portrayed by Hartley as a kind of equal exchange of energy, rather than as acts of male seduction. Bill and Kate's exchange of glances when they first meet is one such moment; another is the erotic dance they share during the Sonic Youth-scored musical number. Other characters too form relationships endowed with an authentic erotic charge, or at least a lively ambiguity that signals their potential. Elina and Dennis's complicated connection first becomes apparent in an elaborately choreographed sequence in which Elina moves through the rooms of Kate's apartment hiding from Dennis, the fluidity and comical exuberance of their strange, non-musical dance suggesting a chemistry that neither has yet acknowledged. Later, during the musical number, they perform a much more intimate dance, moving in unison to the rhythms of the grinding, sensual music. (Sadly, Dennis and Elina's potential remains just potential, for at the end of the film Elina leaves with Dennis's father, a man with whom she shares a relationship that, because it is defined by a conventionally gendered student-teacher dynamic, is conspicuously lacking in Hartleyan possibility.)

The characters of Bill and Elina, as well as other more minor characters, the most memorable of which is the broken-hearted, poetically pessimistic sheriff, engage our imagination as expressive elements in *Simple Men*'s ambitiously conceived portrait of the vicissitudes of romantic desire. But it is Bill and Kate who form the emotional focus of the film, and it is through their relationship that Hartley conveys to us in the most unusually vivid and immediate way both the human potential for loving connection and the human fondness for distorting fantasies that only block connection. Along with Audry and Josh, Maria and Matthew, and (to some extent) Jude and Sofie, Bill and Kate demonstrate the radical possibility of the romantic comedy coupling. In Hartley's hands, the central couple's dance of desire becomes something more than charming spectacle, prompting us to question many of the beliefs about gender, power and intimacy that so often underpin commercial romantic narratives, and stirring in us a longing to grasp what is real and important about true romantic love.

Hartley's early encounters with the romantic comedy tradition yielded a group of films whose power and depth have rarely been matched in the worlds of either mainstream or 'independent' romantic comedy in the decades since, and indeed none of the films from Hartley's later career is animated by the particular form of magic that animates, say, *Trust* or *Simple Men*. From the mid-1990s onwards, Hartley shifted away from the romantic comedy form to develop a varied, lively and often confounding body of work the impact of which on audiences and film culture has been, on the whole, limited and fleeting.[13] But his most successful early films endure today as pleasurable and profound classics of modern cinema – classics that earn their status not by appeal to nostalgia or simple sentiment (always anathema to good art in Hartley's view) but by engaging us in a complex, difficult but ultimately cheering meditation on the deepest mysteries of human reality.

Notes

1   Berrettini makes this point in a chapter on *Trust* in his book *Hal Hartley* (2011: 20). The chapter also includes a sensitive discussion of the abortion clinic scene (20–1).

2   My wording here is influenced by Kathleen Rowe Karlyn's characterisation in a perceptive essay that discusses *Gas Food Lodging* as a film that challenges 'the conventional belief that femininity simply "is", it doesn't grow or change' (1998: 182).
3   In my description of this scene I am indebted to Steven Rawle, who writes that *Trust*'s final tableau 'leaves Maria (Adrienne Shelly) suspended ambiguously between states' (2011: 73).
4   Fantasy also has a positive role to play in romantic love, of course, as Noël Carroll has discussed in relation to *Vertigo* (2007: 101–7). As Carroll puts it, healthy romantic fantasy 'has a basis in reality – a basis in the real potential of the beloved'. Pathological romantic fantasy, by contrast, 'involves a denial of the uniqueness and particularity of the beloved' (2007: 110). The kind of fantasy that both Jude and Sofie let dictate their behaviour is patently pathological.
5   The full Anatole France quote, from the novel *The Gods Are Athirst* (1912), is: 'Yet, every now and then, there would pass a young girl, slender, fair and desirable, arousing in young men a not ignoble desire to possess her, and stirring in old men regrets for ecstasy not seized and now for ever past.'
6   My understanding of the potential of unconventional film images and sounds to touch spectators at a profoundly meaningful, non-rational, 'subconscious' level is influenced by the work of Martha P. Nochimson, particularly her breathtakingly insightful book *Screen Couple Chemistry: The Power of 2* (2002). Nochimson's ideas in *Screen Couple Chemistry* about energy and its centrality to the most resonant of onscreen romantic pairings have also informed my discussions of Hartley's couples in this essay.
7   In an interview for *Cineaste*, Hartley explains how the dance sequence in *Simple Men* was developed from the dance sequence in *Surviving Desire* (as well as the choreographed violence in the 1991 short film *Ambition*), suggesting that *Simple Men* was made after *Surviving Desire* (or at least while it was in production); see Fried (1993). Part of Hartley's account is quoted in Berrettini (2011: 27).
8   Lesley Deer refers to Kate as an 'Earth mother' in the chapter on *Simple Men* in her doctoral thesis, 'The Repetition of Difference: Marginality and the Films of Hal Hartley' (2000). Steven Rawle uses the same term in his discussion of *Simple Men* in *Performance in the Cinema of Hal Hartley* (2011).
9   My reading of Kate's character is influenced by notes on Hartley's first three features that Diane Negra kindly shared with me when I was writing my doctoral thesis (published in 2011 as *The Cinema of Hal Hartley*).
10 My description of Hartley's shot sequence here is based on a much more detailed analysis by David Bordwell (2005; reprinted in this volume).
11 A view of *Simple Men* as contrasting strong femininity with problematic masculinity is offered by Geoff Andrew, who writes that 'the men are confused, and lack control of their emotional lives, whereas the women know what they want and are not prepared to accept anything less' (1999: 298), and Steven Rawle, who writes: 'We often find Hartley's films featuring female characters of stability and

control, while men remain, as is stressed by the title of the lm, simple' (2011: 141).

12 For Hartley's discussion of his casting of Sillas and her performance, see Hartley 2002: xxviii.

13 Hartley's next feature after *Simple Men*, *Amateur* (1994), centres a romantic relationship but adopts a dark, tragic tone quite distinct from the romantic-comic tone of the early features. In the three-part omnibus film *Flirt* (1995), Hartley shifts focus from the central romance to the film's own narrative design, creating a giddily self-conscious experiment in form in which the emotional textures of the characters' relationships are pretty well beside the point. Many of the later films move beyond both romantic comedy and romance to very different generic realms (horror/fantasy in the case of *No Such Thing* [2001], science fiction in the case of *The Girl from Monday* [2005], the spy thriller in the case of *Fay Grim* [2006]).

CHAPTER SIX

A New Man: The Logic of the Break in Hal Hartley's Amateur

Daniel Varndell

'I thought the pen had been a good pen', Joseph Conrad writes of the pen with which he had written his earliest stories, now kept as a memento of his youth on which he hoped to be able to look with 'tender eyes' as he and his writing matured into old age. Having found his good pen a permanent resting place in a wooden bowl containing other bits and pieces – the 'minute wreckage that washes out of a man's life into such receptacles' – the mere sight of it was enough to bring about an immense feeling of satisfaction until, one day, Conrad 'perceived with horror' that a second *identical old pen* had found its way into the wooden bowl. The two pens were indistinguishable, and his memento was hopelessly confused with a meaningless impostor. While Conrad's memento was not exactly lost, its confusion with the double left him with a strange feeling of discomfort. Only one solution was found to be satisfactory: 'It was very distressing, but being determined not to share my sentiment between two pens or run the risk of sentimentalising over a mere stranger, I threw them both out of the window into a flower-bed – which strikes me now as a poetical grave for the remnants of one's past' (1937: 57–8).

It is from the discarded remnants of the past that Hal Hartley's *Amateur* (1994) begins when, having been similarly thrown out of a window by a woman who hesitates briefly over his body before running away, the film's hero (Martin Donovan) awakens with total amnesia. A stranger in the purest sense, this man picks himself up from amongst the fragments of broken glass and staggers into a nearby café where he meets Isabelle (Isabelle Huppert) – a former nun now writing bad pornography – who, believing herself to be on a mission from God, resolves to help him uncover his past. However, as the picture of his nasty, brutish personality comes slowly into focus, the criminal this man – we later learn is called Thomas – used to be proves difficult to reconcile with his post-amnesia 'goodness' as he becomes increasingly confused with his own meaningless impostor. Concurrent with Thomas and Isabelle's investigation, the woman who pushed him – Thomas's estranged wife, Sofia (Elina Löwensohn) – gives her own account of the crimes her husband committed against her. The two narrative threads dovetail in the middle of the film, as Thomas, reunited – if not reconciled – with his wife, is forced to confront his past. This essay argues that *Amateur* is a film about figures who experience the effect of being caught 'in a break', so to speak. While Thomas 'breaks down' as a result of his amnesia, Sofia 'breaks away' from her old life as a porn star in Thomas's violent film productions in the hope of starting her life over – to become, as she puts it, 'a mover and a shaker'. In both their cases, the question comes down to the possibility of seeing the world anew, and acting differently in relation to it, as we commonly mean when we speak of '*making* a break (for it)' – to *make*, rather than simply let, something new happen.

This essay establishes this 'logic of the break' as *the* Hartleyan idea, the understanding of which gets us to the very heart of his cinema. For it is the experience of being *in* a moment of crisis or rapture that his characters' worlds appear to us so familiar yet at the same time utterly foreign; standard genre tropes are rendered uncanny by virtue of their existentialist framing while comedy dialogue is undercut through deadpan delivery, by characters in situations that seem hopelessly absurd (in his 1995 review, Roger Ebert suggested watching *Amateur* with the sound off to illustrate how far Hartley's manipulation of genre is effected by his idiosyncratic dialogue and use of alternative rock music). Hartley's cinema is dominated by the figure of an irreconcilable 'two' where the unity of a singular truth is refused, denying an easy exit. Rather, the act of breaking in *Amateur* is something like a productive haemorrhaging, where one makes a break in order to disturb or interrupt the vicious circle of an unhappy or unfulfilled life. While its effects, to be repeated, tend to be similarly difficult and disturbing, it is only by making a break – moving beyond a difficult past – that one can begin again. To truly start over one must be prepared to move the entire frame through which one sees things, to shake (up) one's perspective. After all, our most painful memories render us in our most reflective moments captive to a framing of the world that sometimes, perhaps, it might be preferable to break away from. In this way, one's ability to forget becomes a *positive power*, but one requiring the resolve needed to discard one's souvenirs of the past.

Total Recoil
In his autobiography, *My Last Breath*, Luis Buñuel muses on his mother's dementia, and remains thankful that he has so far managed to keep this 'final darkness' at bay, for a 'life without memory is no life at all … Our memory is our coherence, our reason, our feeling, even our action. Without it, we are nothing.' Buñuel continues: 'I am the sum of my errors and doubts as well as my certainties … the portrait I've drawn is wholly mine – with my affirmations, my hesitations, my repetitions and lapses, my truths and my lies. Such is my memory.' The horror of losing one's grasp on the past is not just that of losing one's composure, but one's very consistency. 'I can only wait for the final amnesia', Buñuel concludes, 'the one that can erase an entire life' (1994: 4,

6). In this powerful description, Buñuel shifts from the distressing physical oblivion of dementia to the existential crisis at the heart of another type of oblivion, the one towards which all life tends. Might there be a moment, Buñuel implies, where one became conscious enough of this second, inevitable, oblivion such that the 'sum' of one's errors and doubts – belonging only to oneself – suddenly aroused a great feeling of disappointment at the life one had lived, perhaps even *shame*? What might one conclude – drawing one's last breath – about the kind of life one had led? In *The Myth of Sisyphus*, Albert Camus suggested that it is in such moments that we experience the beginning of an absurd thought, that

> beginning to think [in this way] is beginning to be undermined. Society has but little connection with such beginnings. The worm is in man's heart. That is where it must be sought. One must follow and understand this fatal game that leads from lucidity in the face of experience to flight from light. (2005: 3)

What Hal Hartley conceives in *Amateur* (and it is undeniably a writerly conceit) is a figure who collapses into one of the two types of oblivion described by Buñuel. A figure whose amnesia constitutes both a life suddenly eclipsed by physical trauma, as well as the dawning realisation that the portrait of his past self is not only 'wholly' his but is a portrait he cannot recognise himself in, and worse – it is a portrait with which he is disgusted to his very core. But this 'doubting Thomas' also experiences the kind of oblivion described by Camus, for having discovered this about himself he enters a 'fatal game' tempting him into a 'flight from light' that could just as easily see him escape into the shadows of ignorance facilitated by his amnesia as confront this difficult truth.

There is a gap, however, between the oblivion that wipes Thomas's memory and the oblivion that confronts him with the truth of his past crimes, both of which anticipate the final oblivion of *grand mort* – his death at the end of the film. As he very slowly picks himself up from the ground at the beginning of the film, a voice-over prophesises the final scene – 'And this man will die. He will. Eventually. He will die, she repeated. And there is nothing any of us can do about it.' At first, this portentous voice seems to emanate from the narrative of Hartley's story itself. However, a sound bridge soon synchronises two spaces: the noise of rain droplets running off a nearby gutter combined with street babble merges with the echoic sound of a typewriter key being punched. A cut reveals the speaker, Isabelle, a writer busily typing out – while reading aloud – her pornographic fiction in a nearby café. The Sophoclean words heard in the voiceover shift in tone as Isabelle's narrative abruptly departs from the style of her poetic prophesy to describe a crass sexual encounter in which her hero's penis is – to the disgust of the other diners – compared to a 'piece of two-by-four'. Hartley's dialogue is replete with such bathetic non-sequiturs, in which a weighty existentialist form frames standard generic content and secret truths are explored through the banalities of the quotidian. Soon after this scene, Thomas entertains himself while Isabelle works, and meets a schoolboy whose copy of *The Odyssey* he briefly exchanges for a porn magazine, eliciting the boy's knowledge of 'Sofia Ludens', a porn star whose name seems to trigger in Thomas's dreams the stirrings of his dormant memory. With this clue, Thomas and Isabelle find out where Sofia lives and discover the broken glass shattered around the street where he fell. It is in this same place that he awoke as a 'new man' that Thomas experiences a 'dreadful shipwreck' – as Dr Jekyll describes his realisation of the existence of Mr Hyde – when the weight of his past comes crashing down on him. He enters Sofia's apartment, and with just the barest of facial expressions and a typically understated exclamation – 'shit' – Thomas experiences a kind of 'total recoil' when confronted by the proof of his violent nature (he holds in his hand a Polaroid image of a facially disfigured woman used to make the stars of his porn films compliant with his demands as a producer). This moment marks the middle of the film, and is the precise point at which Thomas experiences a second loss – a *petite mort*, as the French call such 'little deaths' – this time not of memory, but of *innocence*. 'I'm the same man you knew yesterday', he later insists to reassure Isabelle. *Not* the same man, that is, that *Sofia* knew (the day before) yesterday. This moment of 'total recoil' in the middle of the film marks the precise moment that Thomas is beginning to *think* in the sense Camus intends; he is undermined and so, for a second time, he breaks.

'If I accuse an innocent man of a monstrous crime,' wrote Camus, 'he will reply that this is absurd.' The indignant response of one so accused, Camus continues, has a comical edge on the basis of the 'antinomy existing between the deed I am attributing to him and his lifelong principles' (2005: 28). Thomas belongs to a rich line of absurd heroes so accused – the work of Dostoevsky and Kafka is replete with such figures – whose only hope is that they might discover some meaning behind these accusations, and, if at all possible, search in this understanding for some form of redemption. Thomas's condemnation echoes that of K. in Kafka's *The Trial* who, following a lengthy and esoteric arraignment, is led out to the suburbs by two gentlemen who carefully place his head on a stone and stab him in the heart with a butcher's knife. As he bleeds out, K's final words gasp from his mouth, commenting on the shame of it all – 'Like a dog!' But Thomas belongs just as much to the rich line of classic film noir heroes similarly condemned for crimes of which they are *in reality* fully guilty, but whose 'lifelong principles' seem no less incommensurate with such criminality. In contrast to the absurd hero, it is the job of the noir hero to settle his own 'account' (in the sense both of paying his debt and telling his story), as Walter must in Billy Wilder's *Double Indemnity* (1944) – a paradigmatic case – the end of which comes when, having recorded his confession onto a tape machine, he is finally disburdened of his suffering (whereupon he perishes). In his last moments, it is suggested to K. in *The Trial* that he should take the knife from his executioners and end his own life. K. refuses this offer – how can he authenticate the punishment with his acceptance of it when the law has been so manifestly inadequate in bringing the case against him? By contrast, with Walter in *Double Indemnity*, no trial is necessary – in the 'eyes' of the law his confession puts him back 'on the record' following his crimes (we realise the film itself *is* this confession), thereby straightening the 'kink' introduced by the femme fatale (after all, the downfall of the noir hero is sealed with a kiss). Thomas is neither one nor the other character type alone, just as *Amateur* itself seems caught between two genres.

Drawing attention to the film's 'strange, discomfiting character', Sebastian Manley points out that the style of *Amateur* was one of the biggest problems for reviewers. In one of the more critical reviews explored by Manley, Jonathan Romney complains about 'a strange disjunction of tone that doesn't quite add up', to which he adds: 'You could read *Amateur* either as a wilfully nasty piece of noir or as an absurdist comedy, but try to put the two together and they refuse to gel' (quoted in Manley 2013: 66). But this refusal to 'gel' is Hartley's greatest achievement here. It is a question of confronting the deadlock experienced as a result of reaching an impasse in one's life. Such an impasse is described by the eponymous hero of W. G. Sebald's masterpiece, *Austerlitz*, where,

> like a tightrope walker who has forgotten how to put one foot in front of the other, all I felt was the swaying of the precarious structure on which I stood, stricken with terror at the realization that the ends of the balancing pole gleaming far out on the edges of my field of vision were no longer my guiding lights, as before, but malignant enticements to me to cast myself into the depths. (2002: 173)

Amateur's 'guiding lights' – classic detective clues – are transformed in the second half of the film into 'malignant enticements': the enigmatic name 'Sofia Ludens', whom Isabelle initially seeks to protect *with* Thomas, must be latterly protected *from* him; a photograph Thomas takes at the police station to file him as a 'missing person' becomes his mug-shot; a razor blade he finds among his possessions is no longer an instrument for shaving but a weapon used to threaten women. What each of these examples illustrates is the shift from 'in-itself' to 'for-itself' – David Hume's famous thesis in which 'repetition changes nothing in the object repeated, but does change something in the mind which contemplates it'. The shift from in- to for-itself marks a break following which familiar objects are rendered 'strange, discomfiting' via a crucial shift in the subject's position and relationship to the object. Steven Rawle makes the point that it is through repetition that Hartley introduces the weight of the absurd into generic codes. Rawle writes that it is in the repetition of key phrases that Hartley illustrates the 'inadequacy of language': 'Thomas is not necessarily Thomas: Thomas was a violent criminal who exploited and abused women, but the amnesiac Thomas in the film is a newly formed subject untainted by the sin of his past incarnation' (2009: 64). The moniker 'Thomas' therefore fails. While we learn his name early on, Thomas spends the first half with no name. Might he not have picked a name at random? And, even upon learning his old name, might he not have kept the new one? It is in error that one insists on reintegrating the new subject with the old once it is discovered that they are essentially the same. For Rawle, the error is in this word 'same', which works to deny that a transformation of any kind has occurred. Perhaps the more nuanced observation then is that the 'mind' which perceives the object also *constructs* it (which is to say, the twist on Hume's thesis is that the object *is* in a sense different).

We learn at the end of the noir narrative that what we have effectively been witnessing is the condemned man in the act of confessing. In *Amateur*, Thomas cannot confess, but is nonetheless indicted. 'I'm sorry', he tells Isabelle at the end of the film, but for what he still cannot be certain, as she ruefully points out to him. Thomas can neither atone for, nor reconcile himself with, the crimes of his shadow any less than he can be punished, that is die, in this other's place. Nonetheless, such narratives demand that the criminal pay with his life. Yet Thomas's situation is much closer to Kafka's K. than Wilder's Walter. This does not, however, mean that the 'nasty noir' side of *Amateur* can be summarily dismissed. Thomas becomes a highly moral detective of the soul haunted by another Thomas whose crimes disgust him no less than they disgust us. It is here that Hartley's film avoids 'dwelling with pleasure', as Jekyll puts it, on the daydream that the two Thomases might be somehow separated, allowing us to simply identify with the good side. When Jekyll confesses in Stevenson's classic story, there is no final reconciliation: 'And thence,' so Jekyll pleads, 'when the night was fully come, he set forth in the corner of a closed cab, and was driven to and fro about the streets of the city. He, I say – I cannot say, I' (2012: 1717). This disjunction between 'he' and 'I' constitutes a gap that cannot be closed. However, as the next two sections will show, it is through Sofia and Isabelle that Hartley illuminates the path towards the film's *acceptance* of Thomas as a new man.

A Bright Gleaming Beam of Light

Prior to his experience of the 'little death', Thomas spends his time in a rather contented ignorance, somewhat aimlessly wandering around trying to find clues to jog his memory. Through a key narrative departure however, Hartley introduces Sofia through the barest of chance encounters. The connection comes as Sofia is forcibly ejected from a cinema for sleeping, rebuked by an usher with the same words – 'This is not a hotel' – used to chide Isabelle in the café after she annoys the other diners with her porno-poetry readings. Isabelle, dismayed at Sofia's bedraggled state, immediately resolves to help her. However, while she is set up as the enigmatic Sphinx whose secret holds the key to unlocking Thomas's past, the narrative shifts its focus to Sofia herself as she first tells her story, and then puts into effect her own plans to make a break. Thomas, she discovers, was in the process of blackmailing his former employers – an international business organisation with political connections – by threatening to publish the details of illegal trading contained on a series of floppy discs. Sofia decides to put the same plan into action. 'Why shouldn't I?', she tells Edward (Damian Young) – Thomas's former accountant (who is in love with her) – before revealing to him the full extent of Thomas's horrendous crimes against her: at twelve years old she was seduced and drugged by Thomas and forced into the porn industry, coerced and threatened with disfigurement should she try to leave. Having been initially cast as a femme fatale (by the way she dresses and is shown to manipulate men), Sofia is quickly recast as a femme *attrapée* – a 'trapped woman' who wants to empower herself and become 'a mover and a shaker'.

In his review of the film, Roger Ebert praised Hartley's refusal to conform to genre stereotypes, observing that his cinema is all about characters who surprise themselves by 'changing their natures'.

It's as if all the characters were a little dazed – by a blow on the head, say – and have awakened to find themselves assigned names and identities, which they dutifully try to portray, until as their heads clear and choices become visible, they realize that nothing in their lives is obligatory, and that they have the freedom to become someone else, completely. (1995)

However, this freedom is by no means as easy as Ebert seems to imply. Sofia's plan backfires when, having set up a meeting at Grand Central Station to collect her million dollars in exchange for the discs, she realises her mistake: two ruthless gangsters – with no intention of paying the money – turn up and Sofia panics. While she manages to escape in a cab, Sofia desperately witnesses Edward being beaten and bundled into a car by the gangsters – ironically both are accountants too, albeit with a penchant for torture and murder in addition to balancing the company's books. This scene is Sofia's own *petite mort*, as her crestfallen expression indicates. While she clearly doesn't love Edward in return, she is mortified to see him kidnapped as a result of her attempt to make her move. With her escape plan also having failed, Sofia's newfound confidence in herself evaporates. As it dawns on her that she cannot escape from her past so easily, Sofia's expression is – like Thomas's 'shit' – that of someone suddenly awakened as to the absurdity of their impossible situation. Far from feeling the freedom described by Ebert, this is, rather, the experience of the walls closing in.

In this scene outside Grand Central Station, Sofia shifts from an experience of the world in which she feels 'not quite there yet' to one in which she is suddenly confronted with the realisation that she is 'no longer *in* it at all'. From the hopeful expectation of a new freedom to the crushing disappointment of its sudden loss, Sofia sees the situation clearly as if for the first time. 'There is another blow,' F. Scott Fitzgerald says of such experiences, 'that comes from within – that you don't feel until it is too late to do anything about it, until you realize with finality that in some regard you will never be as good a man again' (1993: 69). And, so, 'like an old plate', such people 'crack'. Awakened to the absurd reality of a senseless world in which the bad guys are accountants whose balancing of the books brings with it so much injustice, Sofia is reduced – like Kafka's K. – to a figure who, moments before she is due to be executed when these gangsters find her in her apartment, looks with an expression that seems to convey the same grim resignation – 'Like a dog!' Brimming with yuppie aplomb, one of the accountant-gangsters threatens to torture her to find out what she knows, but a physical blow would make little impact next to the blow already struck from the inside, in what she perceives as her betrayal of Edward.

Feeling hopelessly forsaken, Sofia plunges headlong into a deep and lasting melancholia of the type described by Freud in which 'the shadow of the object fell upon the ego' (2001: 249). Confronted with the knowledge of the absurdity of one's life, Camus offers a choice: one can either forget what one learned in one's 'awakening' and return to ignorance or else remain in it. If one chooses the latter, one faces another choice: one must either 'die or else reverberate' (2005: 27), as he puts it. Sofia almost resigns herself to death. Hidden away, Thomas turns as if to leave her to this fate, but stops. It is the first point at which, having recoiled from the truth about who he was, Thomas *affirms himself* by acting to save Sofia, effectively saying 'yes' to the new man he had already become. For Thomas it is a question of how he should treat other people. He already knows that he does not have to live the way he did or treat people the way he used to, but the freedom to change is nonetheless more difficult to put into practice than he might have thought. Aristotle said that one had to make a practice of virtue such that one acted well in a situation out of *habit* (and habits are all that remain of the old Thomas). Truth, in the first half of *Amateur*, can be thus conceived as the conformity of one's desire to know with the object of knowledge (the simple question, 'Who am I?') In the second half of the film, however, this truth is the conformity of one's desire to know *with itself* (the more reflexive question, 'Do I still want to know who I am?'). In addition to wanting to know, Thomas must now justify his resolve to know. Out of this a new set of standards can be put in place, standards against which his actions can now be measured. While his fruit ripens late, it ripens nonetheless.

But why act in this moment? Why affirm himself at this point, when for much of the film he has been living as if he too were a condemned man? As Murray Pomerance notes of the Jekyll and Hyde archetype, a small gap always separates the death of the monster from the demise, moments later, of his good alter ego: 'The monster perishes at the good man's hands, reconverting to a shining exemplar of sweetness and light just as, with the girl he craves gazing tragically on, he takes his final breath' (2013: 107). Law and order is restored as his debt with society is settled, even while it is the good man who pays for the crimes of his shadow with his pound of flesh, a wound from which he will not recover. Yet, as Pomerance implies, we should not underestimate the power of this gap separating the two deaths for it is in-between that the loving encounter, however brief, nonetheless *takes place*. This encounter distinguishes this kind of death from a suicide driven by total despair at the impossible situation. While the latter aims precisely at the comforting oblivion of death, in the former such a mind resists. It is a grip on life that is to be found, Camus insists, 'at the extreme limit of the condemned man's last thought, that shoelace that despite everything he sees a few yards away, on the very brink of his dizzying fall. The contrary of suicide, in fact, is the man condemned to death' (2005: 52–3). To focus on a shoelace in one's final moments – much more to focus on the face of one's beloved – is to resist the 'flight from light' and insist – no matter how short-lived it might be – on the truthfulness of the loving encounter. Given a simple glance will suffice, it can never be too late or too soon to transform this moment from one of despair into one of hope, to charge one's final moment with the weight of an eternal truth.

Just prior to the point at which Thomas and Sofia's worlds collide once again, as Thomas and Isabelle arrive at the apartment and discover the broken fragments of glass scattered around the spot where he fell, they find themselves lit by a deep blue neon light reminiscent of adult store windows and sordid hotel signs. This unreal luminescence points to yet another ironic disjunction: that it is bathed in the seedy lighting of a world in which one expects only the most casual and fleeting of human interactions that Thomas and Isabelle realise that they have fallen in love. So Thomas falls again, in the same place he suffered the trauma which clouded his memory.

Nietzsche describes this process of thinking and reflecting on the unhistorical interruption to one's life in which one's own personal history is briefly suspended. It is 'only through the appearance', Nietzsche says, 'within that encompassing cloud of a vivid flash of light – thus only through the power of employing the past for the purposes of life and of again introducing into history that which has been done and is gone – did man become man' (1999: 64). This beginning of a new historical moment is what compels Thomas to act, but it is a moment that has nothing to do with his returning memory; rather, it is a moment rooted in love.

Forgive-Me-Not – 'Eventually'
The importance in Hartley's films of such delicate 'moments' – nuanced gestures and subtle looks – cannot be overestimated. In *Stranger than Paradise*, Geoff Andrew distinguishes Hartley from John Sayles, Jim Jarmusch and Todd Haynes by pointing out that 'it is as if Hartley is constantly reworking his material, refining his art, trying to find fresh ways of looking at the same handful of subjects that obsess him' (1998: 281). In the preface to the screenplay of *Flirt*, Hartley quotes Jean Renoir's statement that 'everyone really only makes one film in his life, and then he breaks it up into fragments and makes it again, with just a few little variations each time' (Cardullo 2005: 113). A similar sentiment was echoed when Hartley met and interviewed Jean-Luc Godard, whom Hartley described as sharing his 'urge to see new'. Hartley made this observation about using film to 'see new' in response to his interviewee's (rather belligerent) provocation that he, Godard, was 'younger' (than Hartley) because he was still making his 'first' film, while Hartley was 'older' because on his fourth. Hartley respectfully countered that, on the contrary, he too felt like he was still making his 'first' film; hence the title of his new work, *Amateur*. To make again (as if for the first time) one's first film, to see the world (once more) through fresh eyes clearly has its appeal. Yet the word 'amateur' implies a certain naiveté one might seek to overcome: a sharp picture is surely preferable to a blurred one, and is not professionalism the act of *honing* a craft?

Peter Bowen reports that Hartley imagined an alternative version of the film titled *The Professional*, which would 'deal with the implication of submitting your own personal morality to standards which don't personally have anything to do with you' (1995). 'I feel things, but I don't know what they mean', Thomas says. Yet Thomas used to be a professional. It is with Isabelle, however, that we find the real amateur of the film and who, despite her inexperience, insists on writing pornographic stories that no one, according to her editor, wants to read. 'I'm mediocre', she complains to Thomas, yet this is far from a simple word for Hartley, who stated that the feeling of being mediocre reflects 'the way I feel most of the time, sort of confused about what ... "competence" refers to' (quoted in Johnston 1995). There is, however, a second meaning to the word 'amateur' which is to be an 'enthusiast or admirer', one who does something out of *love*. Hartley explains his fondness of an anecdote from the annals of film lore, an anecdote 'about Hitchcock once dismissively calling Charles Laughton an amateur. Laughton responded, "Well, I love my work." That is the meaning of the word I intended. You know the root of the word is "one who loves"' (quoted in Bowen 1995). An amateur is one who pursues a craft as a lover of that craft. Perhaps this is why Hartley sits so comfortably outside of the mainstream of filmmaking as a business and industry, one full of accountants. Moments like the one Pomerance describes of the lovers' gaze prior to the point of the good man's death cannot be accounted for because they carry a different weight for the lovers than for those outside of it (which is everyone else!). The words 'I love you' remain banal, clichéd, outside of this loving encounter. It is clear that Hartley has little interest in using accountants to balance his books, preferring instead the intimacy of the private moment.

So the 'account' remains unbalanced, dominated as it is by amateurs who in the second half of the film go on the run up in the country to escape one of the gangsters (the other of whom, having been surprised by Thomas and Isabelle's intervention to save Sofia, toppled comically out of the apartment window, the same window – still missing a pane of glass – out of which Thomas was pushed). An awkward silence ensues as Sofia remains reluctant to reveal to Thomas the details of his past. Exasperated at her silence, Thomas pleads with her, to which she replies 'Why should I?' – her face, frightful yet scorn-filled, wordlessly condemns him. It quickly dawns on us that Thomas might not discover the knowledge he needs to break with his past. 'I can't forgive you', she tells Thomas, 'I can only forget' ('and I don't want to', she adds).

In her section on Hal Hartley in *Fifty Contemporary Filmmakers*, Lesley Deer states that *Amateur* ends on this ambiguous note: Edward – now raving mad having been tortured by the gangsters – turns up having escaped from police custody by wounding an officer, trailing what seems to be the entire police force in his wake. Sofia decides that the only way she can truly start over with her life is to tell Isabelle the truth about Thomas, thereby offloading her burden. Soon after, Thomas anxiously waits to see how Isabelle will react to this knowledge of his crimes. Finally, after looking unsure about what to do, she turns and asks, 'Will you still make love to me?', to which he humorously responds, 'Eventually' – a reference to their numerous failed attempts to make love throughout the film (for all Isabelle's talk of sex, there is a distinct lack of it in Hartley's film). Mistaken for Edward, Thomas is shot in the chest by a young and overeager police officer. Hence, while Thomas's redemption comes through Isabelle's demonstration of her love, trust and forgiveness, Deer points out that Hartley's refusal to end with the restoration of his memory ensures that the question mark hovering over the authenticity of his 'goodness' goes unresolved. 'Although amnesia allows him to shed an identity and become good,' Deer suggests, 'we are never given the opportunity of discovering whether Thomas is temporarily or permanently redeemed by his amnesia' (2002: 167). The problem raised by this suggestion is twofold. First, to what extent is one indebted to one's past? And second, to what extent is one indebted to those from whom one receives forgiveness?

On the first point, one must pay close attention to the words Thomas and Isabelle use in this final scene. 'I know this man', Isabelle defiantly states while she cradles her dead lover, her tearful expression nonetheless restrained in the face of such a catastrophic misfortune. Mark L. Berrettini emphasises that the repetition of 'this man' from her opening condemnation of him ('this man will die') creates a 'fold back onto the film's opening' (2011: 39). But another repetition in this final scene redoubles this folded speech. In the preceding moment, Thomas replies to Isabelle's question about making love with the word 'eventually', which brings the wry smile of a shared joke, a little grin, a moment of relief. They kiss, and as Thomas leaves we begin to realise where else in the film we have heard this word 'eventually': Isabelle's augur, which opens the film, when she said 'And this man will die. He will. Eventually. He will die, she repeated. And there is nothing any of us can do about it.' *Eventually*. On this implication Hartley gambles his entire film. We realise that we are witnessing the moment Pomerance described as the point at which the condemned man locks eyes with his lover one last time, whose gaze he holds long enough that the executioner's blade gets caught in Zeno's paradox of infinite regress – a brief moment interrupted by the weight not of the past, but of the future. It is a promise that stands, perhaps, for the paradoxical sense of being 'at eternity'. As Thomas and Isabelle embrace this last time, Hartley cuts first to Edward, who is no longer raving but calm and asleep, and then to Sofia, who is also resting peacefully. With Thomas's reply, the anticipated resolution seems to have arrived – a promise is made to the future, just as his debt to the past seems to have been settled.

On the second point, related to the first, one perhaps wonders what Sofia meant when she told Thomas that she could not forgive him, 'only' forget. Once again, it is Isabelle whose 'pornographic' fiction points to the underlying truth of the situation. 'In even the smallest things', Isabelle writes, 'she saw the pointlessness of hope, the impossibility of forgiveness.' When Isabelle and Sofia speak of the impossibility of forgiveness, it is easy to miss the great and wholly positive leap into the future that this implies. To forgive implies that the misdeed is *not* forgotten, but lives on in the memory – 'I forgive you' really just renews and strengthens the debt owed by the debtor – hence, the oldest philosophy, Nietzsche says, tells us that 'If something is to stay in the memory it must be burned in: only that which never ceases to *hurt* stays in the memory' (2010: 38). The oldest philosophy to which Nietzsche unsurprisingly refers is Christianity, in which the ultimate debt – sin – owed by the ultimate debtor – man – to a creditor who pays this debt off Himself by sacrificing His only son on Earth, indebts us at an even higher level (where the interest rates fluctuate according to the apostasy of the times). For Nietzsche, in giving up on one's memories that continue to smoulder, one acts to move on from that which hurts. Such a figure possessing the *will* to forget would experience a revaluation of everything they previously held dear; such painful memories would hardly carry the same weight they had before given the one who held on to them so tightly is, in a manner of speaking, no longer around. One steps out of the circular boundary around which one's memories have been so tightly circulating, and experiences the present with a perfect weightlessness, a condition beyond the calculations of society's notion of justice in which one becomes 'narrow-minded, ungrateful to the past, blind to dangers, deaf to warnings, one is a little vortex of life in a dead sea of darkness and oblivion' (1999: 64). While Sofia cannot quite will herself to move on in this way ('I don't want to'), she effectively achieves the same goal by entrusting Isabelle. We should be in no doubt whatsoever as to the importance of her gift, which aims neither at prolonging Thomas's suffering nor punishing him; rather, by passing on this knowledge, Sofia empowers Isabelle with the authority to forget, thereby offering Thomas *his* right to forget, move on and become a new man.

We must learn how to embrace our *plastic power*, Nietzsche suggests, which is 'the capacity to develop out of oneself in one's own way, to transform and incorporate into oneself what is past and foreign, to heal wounds, to replace what has been lost, to recreate broken moulds'; to be capable of such 'plasticity', for which the capacity to forget one's past is essential, is to become one of those who, as Nietzsche continues, 'are so little affected by the worst and most dreadful disasters, and even by their own wicked acts, that they are able to feel tolerably well and be in possession of a kind of clear conscience' (1999: 62). To take a counterexample, one need only look at Leonard Shelby's (Guy Pearce) final words – 'Now … where was I?' – at the end of Christopher Nolan's amnesia-noir, *Memento* (2000). Leonard is, like Thomas, a criminal whose amnesia enables him to believe that he is a good man – a detective avenging his wife's murderer. Yet unlike Thomas, when the truth briefly appears to him in a rare moment of lucidity, Leonard allows himself to forget in the full knowledge that he will return to his deadly game of revenge (in which he is both the animal caught in the hunter's snare *and* the hunter setting the traps). 'Now… where was I?', Leonard asks. So, he spins off once more to get another tattoo on his body, which we realise is not a record of the 'facts' of his case, but a record of the murders he has notched up.

By contrast, the kind of forgetting Hartley ends his film with is the second, *willed* and active forgetfulness from which one derives 'a little peace, a little *tabula rasa* of consciousness to make room for something new' (Nietzsche 2010: 35). If a thing must be burnt in so that it stays in the memory then *Memento*'s Leonard is one who gets his 'hurt' inked in to compensate for his amnesia. Hartley's amateurs, by contrast, opt for the peace of a forgetful oblivion that must be willed as such. As with Ursula Brangwen in D. H. Lawrence's *Women in Love* – who declares of the sudden rush of an unwanted childhood recollection:

> Oh God, could she bear it, this past which was gone down the abyss? Could she bear, that it had ever been! … There was a shadowy unreal Ursula, a whole shadow-play of an unreal life. … What was this decree that she should 'remember'! Why not a bath of pure oblivion, a new birth, without any recollections or blemish of a past life. (1971: 399)

Yet this desire for a new life is not easily come by as Ursula, tormented by her memory of home, illustrates. And Sofia shows only too well that it takes no small amount of effort to give up one's hurtful memories of the past. But give them up she does. It is forgetting, not forgiveness, which leads to redemption in *Amateur*, for 'a living thing can be healthy, strong and fruitful only when bounded by a horizon' (Nietzsche 1999: 63). Thomas's 'eventually' marks this horizon, and it is a horizon whose 'fundamental mood' – prior to his death – is *cheerfulness*, of confidence in the future even – perhaps *especially* – when that future is uncertain.

On the Verge

In *The Forgetting* (2003), David Shenk records a touching anecdote about Ralph Waldo Emerson who – aged seventy-six and suffering from severe memory loss as a result of advancing dementia – gave the same paper on 'Memory' he first presented twenty-two years prior. Shenk notes that Emerson's choice of material was sharply ironic: in the context of his own failing memory, Emerson spoke the following words on his subject:

> Memory performs the impossible for man by the strength of his divine arms; holds together past and present, beholding both, existing in both, abides in the flowing, and gives continuity and dignity to human life. It holds us to our family, to our friends. Hereby a home is possible; hereby only a new fact has value. (Quoted in Shenk 2003: 101–2)

'How poignant, and how awful,' Shenk comments, 'that as Emerson read aloud these evocative words, his own memory was broken' (2003: 102). Yet can we imagine a more powerful or resonant performance of the paper's original subject matter? Certainly, these words would have been meaningful when Emerson first read them 1857, but against the context of his condition in 1879 those same words are *infinitely richer*. While Shenk is right to point out that the double declaration elicited by the tragic context – well known to the small private audience respectfully gathered to hear him speak – must have pushed to the limit the poignancy of his delivery, we might also suppose that his choice of material had the most *disarming* of effects. After all, nothing would have disgusted Emerson more than to see in the eyes of his listeners the pitying expressions of those sympathetic to his growing reliance on family members to remind him of his place in his script – to manage, as Irving Goffman put it, his 'spoiled identity'. As a champion his entire career of individualism and self-reliance, the old transcendentalist's choice of essay foregrounds the stigma of his condition in a way that enriches, rather than diminishes, his material.

This is what Nietzsche means when he speaks of 'noon' as the 'stillest hour', which, Alenka Zupančič argues, is the figure of 'two' in which one exists only as a lost or incongruous antecedent, in some other time – a person who haunts 'from elsewhere'. Such an individual – as with Emerson – cannot overlap completely with this figure from the past who is, so to speak, 'found missing'. But it is in the difference between the two that a far greater impact can be felt. Nietzsche's 'noon', for Zupančič, is the figure of this logic of the break, as she explains:

> Midday is *not* the moment when the sun embraces everything, makes all shadows disappear, and constitutes an undivided Unity of the world; it is the moment of the shortest shadow. And what is the shortest shadow of a thing, if not this thing itself? [...] The thing (as one) no longer throws its shadow upon another thing; instead, it throws its shadow upon itself, thus becoming, at the same time, the thing and its shadow. (2003: 27)

At noon, far from being exposed and out in the open, such figures are 'dressed in their own shadows'. Thomas is a pornographer, after all, who can't even rent a dirty movie – 'You're a pretty naive guy' is how the video rental clerk describes him when he tries to rent one of his own productions! Thomas's naiveté stems from being an outsider in his own body, one who knows nothing and no one in a town where he used to know everything and everyone. Thomas is reborn as a 'native' (naive, *naif*, originates in the Latin *nativus*) and there is no Archimedean point from which he can effectively 'see himself'.

Let us conclude by returning to Conrad's confusion between his good pen as a souvenir of the past and its pretender. The presence of the latter resulted in the loss of Conrad's emotional tie to the object, but its ejection out of the window finally severed the tie *to the past itself*. Once ejected, he managed to breathe once more, feeling fine. Better, in fact – his next effort at writing was something of a 'departure' given he found himself in a 'very different atmosphere', one with a different *moral* attitude. 'I seemed able to capture new reactions, new suggestions, and even new rhythms for my paragraphs.' Conrad concludes this point, however, in a far more ambivalent way:

> For a moment I fancied myself a new man – a most exciting illusion. It clung to me for some time, monstrous, half conviction and half hope as to its body, with an iridescent tail of dreams and with a changeable head like a plastic mask. It was only later that I perceived that in common with the rest of men nothing could deliver me from my fatal consistency. We cannot escape from ourselves. (1937: 58–9)

One fancies oneself a 'new man' but instead experiences the wrenching return to the old self still beset by all the usual foibles. But is there not another layer to what Conrad is saying here? One cannot get to the birth of an idea because the act of thinking *changes* the thinker; hence, one reflects on the process, but is already a different person because of the consequences of the thought. What one perceives as a return to a 'fatal consistency' is really the readjustment of one's horizon to the new frame through which one perceives. From within the perspective of the break this new frame appears as something radical and exciting, whereas afterwards, when fully reintegrated, one finds oneself confronted once more with familiar problems. It is for this reason that one must continually prepare for a new departure to challenge one's moral attitude to 'see new'.

To experience the world as such is to experience it, as David Farrell Krell put it, 'on the verge': 'To be *on* the verge is to tend to presence principally in the modes of absence, evanescence, failure to remember, and oblivion. A script at the limits of legibility, the opacities of a vagrant spirit, a temporality of mortal transience, and an affirmation without nostalgia are the verger's only sources of light' (1990: 166). To be on the verge, in this sense, is to be decentred in relation to the origin of one's memories, reminiscences and writings; to be as far from anamnesis as possible, such that when one does experience a flooding back to oneself following a radical departure, it is with the feeling of unfamiliarity, as when one returns home having spent time in a foreign country. Hartley is one such verger. His first film away from his own native Long Island introduces a New York on the margins, estranged from itself. Emmanuel Levinas describes this sudden experience of estrangement in and from the familiar world in which 'illuminated objects can appear to us as though in twilight shapes. Like the unreal, invented city we find after an exhausting trip, things and beings strike us as though they no longer composed a world, and were swimming in the chaos of their existence' (2005: 31). Hartley's New York is presented as though it has been similarly invented. No one seems 'at home' here, but then perhaps they didn't much in his Long Island films either.

* * *

So, the stage sets fall down and, as Arthur O'Shaughnessy poeticised in his *Ode*, it is the 'movers and shakers of the world' who caused them to fall. They are 'world losers and world forsakers' who, in dreaming the dreams have such a force of passion that they overturn the past itself, conquering crowns and trampling whole empires underfoot. It is in even the smallest movements of such individuals – a push out of a window, or posting to a publisher an envelope containing floppy disks – that such worlds crumble. One breaks on the smallest detail in a Hal Hartley film, for his absurd characters are nothing if not awakened to the subtle power of the *nuance*: such figures can shake the very foundations of the world in which they live through little more than a word or a gesture – a look that says 'I need to tell you something', a wry smile that says 'all is forgotten'. The pornographer king is dead, but risen in his place is a new man capable of turning his life around, rejecting his crown. Recidivism is not an option for this man, and the 'total recoil' he experiences when confronted with his past actions ensures that re*call* is strictly unnecessary, not just for himself but for those who have the only claim to demand justice. And these figures – Sofia and Edward – end the film resting, finally at peace with the new state of things. Hartley's film ends, as his films tend to, not back at the beginning, but at *a* beginning. These critics who felt cheated by the end of the film have missed the point of its strange, discomfiting style. *The old Thomas is already dead*; he was dead even before the opening scene. What we have witnessed in the film is nothing less than the difficult birth of a new man, for whom breaking in two was a most momentous of events leading him to true love, a love enabling those against whom he had transgressed the opportunity to give up their hold on the hurtful memories that were stopping them from starting over. When he is killed in the final scene, his death should strike us fully unjust. Thomas finally 'pays' with his own pound of flesh as Isabelle remarks, 'I know this man', not yet ready to use the past tense. Either way, Thomas is killed 'Like a dog!', as that other writer of the absurdity of modern life put it, a writer in whose company Hal Hartley most deservedly belongs.

CHAPTER SEVEN

Not Getting It: Flirt as Anti-Puzzle Film
Steven Rybin

Hal Hartley's *Flirt* (1995) plays an intellectual game with its viewer. Each of the three episodes in the film involves a similar story: an individual – a flirt – is faced with the problem of whether or not to commit to a lover. Repetition with variation creates a structure abstractly connecting the stories. Lines of dialogue are echoed across the three parts. Decisive narrative moments depicting the flirt's relationship (will the flirt finally commit? Will a jealous lover kill the flirt?) are re-staged by Hartley in different geographic locations and with subtle changes in style and form. Finally, different actors appear in each of the three parts, each with different qualities of personality and presence. *Flirt*, through this framework, implicitly asks its viewers to think through how these variations function meaningfully in the film's overall form.

In part one of *Flirt*, set in New York City, a man, Bill (Bill Sage) equivocates in his commitment to a woman, Emily (Parker Posey), who will be leaving soon on a trip to Paris. In part two, set in Berlin, Dwight (Dwight Ewell) wavers in his commitment to his present partner, Johann (Dominik Bender), a successful German art dealer. And in the third part, set in Tokyo, a Japanese dancer, Miho (Miho Nikaido) finds herself torn between two different men: a filmmaker (played by Hartley himself) and a dance choreographer named Mr. Ozu (Toshizo Fujiwara). In a typical romantic comedy, we would be eager to know the outcome of the decision the flirt makes between her lovers in each of these three episodes: will Bill commit to Emily? Will Dwight stay with the art dealer? Will Miho go for the film director, or the dancer? *Flirt* does offer something in the way of provisional answers to each of these questions, at least in the narratives of Bill and Miho: we at least know, at the end, that Bill will *try* for Emily, for when we leave him, he is grabbing a taxi to the airport, with the intention of flying to Paris to win her; and Miho, at the end of her episode, decides on the filmmaker.

(Dwight's future is less clear.) But the joy of the film is not with resolution or even with narrative itself. Rather, Hartley's interest, and ours, lies in the fresh variations in gesture, framing and movement on display in each of the episodes. Should we remain preoccupied with narrative, it is unlikely we will finally be satisfied, despite the film's provisional moments of closure. It is, of course, not clear at all if Emily will accept Bill once he arrives, and the future of the filmmaker and Miho (although paralleled by Nikaido's marriage to Hartley in real life) is not spelled out in the film. None of the stories, as Hartley presents them, quite commits to a conclusion; the fate of the lovers, ultimately, is ambiguous. They are at the mercy of our interpretations, should we ourselves wish to commit to meaning.

Reflecting upon the film's patterned variations as well as its tantalising ambiguities, Tom Gunning suggests that the film's structure is reflective of the ambiguous status of the flirt as a social type. A flirt is one who vacillates between a play with open contingency and possibility, on one hand, and a final commitment to a particular kind of individual and the particular kind of world that individual orbits, on the other. As Gunning writes, in the film we see 'how the encounter between a contingent reality and a situation that demands a definite decision gives birth to a film – to three films, in fact, and to one total film, which is these three films interacting and playing together' (1996: vii). This encounter between contingent reality and definite decision is, as Gunning's discussion suggests, at the heart not only of *Flirt* but of cinema itself: the film frame seeks to fix, for a moment, an overwhelming and expansive reality that bends and twists in multiple directions. Hartley, throughout his career, has made part of his project as a filmmaker the goal of exploring these tensions between fixed form (the frame, camera position, a precisely choreographed movement) and contingent reality (the quality of light on a certain day; the inflection in the voice of an actor at just this moment; the way the wind blows through a performer's hair). *Flirt* is emblematic of Hartley's approach to filmmaking and storytelling because in this film his game of filmmaking is directly tethered to the game of love. The viewer is witness to how the director's efforts to commit to a reality through his play with the art of cinema are echoed and redoubled in the decisions and commitments his characters are compelled (or not) to make.

Yet is it quite right to describe *Flirt* as a game? What is at stake in describing what is perhaps Hartley's signature achievement in such terms? To describe the film this way is not just to pave the way towards a particular interpretation, in which to simply call the film a game or a puzzle would be innocent enough (that is, to play with the film's patterns and motifs as one might with any film, albeit in a self-conscious manner attuned to the film's own reflexivity). It is also to place the film in a contrapuntal relationship to a recent body of films which are also often described as games or puzzles, but which are nevertheless quite different from Hartley's own notion of what constitutes playful complexity. Thomas Elsaesser has usefully delineated a recent corpus of cinema, emerging in the 1990s and continuing into the new century, that he calls 'the mind-game film', a form of narrative that takes 'delight in disorienting or misleading spectators' – with withheld narrative information (à la *The Sixth Sense* [1999]) or narrative ambiguities (à la *Memento* [2000]) – and that invites the participation of those spectators. These are viewers who, for Elsaesser, 'on the whole do not mind being "played with": on the contrary, they rise to the challenge' of the narrative conundrums and challenges to classical form that puzzle or game films present (2009: 15). Most provocatively, Elsaesser suggests that these new narrative 'puzzle films' are symptomatic of a contemporary '"crisis" in the spectator-film relation, in the sense that the traditional "suspension of disbelief" or the classical spectator positions of "voyeur", "witness", "observer" and their related cinematic regimes or techniques (point-of-view shot, "suture", restricted/omniscient narration, "fly on the wall" transparency, mise-en-scène of the long take/depth of field) are no longer deemed appropriate, compelling, or challenging enough' (2009: 16). The puzzle films Elsaesser discusses play with this 'crisis' through various repeated features, and they include films such as *Lost Highway* (1997), *Dark City* (1998), *Run Lola Run* (1998), *The Matrix* (1999) and *Donnie Darko* (2001): deluded, confused or 'tricked' protagonists, who are presented with an overwhelming complexity of narrative events that to some degree mirrors the viewer's own engagement with the game; a protagonist who has a friend who is revealed to be, at some point in the narrative, imaginary (*Donnie Darko* and *Fight Club* [1999], as Elsaesser notes, are emblematic of this tendency); characters who question the ontological status of their reality, or their identity (*Blade Runner* [1982], *Total Recall* [1990], *Minority Report* [2002]); and so on.

It would be simple enough to point out that Hartley's *Flirt*, despite its own status as a kind of small-scale, three-piece cinematic jigsaw, contains none of the features of the aforementioned puzzle films. The protagonists (Bill, Dwight, Miho) are not quite deluded, or confused, in the spectacular manner of the heroes of the puzzle films; they are, instead, merely riddled by the sufficient-enough complexities and ambiguities of everyday life and love. They do not have any imaginary friends (their lovers all really do exist); and if they question the nature of their identity or their reality, it is only in response to the reality and identity of a lover to whom the question of commitment signals, nevertheless, a certain groundedness. In other words, they are struggling with a commitment within *this* world, not with the question of whether or not they or the world as such exists. And, indeed, while the aforementioned mainstream puzzle films tend to suggest that classical traditions of cinematic style are no longer sufficiently challenging or interesting on their own terms, *Flirt* assumes a viewer who will find questions of style and its variations inherently thought-provoking. Indeed, *Flirt* desires a viewer who will, as I have suggested from the outset, find questions of how to 'commit' to a reality in front of the camera, through choices in framing, colour, performance and so on, to be as interesting as the various romantic goings-on coursing through Hartley's plots.

What I want to propose, then, is the idea that *Flirt* is ultimately not so much a game as it is an 'anti-puzzle' film: a film that presents pieces of an ostensible puzzle only to assert that the point is to *not* finally put its pieces together at all. Elsaesser's puzzle-film spectators delight in locating and sharing their interpretations and 'solutions' to the various ambiguities presented by the narrative complexities and 'brain teasers' in certain contemporary films (often, they share these experiences or interpretations of the films on blogs or online fan communities), despite the fact that several of these films 'do not add up' – they present conundrums or ambiguities that cannot finally ever be solved or fully thought-through (the films of David Lynch are especially notable in this regard). *Flirt* never quite 'adds up' either (either in its individual sections or as a larger collage), but I take it as significant (and not at all to its detriment) that it has not quite inspired the torrent of online comment or interpretation that the films Elsaesser discusses provoke. This is because the question of 'adding up' or not is not on the film's agenda at all. The game or 'puzzle' it presents to us is not one that can be solved, nor the kind that yearns for endless commentary as a kind of solution – it is not the kind of game that thrills or overwhelms. But it is a game, I contend, that offers a much more grounded and relevant vision of human relationships than most of the razzle-dazzle puzzle films, a vision in which not finding the solution, not adding up the score or articulating the meaning, and, indeed, perhaps not even getting what one desires or finally wants, is the entire point of the game.

Flirting with a Puzzle
The puzzle film, it would seem, is all about 'getting it': if not arriving at a final, polished solution, then at least articulating a provisional one that positions one's interpretation discursively and pointedly. In a way different from the interpretations that accompany discussions of films such as *Fight Club* and *Memento*, writers on Hartley have often displayed this anxiety over 'getting it', either in the presentation of an interpretation of a film or in the suggestion that only certain kinds of viewers will finally 'get' what Hartley is up to. The latter position is saliently articulated in many reviews appearing around the time of Hartley's emergence as a new director on the indie scene, often by critics seeking to position themselves as 'hip' or 'visionary' enough to understand Hartley's work. In Jason Davids Scott's contribution to this volume, which thoroughly analyses critical discourse surrounding the release of Hartley's early features, we often find the critic positioning herself as the one who 'gets it', or at least the one in charge of marking the boundaries of the community populated by those who do. These are familiar critical parries – the critic staking out a position of distinction in her tastes, in order to establish that position as the one from which to declare who will 'get' Hartley and who won't. If these critical positions don't amount to either interpretations or substantial descriptions of Hartley's aesthetic, they nevertheless still do amount to a declaration that a position of 'getting' Hartley might be won if the critic's sensibility or 'wavelength' is shared – a wavelength and sensibility that, presumably, the director himself also occupies.

That a film might have to win over a viewer, however – and this language of flirtation appears explicitly in one critic's suggestion that Hartley's films may not 'woo' everyone (see Gillespie 1994) – reminds us that for the flirt, wooing and winning over may ultimately not be connected to 'getting it' at all. This is an idea that Adam Phillips explores with great perspicuity across two books exploring relationships between psychoanalysis and art. In the first of these books, *On Flirtation: Psychoanalytic Essays on the Uncommitted Life*, Phillips positions the very act of flirtation as a 'transitional performance' that always and perpetually attempts to 're-open, to rework, the plot' (1994: xxv) – deferring final commitments and declarations of virtue in favour of a life lived in and through contingency. Although on some level Phillips is concerned in his work with *actual* flirtation – that is, with the experience of two potential lovers circling around one another – flirtation opens up as a more extended metaphor in his writing, a device he uses to encourage the reader to recognise that the contingency of all experience works to productively unsettle previously articulated preferences and commitments. In other words, for Phillips, flirtation – that which 'eroticizes the contingency of our lives' and a mode that functions as 'the art of making ambivalence into a game, the ironic art of making it a pleasure (or at least an excitement)' (1994: xxiii) – is not a moment of life that one passes through on the way to commitment, but a key to living: a way to keep thoughts and emotions in play, before they are assigned to and deadened through instrumental and committed use.

In a later book, *Missing Out: In Praise of the Unlived Life*, Phillips connects these ideas to the act of making meaning, a concern that has a more direct connection to the interpretation-filled world of film studies and to the games and pleasures of film discourse that lingers over puzzles. Phillips frames meaning, or understanding, as the 'it' – the thing all of us are anxious to be sure we *get*; this is the kind of anxiety, I would suggest, that drives those to declare their various ways of 'getting' the kinds of films routinely described as puzzling or like games. 'Not getting it', Phillips writes, 'whatever it is, means being left out; left out of the group that does get it, and exempt from the pleasure that getting it gives' (2013: 34). Phillips connects this idea more generally to the idea of 'getting it' in our lives – the feeling of lack, that there is something missing, an 'it' that only acquisition will serve to overcome. 'Whatever the "it" is – the joke, the point, the poem – we would rather get it' (2013: 37), precisely because 'getting it' proves we are in the game, functioning as an 'I' who not only knows the stakes, knows how to win, but knows what to want and how to get it. Yet Phillips suggests, in our encounters in life as well as in art, 'not getting it', and not worrying about getting it or declaring one's having gotten it, may in fact be more pleasurable, more enthralling, more satisfying:

> Meaning is imposed wherever experience is disturbing; which is why the psychoanalyst – another 'modernist' artist – wants to talk about what the patient says, not what he means. The audience cannot work out what the artist needs or wants from them; and that may be the point, the artist herself may not know. Either not getting it becomes, in the glib sense, getting it ('the worse your art is', the poet John Ashbery remarked, 'the easier it is to talk about'); or, in the audience being actively prevented from getting it, something else becomes possible in relation to it. Not being able to find out what the writer wants from the reader – exhausting the possibilities of the reader getting it – forces the reader, if he is sufficiently intrigued, to do something else. (2013: 44)

'Getting it', for Phillips, is a moral pressure, driven by the super-ego: to get it means we can safely and confidently become part of a group (that group which 'gets' Hartley, for example, in the critical discourse; or lovers defining themselves through the formation of committed couples). We do not want to be humiliated by not getting it; so we work to get it, or, within the discourse of the puzzle film I have cited above, to offer a socially reasonable and acceptable interpretation of what 'getting it' might amount to for a fellow community of viewers and readers. Yet throughout his work Phillips encourages us to imagine life with this pressure released, 'a life in which there was nothing to get because what went on between people, what people wanted from each other, couldn't possibly be phrased that way. Our lives would not be about getting the joke or the point. Or, to put it slightly differently, there would be other pleasures than the pleasures of humiliation' (2013: 48). These are the pleasures – the pleasures of deferring meaning, and of not much caring whether one 'gets it', finally – with which Hartley's *Flirt* engages.

Flirt, then, finally shows us that not getting it is, or can be, a pleasure. To grasp what might be won in giving up on the idea of finalising meaning or affirming commitment, I suggest, it is important to relinquish the moral demand that we finally 'get' what each of the three narratives in Hartley's film collectively amounts to – that is, we give up any notion that the endings of the three stories in *Flirt* cleanly or sensibly 'fit together' or arrive, separately, at finalised moments of rounded narrative clarity. This goes beyond stating that the ends of the films are ambiguous. Rather, it is to become more closely attuned to the manner in which they animate ambiguity: how Hartley's framing choices rigorously commit to a certain image and a certain sound, in the waning moments of each of the three episodes, while at the same time opening us up to precise details (of movement, colour, gesture, setting and more) that slip beyond the meticulously chosen borders of Hartley's frame in their evocative and associative qualities. To key in on these subtle pleasures – darting away from the superego's demand that the viewer 'get' a final satisfaction in our relationships and in our lives, or in our narratives – it is useful to begin an analysis of the film by focusing first on the endings of each of the three episodes. This makes sense as a starting point: in most conventional films, the ending is where we go to 'get it' (the solution, the meaning, the closure, the satisfaction). So I want to proceed not by beginning with the ends of the *narratives* told in each of the three episodes in *Flirt* but rather with the *images* that punctuate each of those stories. In images and sounds, I think, we will more vividly find those details that finally establish *Flirt* as an anti-puzzle film: the sort of movie that ends by confirming that life is to be lived not to 'get' a final meaning but rather to find pleasure in moments and in details that exceed and slip away from certainty.

Bill and Emily

The end of the first part: a taxi cab, its windows and doors encrusted by half-melted ice on a cold evening. Bill is inside: despite the blood on his shirt, which the cabbie has noticed, he wants a ride to the airport so he may make it to Paris, presumably to reunite with Emily, commit to her, perhaps marry her. But none of this is stated directly in this final shot of the taxi and *Flirt* up to this point gives us no reason to suspect any of this will quite work out the way one might anticipate. Throughout the first part of *Flirt*, Bill has been subject to any number of contingencies that suddenly redirect his course. During an argument with Emily, in the first scene, she comically pushes him out of the frame, sending him crashing (offscreen) into a pile of dishes. While waiting by a phone booth, later, to call Emily, he lends a quarter to a young woman presently occupying the phone, the handing of a coin transforming into a caress as Bill's fingers linger for a moment on the tips of hers, a gesture that Hartley highlights in a close insert shot of two hands (throughout the film's repetitions and variations, the most intimate and sensual moments of contact or discovery will often occur while waiting or preparing to use a public phone). Later, in a bar, Bill will be accosted by Walter (Martin Donovan). Walter brandishes a gun, and is prepared to kill himself, or perhaps Bill, whom he suspects is having an affair with his wife. During a struggle for this gun, Bill will be shot across the side of the face. In a film in which strangers transform moments of violence into musicals – after Walter plugs Bill, an unnamed woman sitting at the bar launches into an awkward dance – any intention to commit to anything (to a woman, a phone call, an act of violence) brushes up against the vivid variety of lived experience, and the strange and random patterns shaping experience's path.

And yet that taxi cab door: Hartley (and Bill) have committed to it; it is the final image of Bill's story, the one that declares (with Bill's confident slam of the door) the character's newfound commitment, his plan to fly to see Emily. Yet what moment will come next, if the story were to continue? Like so many of the images in Hartley's films, the image of the taxi is presented to us with a forcefully paratactic logic: its causal connection to the images preceding it is less strong than its power as a moment and as an image, framed in a particular way. Although the separate stories in *Flirt* each flow more or less continuously, Hartley does not render his editing or his imagery invisible; his cinematic strategies do not merely sink behind or become absorbed in the weight of a narrative moment. Instead, narrative trajectory and traces of character psychology and motivation pulse quietly, nearly invisibly, *behind* the image, while the density and vividness of the image itself – and the multiple and various possibilities of

Fig. 7.1: Parker Posey as Emily in *Flirt*

close attention it presents – alert us to the larger possibilities of a life that might defer those quietly lingering commitments in favour of new or other ones.

The film's astonishing first shot (Fig. 7.1) prepares us to arrive, some twenty minutes later, at the final shot of the taxi cab with this sensibility: a high-angle shot of Emily, lying down in bed, covered up to above her chest with bedsheets, arms splayed across the mattress. She is looking directly into the camera but her head, hanging over the edge of the bed, appears to us upside-down, whatever invitation to connection invited by this gaze immediately deferred by the strangeness of seeing her hair below her eyes, her chin above her lips. This tension between erotic invitation on one hand and estrangement on the other is echoed in the position of her arms, her left arm extended fully outwards, across the bed, and out of focus, her right arm bent at the elbow and extending towards the camera (and towards Bill, who, we will soon learn, lingers out of frame), with reticent fingers nevertheless creating a fore-shortening effect. No other image in *Flirt* couples better intimate commitment with its accompanying deferral, the welcoming gaze with a gesture of estrangement. The camera movement that begins a moment later only complicates the effect: tracking rightward to turn Emily rightside-up, to 'get a better look at her', at the same time it loses the connection it had, breaking the intimacy of eye contact as it conventional-ises its view. The cut to Bill, in the next image, only serves to remind us how intensely this first image, with its suggestiveness and its reticence, stands apart from narrative flow: when first seen, Bill is standing some ways away from the bed, leaning against a refrigerator, his arm raised as if to shield him from the complicated gesture of inti-macy and connection at play in the preceding shot. No doubt, before this moment, the two have had sex, perhaps a date, a provisional commitment and connection at a particular time, day, and place. There is no reason to suspect that what Bill is heading towards in the taxi at the end of the film are anything other than more moments such as this one: intimate connection coupled with the uncertainty, the palpable presence of other possibilities, that attends all such bonds.

Dwight and Johann

The final image of *Flirt*'s second part, which transfers the same set of circumstances to Berlin, strikes a somewhat different note. Dwight, like Bill, has suffered an injury to the face after an altercation with a gun. In the final image, after he stumbles out of the hospital, he walks to a snack bar as Hartley's camera follows him. He places a few coins on the counter, but it is not enough to buy anything, so the employee hands him his money back. After this, Dwight steps to the edge of the snack bar, and the right side of the frame, while another man, in a polo shirt and a green jacket, standing on the opposite side, enquires about his injury. Here the viewer learns, as the man in the green jacket does, that it is Greta, the wife of his lover, who has shot Dwight. Then, a tender gesture, and perhaps the beginning of a new and amorous connection: the man steps forward to offer Dwight his jacket, placing it around his shoulders. Dwight accepts this gift, and walks to the other side of the frame, stepping closer to the camera and leaning against a yellow pole. He glances back at the man and smiles, with a laugh: it is unlikely this friendly fellow is the type of lover he would quite go

Fig. 7.2: Dwight Ewell in *Flirt*

for, yet he appreciates, in this moment, the tenderness. Dwight glances out of frame, looking left and right, as the smile falls away from his face (Fig. 7.2; no doubt, with this injury, it is a painful struggle to smile). Fade-out.

What does it mean for the flirt to struggle to smile, and finally to frown? The smile would seem central to the flirt's operations: it is the invitation for connection, the overcoming of estrangement. But all this depends on the way the flirt has previously moved. Dwight's injury, I contend, is altogether more jarring at the end of this second episode than Bill's is to the first: the bandage, compared to Bill's, occupies a much greater portion of Dwight's face, and Dwight's smile, flowing so effortlessly earlier in the story, is restricted here. Bill is, comparatively, quite rigid: hiding himself behind a refrigerator while his lover attempts to woo him to commitment, and keeping a rather static expression glued to his face at all times (does Bill experience joy with Emily? The viewer, gazing upon his poker face, wouldn't know it). Miho, the final episode will reveal, is more dynamic than Bill: she is a dancer, and can move – but in a staccato, cautious way, slipping in and out of the alleys and streets of Tokyo with stealth. Dwight, by contrast, is throughout his episode the most playful of *Flirt*'s characters, finding pleasure in handling the objects that he finds around him (and, indeed, in offering himself as an object – as one who is open to being handled). Examples abound: flipping through magazines, in the story's first sequence, while Johann discusses commitment; occupying his hands with a cigarette while he discusses, with a friend, Johann's intentions to leave Berlin for New York; leafing through yet more fashion magazines while discussing his future with another lover. And Dwight goes further than this, offering himself as an object: he walks through the city of Berlin with the most delectable fashion sense in the entirety of *Flirt*, his vivid yellow-and-black shirt, gold belt and leather pants complemented by a suede peacoat. And because he presents himself so, he is himself opened to being handled: by the woman at the phone booth, who clutches his groin as she leaves; and by the man in the fantasy he recounts to the doctor and the nurse as he lies on the surgery table near the end of the film, the man who holds his cock in his hands.

Dwight moves here so effortlessly through the world, finding new things to play around with everywhere he goes, and offering himself to a select few as one who might be played with, that it comes as a shock – even though we are prepared for it by knowing that the narrative event must be repeated in this second episode – when he is shot by a jealous lover. Dwight's dexterity and his inventiveness, his absolutely confident status as a flirt, are the qualities that strike throughout the story; more than Bill and Miho, who are at times uneasy in their movements, Dwight seems perfectly at ease with his flirtatious existence, up until the end. His playful ability to find something pleasurable to touch, and his striking ability to continue to imagine such powers of touch even as he is restricted on the white slab of an operating table, is part of what makes the final frame of this episode painful, too, for the viewer who has developed a connection to him and his flirtiness. His very way of moving through the world, of playing physically with its contents, has been stopped short by an injury causing pain in a body dedicated to pleasure. At the end of his story, he is left in a state of suspension. Perhaps appropriately, *Flirt* leaves its most flirty character without finally committing to a narrative end for him.

Miho and Hal
The third and final sequence in the film, which revolves around Miho, is the longest in *Flirt*, and the one which takes the greatest liberty in its variations and departures from Hartley's general schema. Hartley's very presence in the episode as an actor signals that its method and concerns are ultimately somewhat different than the preceding two narratives. Nevertheless, it ends with a final image that once more questions final commitment. Miho, a dancer, is leaving the emergency room of a Tokyo hospital. Like the other flirts in the film, she has been injured with a gunshot, shortly after a scuffle in an earlier scene with Yuki (Chikako Hara), the wife of Mr. Ozu. Here, in this last scene, Miho is about to make a phone call. She is interrupted by the sight of one of her lovers, an unnamed character played by Hartley (in what follows, I will refer to this character as 'Hal'). He is asleep – or seems to be – in the waiting room (Fig. 7.3). She goes over to his side; resting next to him is a sky-blue film can which contains the original negative of the film he has been in Tokyo to make. It is difficult, however, to imagine Hartley here as asleep, not only because we can imagine Hartley himself, fully awake and alert to the various possibilities open to him as a film editor, looming over this shot in the editing bay where he edits the film we are watching; but also because his figural position in the frame looks distinctly poised and summarily uncomfortable. No one sleeps like this, not in movies, or at least not comfortably. Miho's arrival, and her gesture of placing his arm around hers, is not enough either to wake him from this contrived sleep. This final shot is an especially reflexive image, one that, as I have tried to describe, draws our attention explicitly to the making of the film we are viewing: the film cans in the frame are those belonging to a project called *Flirt*, as if to remind us that the finished status of the film we are watching is in fact refracted within the frame of the film itself, a story world in which the finished

Fig. 7.3: Hal Hartley and Miho Nikaido in *Flirt*

Flirt of our world remains, in fact, unfinished, its final reels not unspooling in front of us presently but rather stored away in the film cans Hal uses as a footstool in his fictional slumber.

The reason Miho sits next to him now is because of an accident, a violent injury that has more than a little to do with the film cans we see in the final shot. Miho, earlier in the episode, has been in the centre of a love triangle. A dancer who has made intimate bodily contact with her choreographer, she flirts with Mr. Ozu. Yuki, a co-star in her dance and just as intimately attuned to her ways of moving, accuses Miho of being a flirt. Elsewhere, we have seen her with Hal, who insists on asking her to commit to their relationship together. (Symbolically, this line of the story suggests something of an uncertain but still potentially quite productive relationship between the art of cinema and the art of dance, two sensibilities that Hartley's choreographically-minded films have, throughout his career, attempted to unify.) The first time Hartley as 'Hal' is seen in the film, he is in his editing bay: the shot is composed with his Japanese editor, known only in the script as 'Hal's assistant' (Masatoshi Nagase), in the centre of the frame; he cuts and splices – again, the film we are presently watching – as lines of 35mm cross diagonally, up and down, in the foreground of the shot. When Miho arrives for the first time to speak with Hal, her filmmaker-boyfriend is on the line with someone else. If Miho is a flirt, Hal is not: he is barking answers to unheard questions to someone, likely a producer, or perhaps his former lover back in America, on the phone: 'No. No. Uh, no. No.' These direct, unambiguous responses parallel his own unambiguous demand that the flirty Miho commit, finally, to him and to their relationship (and perhaps also to his art of film). His demands are as precise as the framing of the shot in which we hear them, in which the constant spool of moving celluloid frames *within* the shot is placed into counterpoint with the static and firmly committed framing Hartley chooses in filming this moment.

Yet for all this rigorous commitment, Hal leaves one film can behind. Later, Miho will find it – forgotten by Hartley on his way out of Tokyo – in the city streets. This film can in tow, she is on the run from the police, after an initial spat with Yuki and Mr. Ozu. The police follow her to her choreography studio. They find Miho and Yuki in an embrace, a kind of reconciliation – perhaps a narrative conclusion?

Not quite. One of the cops knocks over the film can. The sudden surprise of this sound triggers Miho's finger, which still rests on the gun, and she accidentally shoots herself across the side of her cheek. This is what brings her to the hospital in the film's final sequence. Like Bill and Dwight, she will be encouraged to think about something else as doctors administer painkillers and perform surgery. But where Bill and Dwight spoke words of their distractive imaginings, here Hartley cuts to a shot of what Miho is presumably thinking about: Hal and her in bed, in the early morning, her hands removing his watch from his wrist and placing it on her own, as the sound of a babbling brook is heard offscreen. The bedsheets remind us of the opening shot of the film, of Emily gazing up in bed at Bill, but with an important variation: here the couple are together in bed, and here the image is meant as a respite from pain, a distraction from the kinds of injuries that might befall any of us accidentally on any day. Does this mean that Miho's flight from pain will involve, finally, commitment with Hal? Her mindscreen here, as well as her position next to Hal in the final shot of the film, would seem to suggest so. But *Flirt* remains unfinished. Hartley steadfastly reminds us of this, not only with his sleepy presence in the final shot – can a director with his eyes closed ever quite finish a film? – but, more importantly, with those film cans inside the final shot itself, those film cans which might have led us to believe, in a more conventional or more narratively-driven film, that they contained all the answers to the film's enigmatic puzzles. The film can motif is a reminder of Hartley's insistence, finally, that we stem the tide of puzzle-unlocking discourse in favour of life's more ambiguous, and less philosophical, pleasures. The mysterious briefcase in *Pulp Fiction* (1994), or the box in *Mulholland Dr.* (2001) – these are the cinematic motifs that lead us to unlock puzzles and contemplate a complete picture of all narrative connections. The film cans in *Flirt* offer no such promise. They playfully tuck away all the pieces we might need to put together such a complete picture. Instead, the very title of the film they contain reminds us of the pleasures to be had when we forego commitment in favour of ongoing play.

Conclusion

In this essay I have tried to highlight a few vivid moments from *Flirt* that capture the different embodiments of flirtation at play in each of the stories. By beginning my discussion of each variation with the final image of each episode and then finding resonances with that image in earlier moments, I hope to have offered one way of looking at the film's understanding of life as a series of contingent resonances and encounters that finally slip away from the conservatism of commitment or finally rounded meaning. To look at *Flirt* repeatedly is to every time notice new connections and evocations, and to be reminded again of those pleasures to be found in slipping away.

CHAPTER EIGHT

Poiesis and Media in The Book of Life and No Such Thing

Fernando Gabriel Pagnoni Berns

In *The Book of Life* (1998), when Jesus Christ (Martin Donovan) presents himself as D. W. Griffith, the gesture is not innocent. Griffith (1875–1948) is widely known as the father of modern cinema, an early pioneer of the narrative film (see Gunning 1994: 130). The classical narrative film he helped devise forms a fantastic world that tries to resemble our own world as we know it but with its own rules of composition in the creation of a particular diegetic universe. Griffith, like God, was a creator of entire lives and worlds.

The ability of humans to create and recreate their existence through poiesis has been a constant through human history. Poiesis is, unlike *theoria* (knowing by observing) and *praxis* (knowing by doing or acting within a moral code), is a form of activity that creates an object that is different and distinct from the creating subject. It is 'this objective character of the poetic object that opens up a fundamental ambivalence' (Colebrook 2008: 99) that invites philosophical reflections and readings. Poiesis is creation, the product of humans; the word 'poiesis' refers to both the poetic object and the process that made it. It implies autonomy from reality, so narrative cinema, even if mimetic in its depiction of the world, works following its own rules and norms of order and intelligibility. Poiesis refers also to the ability of creating in the arts, but creating without any authentic imitation as the ideal (see Kirkeby 2000: 188). Still, poiesis does not refer exclusively to the arts: more broadly, it refers to any action (and the product of that action) that both transforms and continues the world. In short, poiesis is the act of creative making.

Hal Hartley's films explore the human capacity to create self-sufficient worlds, whether these be the worlds of film itself or the cosmologies of different religions, both works of human poiesis understood as the principle that 'we can know only what we make ourselves' (Kahn 2014: 3). His films contain several characters who have lost their identity and must undergo a process of reconstruction (see Berrettini 2011: 37), such as in *Amateur* (1994) or *The Girl from Monday* (2005). These characters have the opportunity to recreate their lives and their worlds. This leads to the problem that with creation comes great responsibility, as observed by characters in *The Book of Life*. Both this film and *No Such Thing* (2001) speak of man's ability to invent worlds, to the point that the latter can be taken as a continuation of ideas foregrounded in the former. *The Book of Life* tells about the coming of the millennium and the possibility of mankind's redemption by means of their ability to create and to re-shape themselves. The danger of potential alienation provoked by the omniscient presence of global mass media lurks throughout the film. *The Book of Life* asks what the fate of humankind is and, more importantly, queries what exactly humans will do with the means and ability to re-create their world.

The answer seems to come with *No Such Thing*, and it is a hopeless one. After the 9/11 attacks and the fall of the World Trade Center (which *The Book of Life*, with its end-of-millennium paranoia, seems to prefigure) and with the constant repetition of the tragedy in a sort of loop or 'loop-loop' (Friend 2007: 232) on TV, the sense of wonder of humankind, in *No Such Thing*, seems to have died. (Although *No Such Thing* was made before the 9/11 attacks, it speaks presciently of their consequences.) In the film, the media is driven by its ability to shock, embodied in Helen Mirren's character, the director of an empire of mass media constantly influencing consumers' sense of what is of importance. She distinguishes between what is 'breaking news' and what is not. Here, the media is conceptualised as creator and/or re-creator of realities (see Weimann 2000: 4).

The human sense of wonder dies at the end of the film, after Artaud (Baltasar Kormákur, playing a character with a name not innocently chosen) eliminates the last monster living in the ends of Earth. With the death of that capacity also dies the ability of everyone to create, since everyone is a potential artist, as argued by Antonin Artaud. Every human is creative, but she must escape the symbolic (as do the characters without memory) so they, as a plague, can refigure the social fabric. With the death of the monster at the end, this potentiality for wonder and creation dies.

This essay will examine these issues in a close reading of *The Book of Life* and *No Such Thing* following the idea that the former asks questions that the second, already in the new millennium, tries to answer, under the shadow of the mass media in the post-9/11 age.

The Book of Life and the Coming of the End
The Book of Life is the US entry into the multi-film *2000 Seen By* series about the new millennium. Even though the film was made before the 9/11 attacks, the first scenes of *The Book of Life* intriguingly prefigure the terrorist attacks upon the World Trade Center perpetrated in September 2001. The film opens with motifs of religion and airports, a sense of apocalypse illustrated, through digital imagery, in greenishly sick hues. Images of New York City, with an ominous airplane flying close to tall buildings, are especially significant, particularly since the clarity of these images is perturbed

by the static and noise typical of non-professional recording. The use of this 'do-it-yourself' digital video aesthetic retrospectively echoes the incessant repetition of the Twin Towers crumbling, an image recorded by thousands of citizens who filmed the destruction from a variety of angles and perspectives with thousands of cameras, phones and PCs, images later transmitted and retransmitted through the entire world as some kind of fascinating revulsive and traumatic spectacle (see O'Reilly 2008: 195). Through the entire world, eyes were glued to TV screens depicting a horror that obliterated the borders between Hollywood blockbuster and reality, even when everyone knew that what was taking place was entirely real (see Vanhala 2011: 1). *The Book of Life*, a film about the coming of the millennium and the impeding apocalypse, eschews Hollywood spectacle in favour of the inscription of potentially real horrors in its depiction of a possible end to the world. Hartley's eerie prefiguration of events to come is not entirely surprising if we take into account that mass media had a starring role in both the film and the terrorist attacks.

The first shots of *The Book of Life* are filmed using motion blur, a digital technique that appears to smear background colours in the shots (see Brinkmann 1999), giving a sense of immediacy to what is seen. Everything seems to be in constant movement, with a destabilising effect establishing the tone of a world imbued with urgency but going nowhere, as if to signify the coming of the end. Adding to the destabilising effect, the mise-en-scène and cinematography privileges a narrative composition consisting of oblique angles and non-classical arrangements of film space that leave out of the shot important pieces of information (for example, to whom a character is speaking). This compositional strategy has two effects: first, these framing choices help build an apocalyptic narrative of uneasiness which denies any sense of security for both character and audience. Second, these choices serve to foreground the film as film, a work of pure artifice. Even if following the logic of narrative cinema, the composition of scenes, the use of artificial colours, overexposures in lighting (for example, the sun pouring from a window almost covers the entire shot and diffuses our visual grasp of the characters within the scene) and the recurrent use of motion blur create a poetic world which rejects the artifice of reality. Here is a universe which presents itself as filmic diegesis, artistic human creation rather than mimesis.

The second arrival of Jesus finally takes place. He has comes to our world, together with Magdalena (P. J. Harvey), descending as if from heaven (he has come by airplane). Even if immediately recognised by the Devil (Thomas Jay Ryan), Jesus has doubts about himself and about the impending condemnation of the human race. Everyone seems to know what his presence means, except himself. He is lost in the world of men, unsure about how to proceed. As both God and man, he is neither of them. Hartley constructs his Jesus as not that different from the common citizen, as a man who is on the brink of losing faith in God's plans. If people 'question themselves', he, Jesus, wonders about what must be done. The image of a Christian entity arriving to separate good souls from bad ones is complicated in the film, however. Rather than punish the bad ones, this version of Jesus is more interested in the ability of man to construct a whole world without divine intervention, even if that cosmos is full of evil (after all, God creates a world with moral evil as a possibility, too).

Jesus checks in a hotel using this surname: 'Griffith.' As suggested at the outset of this essay, every film constructs a kind of autonomous world, complete with its own rules and norms – in other words, with its diegesis, the imaginary sum of referents within the film, the total world of the fabula (see Casebier 1991: 105). In *The Book of Life*, this principle of cinema is signified by the surname Jesus assumes as his own. As Marilyn Fabe writes of Griffith's narrative style, 'Griffith insisted on the construction of authentic-looking three-dimensional props and sets for his films. He also brought increased realism to the screen by directing the players to act in a restrained, natural, less flamboyantly theatrical style' (2004: 3). In short, according to Fabe, Griffith added verisimilitude to the fictional world of cinema (2004: 11), thus constructing a cinematically intelligible diegetic world. In the metaphor suggested through the use of his name in *The Book of Life*, Griffith might be understood as establishing the basic institutional rules of narrative cinema the same way that God establishes the proper rules of the universe and how it works for Christian theology. Both God and Griffith are mythologically framed as 'world-makers', a world of poetry on one hand and a 'real' world on the other, both equally valuable as universes of knowledge. As Jesus mentions in Hartley's film, he works for He who make the rules of the world.

Both Jesus and the Devil in *The Book of Life* battle for the souls of people in a world in which almost nobody believes in souls anymore. The faith of people seems to be deposited in some other place rather than in the transcendent worlds built by religion. As Hartley's film suggests, maybe faith in the secular world lies now on the power of money, lawyers and media. That is why Jesus manages the last day with the help of lawyers, Satan tempts with money and characters within the film knock down the fourth wall to address the audience (see Fig. 8.1). It must be noted that this latter act is not made solely with the characters speaking and looking directly at the camera. Rather, this direct address often occurs through more covert means, with a character speaking into a strategically situated microphone in some lonely place, for example, a bathroom or empty street. The situation prefigures 'the confessional' format of the television show *Big Brother* (2000–present), in which the different participants attempt to get out of the 'reality' of reality television by speaking directly to the camera (the 'Big Brother') and, by extension, to the audience, in a 'private' mode about their inner feelings. These revelations are understood to be genuine, unmediated by edition or script. Still, these confessions are made not in intimacy but on national TV, so the 'penitent' knows that he or she has the power to manipulate the audience's feelings with the act of confession. This way, poiesis is again brought back to the foreground, here as discourse that blurs the borders of fiction and reality. *Big Brother* presents itself as the unmediated depiction of people living together, as reality without artifice. However, and leaving aside any suspicions of the show's staged and scripted origins, there is not any truth within the show. They are not people behaving as they do in daily life, but people behaving as they do when cameras are watching them. In other words, they are people making poiesis while denying this fact. *Big Brother* is an artificial construct that presents itself as a transparent depiction of another artificial construction: reality. *The Book of Life*, in contrast, foregrounds

Fig. 8.1: Thomas Jay Ryan as Satan in *The Book of Life*

the constructed aspect of mass media, first with the self-reflexive mention of D. W. Griffith and second with the presence of the confessionals that would soon become a staple of reality television.

The confessional moment is also linked to the phenomenon of the talk show that dominated daytime American TV since the 1980s. Confessional talk shows encapsulate a 'tension between commercial tabloid exploitation and the politicisation of the private sphere' (Shattuc 2001: 84), another case of poiesis: supposedly unscripted testimony is shaped to fulfill viewer demands of catharsis through narrative construction and empathy. The confessional phenomenon is thus linked to dramaturgy and theatre, both forms of world-making, to appeal to the audiences' feelings through characterisation and story-telling. This kind of 'unscripted', confessional television appears in *The Book of Life* when Edie (Miho Nikaido), the naïf Asian bartender of the hotel where both Satan and Jesus plays their games, wins the lottery and is interviewed 'live' (by the Devil himself!) on national TV. The scene is filmed in black-and-white to detach it from the main narrative, as part of the cult of transparent confession. The scene, in this context, is simultaneously natural and artificial in its mise-en-scène. However, this piece of 'transparent' narrative is scripted, as is the whole film. The images and discourses of mass media are another form of poiesis, complicated further if talking of 'reality TV', a form that proclaims its nature as unmediated mirror to society. But since the moment in which competitors and/or particular lives are chosen to face the camera in an edited show, there is no unmediated reality but poiesis, creation. Audiences can engage with these supposedly unscripted shows, but they do so with the ability 'to switch from appreciation of these ordinary people and their experiences, to awareness of the staged nature of their experiences created for television' (A. Hill 2005: 177). However, the blurring of the line between reality and fiction goes both ways, since, in *The Book of Life* reality itself seems to be slipping into the realm of mediated fiction: Edie is interviewed but the film never really discloses to whom, nor whom is filming. It appears to be just the Devil playing with people's emotions the same way that media mega-corporations do in real life (as Helen Mirren's character will do in *No Such Thing*).

Mediation, in the form of digital technology, makes another appearance in *The Book of Life* in the form of the Book of Revelations itself: rather than a literal book, here is a computer, a notebook. This brings to mind another type of apocalypse, as Mark L. Berrettini notes: 'We should remember that when *The Book of Life* was produced, real trepidation about the Y2K-induced computer collapse at the new millennium did exist, which for some meant a possible technological apocalypse and for others a time of divine reckoning. Such fears are called up in the use of the Macintosh' (2011: 59). The fact that people felt terrorised by the idea of communications momentarily failing speaks volumes about our society and its dependence upon technology, and connects to the apocalyptic themes of Hartley's film.

To create new worlds we need to use our imagination and free will. That is why, in the film, Jesus ends up dropping the Book of Life, his notebook, into the trash. He is a man tormented by his lack of own will. He must do what his father had asked him to do. In this sense, he is less human, less powerful that the humans that he should condemn to hell or heaven. Both Jesus and Satan, in the film, share the same understanding of the human soul, not as a form of divine transcendence but as the engine for human creation and invention. In this regard, it should be taken into account that in the Judeo-Christian tradition, the Devil is commonly and interchangeably referred to as Satan or Lucifer. But actually, those names represent two different images of the Devil: the name Lucifer (the 'light bearer') signifies the Devil before his fall from grace as supreme archangel of God's army. Satan refers to the Devil after his fall, as a figure of pure evil. Hartley wants to recover some traces of Lucifer, as the entity who gives humanity the fire of creativity through the use of free will and light (Nesfield-Cookson 1998: 45). The Devil in Hartley's film mentions free will as the basis for humanity, even if that could drive them to evil deeds. He mentions with more than a trace of wonder the capacity of humans to 'invent themselves' that enhances life in ways never seen before. Then, it is not strange that Jesus and the Devil agree in their conception of human capacity as one excelling in the creation of worlds, an ability that previously only belonged to God. Of course, among the things created by humans are many stupidities, as both Jesus and the Devil agree, but this capacity is enough to grant them a new millennium.

The film ends and the apocalypse does not come. Humans have been forgiven. At the end, Jesus is 'addicted' to humanity and the Devil is unable to open the Book of Life. Both superior beings have lost some of their divine and fear-inducing power upon humans. The last scene, during which Jesus reflects once more on 'humanity's own god-like self-esteem' and about the capacity of humans to recreate themselves, maybe, as virtual reality in the future, suggests why. The Devil and Jesus have lost some of their appeal because humans hold some divine fire within them too. Human capacity of poiesis, *The Book of Life* suggests, has reached a point in which humans can create elaborate and complex worlds such as cinema, universes that blur the lines between fact and fiction. Humans have some divine traces while truly divine beings are increasingly humanised. As Jesus says, thinking about the potentiality within humans: 'will they become gods themselves?' The gap between the divine and the human spheres shrinks and as a consequence, the apocalypse does not arrive.

It must be noted that this capacity to make life and worlds, as Griffith did a century ago, is not presented as something intrinsically good or bad in *The Book of Life*. Humans recreate their existence through, among other forms, the use and over-use of technology and mass media. The film does not indicate whether or not humanity is dooming itself with these new worlds. Since the Devil functions many times as a sort of television host in Hartley's film, it could be read that reality TV is intrinsically evil, but the latter only if we understood the Devil as Satan rather than Lucifer, the bearer of light. So, the film is ambiguous in its look upon human poiesis. *The Book of Life* celebrates that capacity, but not necessarily its results. A more forcefully negative reflection arrives with *No Such Thing*, a companion film to the themes at play in *The Book of Life*.

The End of Myth in No Such Thing
Thematically, *No Such Thing* follows *The Book of Life* closely, but unlike the latter, the former has been filmed in a more traditional (i.e., mimetic) way. Since the film is related to forms of oral narration, myth and legend, all of them archaic forms of story-telling, a traditional approach is required to tell this story of a monster who is slowly losing his capacity to scare and amaze in a world in which humans are increasingly losing their capacity for wonder.

The film opens with the monster (Robert John Burke) talking within a 'confessional', a thread that continues the theme of confession from *The Book of Life*. The monster talks about his weak condition, since he is only a shadow of his former self. He has retired from 'public life' and hides deep within the fantastic lands of Iceland, landscapes filled with a mythic quality (see Andrews 1998: 169). Even so, the monster cannot truly disappear until humanity completely loses ties with the world of myth, so he surfaces every now and then, scaring with his horrific behaviour and his capacity to exhale fire.

The presentation of the monster and his world of wonder are immediately followed by the current world of myth-making: television and mass media. As in *The Book of Life*, television is presented in all its overwhelming capacity to construct reality, a capacity based exclusively in what sells and what does not. And what sells, as the boss of the mega-corporation of news says, is bad news. The boss, played by Helen Mirren, is uninterested in reality: she only craves the spectacle of tragedy. As she says, the news that her employers offer her is only 'sad, but not catastrophic'. In this respect, the film reminds us how media coverage aestheticises and numbs the viewer's response to global tragedies, and the way those mediated events, in turn, evoke the memory of Hollywood spectacles. As Dean Lockwood says, 'at the moment we cut through reality to the Real, the Real appears at its most staged, an entirely phantasmagorical experience. In effect, the intruding Real is always already plastinated' (2005: 78).

Insensitive and manipulative, the boss played by Mirren in *No Such Thing* is presented as the film's most negative character. The character parallels the Devil in *The Book of Life*, without the potential characteristic of creativity seen in the latter. Like him, she is a host who gives audiences a prefabricated world to swallow, but unlike the Devil, she seems less empathic with humanity. Let us compare what the Devil explains in *The Book of Life* to the character of the boss:

> Satan: What they need and what they want, are two entirely different things. They want divine retribution and they're willing to pay for it. I've been in the advertising business, so to speak, since the beginning [...]. I'm a pro: at telling people what they wanna hear and somehow makin' them think that they've gotta be talked into it.

For her part, the boss in *No Such Thing* only desires to sell prefabricated, regurgitated news that meet the expectations of the audiences. She considers the purpose of a TV news station is to 'put the hand on the worst, the worst possible news' or give segments of 'human interest'. Of course, the media is the entity in charge of electing what is of 'human interest' and how this interest is presented. The ambiguous nature of mass media as a tool for creation of new universes in *The Book of Life* seems to have devolved into pure hollowness and glossy superficiality in *No Such Thing*. Again prefiguring the mediation of the horror of September 11, Hartley does not see mass media as a source of creativity of alternate worlds. In this new scenario, the boss interpreted by Mirren is more evil than the Devil itself. Media is eroding the capacity of myth-making, embodied in the monster, and replacing it with prefabricated wonder without subversive edge.

The other character who, like the monster, seems to belong to a past age of fairy tale is Beatrice (Sarah Polley). A blonde, big-eyed orphan, with her long braids and pale skin, Beatrice is the perfect embodiment of the heroine popularised by fairy tales and commoditised globally by Disney. In brief, she fits perfectly with what mass media traditionally offers as a heroine and/or victim, so her boss (Beatrice works within the same media corporation overseen by the Mirren character) will send her to investigate the rumoured killings performed by a monster in the faraway lands of Iceland. Among the potential victims is Beatrice's boyfriend, so everything fits to create a modern fairy tale of pain and wonder fit for a cynical, contemporary audience.

Traditional myths fulfill the function of explaining how the world works: in this sense, myths reflect 'a given culture's social arrangements' (Leeming 2005: 199). Myths, however, also expand the view of the world beyond the horizon of the local, add scope 'and mystery to a society's world. It is also frequently the case that stories set in the imaginary world tell of events in which the morals of the stories can become lessons about the right and wrong ways of act' (Mack 2008: 9). Contemporary media's powers of world-making through the production of fears, affects and desires, however, does not attempt to explain the world but rather, follows its own market logic and gives more of the same, recycled for the masses and globalised out of proper context. Following this idea, the boss interpreted by Mirren does not know the names of her employees but exploits the tragedy of Beatrice when the airplane that takes her to Iceland crashes, with Beatrice the only survivor. The act of recreating the world by the mass media fails to meet the prime criteria for poiesis: to add something new to the world.

Mass media and the world of 'factual' television recreate and stylise reality as commodity rather than a poetic act or an unmediated display of transparency. One of the most criticised aspects of the over-styling of reality is that it provokes a blur of the frontiers between fact and fiction, desensitising those watching it (see Grindstaff 2014: 23). This lack of sensitivity is evident in the film's airport scene, in which Beatrice is incapable of finding help for a girl in pain. In the scene, a girl crawls on the floor (for unknown reasons) while seated people simply ignore her, as if she were invisible. Nobody seems to see the pain of others in *No Such Thing*. If we keep in mind that the scene at the airport follows that of the boss looking for tragedies to stage on national TV, it is possible to infer that part of the blame for the desensitisation of the public lies in part in the staging of suffering created by mass media.

Beatrice, the only survivor of the crash, rejects the 'help' of her boss (i.e., to tell her story in a sentimental way for the mass-media audience) and after a painful period of recovering from her many injuries, she will encounter another, alternative form of poiesis, one filled with wonder: that of myth in the landscapes of Iceland. It is interesting to point out that before encountering this other world, Beatrice must endure and undergo first a really painful set of operations. The first one will be with anesthesia, but, as her doctor explains, as the process goes on, the drugs will begin to wear off. Beatrice endures, literally, a process of sensitisation, the exact opposite of the American viewers of Mirren's television news station, who become increasingly more indifferent to pain, evident in the airport scene. To get access to a world of myth and legend, Beatrice first has to endure a process that can recuperate her to the world as a sensible human being, even if she already was, until then, truly a caring character. Even so, her goodness is not enough for her to access the world of myth, the universe dominated by the monster. Her companion, her Virgil in this new world will be Dr. Ann (Julie Christie) and that for two reasons: first, because she is, as Beatrice's doctor, the one in charge of taking the girl through the process of sensitisation. Second, because she, even if a doctor (a rational profession), is open to the belief of monsters.

Beatrice comes to Iceland looking for her missing boyfriend but, in an echo of *Beauty and the Beast*, she will find instead the monster. To make the trip, she has left behind civilisation to access this world covered with mist and 'without roads' (thus, almost inaccessible). The people inhabiting the place seem to live in the past: their wardrobe and manners anchor them in a primal world. That is why the American idea of installing a base of missiles within the area is impossible: that zone is a place outside the current world, the last vestige of myth. If it dies, if the monster dies, the capacity of the imagination of humanity dies also and the only thing that would remain is the constant re-creation of the world as commodity.

The monster lies far from human social constructs of good and evil, mercy and bad conscience. To him, killing is just erasing another little piece of humanity, a humanity he sees 'as a plague'. This concept connects with the theatre of Antonin Artaud, the avant-garde dramatist who proclaimed that bourgeois drama and theatre were killing creativity and destroying art and performance with words and mimesis. Artaud conceived the world as heterogeneity: a material-metaphysical and objective-transcendent world. Artaud favoured the fusion of art with life, and saw art as a transformative tool of the world. For Artaud, as for the historical avant-garde artists, it is necessary to dissolve the structures of the established world and art itself. To this end, he proposed the Theater of Cruelty. Theatre is for Artaud a space of connection with the metaphysical realm (see Zarrilli 2010: 518) and operates as *apocatastasis* or return to the origin through two dimensions: as hieroglyph of the founding otherness (to which Western man has turned his back) and a hierophanic, or sacred, space that opposes the organisation of a bourgeois society seen as a plague, a pestilence.

Artaud (Baltasar Komákur) in *No Such Thing* is a scientist, crazy but 'a genius all the same' who is the only one capable of fulfilling the monster's most private desire: death. The monster has lived through human history, becoming weaker and weaker each year, but not entirely dying. Humanity still has the spark of wonder and the freedom for creation and so he survives, but as this power becomes increasingly thinner, the monster gets weaker. The monster suffers crises provoked, in his own words, 'by people, humanity, civilisation', the same recurrent triggers that obliterate the true primal nature of the world, according to Artaud.

The name Artaud does not appear in Hartley's earlier film, *The Book of Life*, but some of his ideas do. The apocalypse as a framing device for the story reminds us of the plague and the end of the world as we understand it. The radio within the hotel's lobby is always turned on, and always tuned to a preacher predicting the coming of the end through a pestilence which will erase the entire world to give place to a brand new cosmos, indifferent to human ego. These ideas follow closely those of Artaud and of poiesis as a plague capable of erasing the senile, fossilised architecture of reality, completely crystallised in a fabric of social constructs that pass for nature. Hartley is not that interested in Christian theology but, rather, in the possibilities of wiping away fossilised forms of being for alternative ways of being human.

These ideas are treated more explicitly in *No Such Thing*. Finally, with the help of Beatrice, the monster will meet Artaud. But prior to the meeting, the monster will come out to be viewed by the public. As a strategy to reach the elusive Artaud, Beatrice, through her boss's media corporation, presents the monster to the audiences, who meet him with mixed feelings. They are more interested in a violent monster who meets their expectations of 'monstrous' than in the deep pain within the eternal creature. The clashing between the world of myth and the world of media, both universes compromised by the slippage between fact (the reality of the existence of monsters) and storytelling (the monster and Beatrice as characters of fairy tales typical of myth but also of mass media) is embodied in Beatrice and her new glossy, glamorous persona. Indeed, Beatrice is literally re-created by the media for the masses as the perfect heroine for TV. Still, the goal is achieved and Artaud is contacted. At the end, Dr. Artaud succeeds in erasing the monster from the world, granting thus his wish of disappearing from existence. The last shot of *No Such Thing* is very telling: Beatrice looks intently into the camera while tears come down from her eyes. She knows very well that what the media is killing is the capacity of wonder, creation and imagination within humanity, now replaced by glittering hollowness, an experience Beatrice knows all too well.

Seen in this light, *No Such Thing* works as an answer of sorts to the questions posed by *The Book of Life* in regard to human capacity of creation. Humanity, indeed, holds the capacity of poiesis, but not necessarily as wonder and fantasy but as repetition that meets expectative, previously prefabricated, bourgeois commodification.

* * *

The Mirren character in *No Such Thing* parallels Lucifer in *The Book of Life*. Both are specialists in giving the audience what they want: narrative (and predictable) forms. The world-making of mass media presents universes that, unlike myth or art, do not explain the world as we know it but rather support clichés and pre-fabricated images that meet pre-fabricated expectations that only accept a very limited range of responses. Even if presented as factual, reality is shaped to fit into structures of dramaturgy and spectacle. The blurring of the lines between television spectacle and reality desensitises toward true suffering in the world. The risk we take in using our poiesis to the extent that we do is that we fail to take full responsibility for the result. In postmodernism, the two concepts, praxis and poiesis, melt together: praxis is poiesis, as we create the world to which we relate as if it were real (see Kirkeby 2000: 188), not in the sense extolled by Artaud as artistic reality (an art full of life) but rather as media that reproduces crystallised forms of organisation of bourgeois society.

The Book of Life celebrates the human capacity to create entire worlds, while *No Such Thing* more forcefully condemns the human proclivity to use this capacity of world-making to desensitise rather than to create a legitimate form of sensitive, rational comprehension. As Peter Murphy and David Roberts suggest, 'the utopia of civilization assumes the power to create worlds. World-making is rational' (2006: 150), a notion that these two Hartley films would seem to endorse. But in a society far from utopic, Daniel Deardorff claims that 'myth, now dead to science, religion, and politics, descends to the living roots in poiesis' (2009: 40). In postmodernity, religion, no longer able to create worlds, itself has been replaced by media (Rothenbuhler 2005: 98). Hartley's films, engaging creatively with these ideas, are radical moves to bring poiesis as creativity back into human history.

Returning to the beginning, how does *The Book of Life* prefigure the terrorist attacks of 9/11? The film talks about the anxieties of the millennium, together with the fears about new technologies and image. In this scenario, myth, as we see in *No Such Thing*, retreats and dies, together with the capacity of humans to wonder. Still, cinema itself holds the power to raise questions and create complex responses that invite reflection rather than the reproduction of patterns. At least that is what the independent cinema of Hal Hartley works to achieve.

CHAPTER NINE

Bodies, Space, and Theatre in *The Unbelievable Truth (and its American Precursors)*

Zachary Tavlin

This chapter analyses the relationship between bodies and space in Hal Hartley's first feature film, and relates his work in this regard to two pioneers of the American New Wave, John Cassavetes and Robert Altman. First, I will provide an extended analysis of scenes from *The Unbelievable Truth* (1989), with special attention to the film's final sequence. Here I will argue that, at a particular crisis-point in the film, Hartley's characters take on the status of bodies moving within a complex choreography, breaking with the bounded, discursive spaces they had been previously caught in. Certain sequences in Hartley's films, heavily choreographed and containing dance-like movements in space, transport these bodies from locations representative of social and psychological repression to abstract planes (represented within the mise-en-scène as beaches, fields, or seemingly uninhabited houses) where pain can be released into love.

Connecting this aspect of Hartley's film to Cassavetes's *Faces* (1968) and Altman's *California Split* (1974), I will then seek to place Hartley's work in a line of American cinema that continually experiments with mise-en-scène. These films take space seriously and, in different ways, construct 'space stages' as a way of transforming (or challenging) traditional cinematic framings of bodies that assume an irreconcilable break between the spatial syntax of film and theatre. Taking a different angle than the oft-referenced influences of European filmmakers like Jean-Luc Godard and Robert Bresson on Hartley's work, I will interrogate the relation between choreography and expansive, abstract space in this line of influence (while noting the differences as well as the similarities between Hartley's films and his American predecessors') and finally suggest, while briefly referencing the work of Fredric Jameson, that Hartley's style and aesthetic can be considered within the context of a particularly American form of postmodernism. As an extension of this investigation, by looking at the historical relationship between space and time and its evolution in the kinds of film Jameson marks as 'postmodern', Hartley's cinematic privileging of space over time can be historicised and considered ideologically, as well as appreciated as an original poetic representation of the contemporary world.

In and Out of Discursive Prison – The Unbelievable Truth
Hartley's films often involve a series of romantic couplings that serve as the formative transaction or feedback mechanism in the shaping of a character's relation to social reality. Romance is, perhaps, the key way a character's self 'takes shape', often with a special emphasis on *taking*: Hartley's lovers (whether successful or failed) constantly give and take emotionally from one another. This dialectical operation of exchange might not be so central in a romance depicting lovers seemingly made for one another, but the central relationship of *The Unbelievable Truth* (or at least what *appears to be* the central relationship, a claim I will problematise shortly) is rather quickly revealed as socially awkward. Josh Hutton (Robert John Burke) is an ex-convict re-entering society after a prison sentence, and Audry Hugo (Adrienne Shelly) is a teenager who has yet to enter society at all, her expected maturation arrested by idiosyncratic visions (or proto-experiences) of nuclear warfare and holocaust, the sounds of bombs detonating in the distance that no one around her can hear (or that everyone around her *refuses* to hear).

At the outset of the film, then, a certain abstract spatial diagram mapping Josh and Audry's respective forms of alienation holds – they both find themselves on the threshold of the social, but on opposite 'sides', one refusing to fully enter and the other scrapping to re-enter. The first shots of the film find Josh on a road that could be almost anywhere in New York state, trying to hitch a ride back to the city, first, and eventually back to his Long Island hometown (that he just left prison and that he's startlingly direct about it provides an initial obstacle to the relatively simple hurdle of sheer spatial distance). He refuses to drive, though as an expert mechanic he knows cars inside and out: he knows all too well how the machinery works in a placid acceptance that mirrors his awareness of the 'machinery' (the *reasons* behind the seemingly unjust breakdowns of central human relationships) of the community he returns to. He sees no real gain in getting back behind the wheel, and it is later revealed that a tragic drunk driving accident started his downward slide that eventually left him behind bars.

Audry, on the other hand, cannot walk the straight line into maturity because her conception of the world is one of imminent annihilation. Or, more appropriately perhaps, she sees the world as already-annihilated, dead to the point that nothing matters, superficial to the point that one cannot have any depth (an awareness that Shelly's flat affect serves quite well). Nuclear holocaust can be read as a form of wish-seeking on Audry's part, as the felt impossibility of a future tense in her life. Receiving admission to Harvard does nothing for her since she does not want to attend college at all, and she ends her relationship with the heavily confused Emmet (Gary Sauer), leaving him (literally) in the middle of the road, nonchalantly and without any external signs of emotional distress. Why would these problems and decisions be worth the common anxiety they often provoke in the non-apocalyptic set when the world is ending anyway?

The ambiguous apocalyptic temporality at the heart of Audry's experience is all the more significant against the background of the well-planned, linear temporalities of the traditional coming-of-age narrative. Much has been made of Hartley's intertitles (drawing somewhat obvious comparisons to Godard), and here their vagary further undercuts their traditional narrative function: 'A Month Maybe Two Months Later' as an ordering signifier provides yet another form of temporal disorientation, one that does not much trouble the viewer's ability to follow narrative chronology, but that instantiates the languor of these two central characters, initially caught in an endless present with no clear future. The order of clock time is the order of the social, of appointments to be met, and neither Josh nor Audry operate primarily on that level. Audry's first scene contrasts the time of the alarm clock with that of the bomb, presenting two temporal interventions, one on the order of regulated time, or *chronos*, and the other as the order of *kairos*, the intervention that suspends or eliminates the effectiveness of the former (social clock time, for Audry, is undermined by the possibility of a *kairos* so destructive it renders the former moot and lifeless).

Late in the film, Audry demonstrates through her attunement to the possibility of nuclear disaster the way these orders of time interact. In photographer Todd Whitbread's (David Healy) apartment, where she temporarily lives, the former explains to her that she has to 'play the game': essentially, she must sleep with him in order to advance her burgeoning modeling career. Todd repeats her earlier claim (in an entirely different context, which I will return to shortly) that 'nothing is got for nothing', a law of commonsense compensation that is drowned out by her reading of the facts of atomic detonation, the brutality of which 'threatens to break through into our normal life at any time'. This 'breaking through' of the *kairotic* moment is here envisioned as catastrophic and messianic; it represents the end of the entire world on one level, and the end of the specifically social world of the *quid pro quo*, of sleazy business and 'the game', on another. The film's *chronos* involves a series of 'deals' based around conditions to be carried out in time, most significantly those between Audry and her father Vic (Chris Cooke), and an entirely different organisation of the social world (eventually depicted spatially) will be a necessary accompaniment to the suspension of that world through love.

A few scenes in the film, an early one where Audry, sitting at the breakfast table, receives a lecture from Vic, and later where Audry, sitting on Josh's stoop, receives a lecture from him on automatic transmissions, involve a related depiction of psychological intrusion. In these scenes, the dialogue seems to jump out on its own in disorienting repetition and overlap, appearing to clutter Audry's psychological space (we are led to assume that this effect is happening inside her head through the representation of disturbance on her face and in her body language). One finds here, particularly in the latter case, a disjunction between language and its corresponding object – Josh's explanation of the function of the planetary gear he holds in his hand leads to Audry's *non sequitur*: 'Will you make love to me?' If, in the film, language and the domain of discourse are associated with *chronos* and the corresponding social world of exchanges, obligations and regulations, these moments allow some insight into Audry's unstable relationship to that world on a level perhaps deeper than her apocalyptic assumptions (often dismissed as a 'phase') suggest by themselves.

That Vic is so determined to convince everyone that Audry's apathetic attitude is merely a phase, to explain through the use of clichés her recalcitrance to his fatherly designs, demonstrates the film's relationship between embodiment and desire. All the forces of this miniature social world initially conspire to define and abstract the forms characters like Audry and Josh take, preventing sexual intercourse and, more generally, the intimacy of touch and the proximity of one to another. These 'forms' are forms of identification: age; gender; occupation (Josh quickly becomes the town mechanic, employed by Vic in order to keep him away from his daughter); pop-psychological assumptions; disciplines of study (Vic refuses to let Audry study literature, pushing for the more practical communications degree); and the inescapability of the past (the presumed manslaughter/murders that led Josh to prison). The most striking example of a surface form working to define the limits of a character is Josh's wardrobe, an all-black ensemble that continually confuses him for a priest. The very first line of the film, spoken by a middle-aged man who picks Josh up on the road from jail, is, 'Excuse me, are you a priest?' Like a number of other categorically confining forms of identification in the film, an outward appearance is taken to imply an inward condition or commitment, a way one 'ought' to be from the perspective of the social order. Further, if one can affect the outward appearance of another (as Vic constantly tries to do), one can supposedly possess them *in toto*.

Vic's policing of Audry's sexuality, significant and interesting on its own, is also the narrative device that 'polices' the forms these characters take in relation to one another. It is the main obstacle that must be overcome for the final, spatially liberating sequence to occur. Vic is the patriarch of advantageous material transactions, often made with his daughter, and these 'deals' are material rather than emotional, the trade of a suburban huckster. His opinion, voiced to Todd at a party, on the evils of the abstraction of credit is betrayed by his propensity to manipulate his daughter emotionally through sorts of 'investments,' particularly by convincing her to go into business with the photographer. He does not 'see' the way he's turned his daughter into an object when he 'sees' her first modeling spread, but as her ads become more risqué the fantasy elements at play become more explicit. Audry is initially 'safe' (from Josh) as a model because her sexual status is one marked by distance (Vic ultimately wants her to become a television broadcaster, another avenue for voyeuristic sexuality). He does not want to see the sexual consummation, remarking to her ex-boyfriend Emmet, who is himself jealous of her new wider audience, that 'it's better than you ogling her in the flesh'. Vic's failure to repress the notion of his daughter's embodiment and maturation, the symptoms of which are his constant bristling at any mention of her sexuality and his anger at catching her first kiss with Josh, result in that series of 'deals' or 'bargains' that keep her under his control *as* a daughter, and as a sexual object *at a distance*, only in the abstract.

Vic's final recognition, upon seeing Audry's arresting near-nude spread, is that his machinations are doomed to fail. This discovery leads to his transition into the role of the donor, granting Josh the money he needs to re-enter the city and fetch Audry. At the same time, Audry must undergo her own process of recognition: earlier in the film, at the moment Audry and Josh's initial courtship breaks down, Vic appears to speak through her: 'People are only as good as the deals they make...and keep', she tells Josh, resigned to the fact that, in large part because of her father's demands, they can never be together. This initial entrapment of narrative commerce in which 'nothing is got for nothing' means that there can be no love in this world, since to love here is to give something you do not have, that you do not possess the way you possess money or prospects (Josh tells her, 'I have nothing', but Audry misrecognises this statement initially as a plea rather than a truth). This law of compensation is the very same sentiment Todd tries to communicate to her in his apartment at the moment Josh is waiting outside, which she then rejects. Audry is no longer Vic's ventriloquist dummy, and if anything, it is Josh now speaking through her: 'I have nothing', she says. She rejects Todd's claim that they had a 'deal' or an 'understanding', any transactional-sexual *quid pro quo*, and in so doing suspends the order of emotional commerce that kept her apart from Josh (wiping it away like an atomic bomb turning a landscape to dust). At this very moment, in an act almost too heavy-handed in its symbolism, Josh throws a book she lent him through Todd's window, breaking his vase as Audry dashes out of her confinement.

The key dramatic development of the film, the engine that both separates and re-joins Josh and Audry, does not take place in traditional filmic space but in discourse, including the cycle of stories told (by often-ignorant, gossiping townspeople) about Josh's past and the 'happy' reveal about the truth of Josh's crime at the end by Pearl (that he, in fact, did *not* kill her father). Hartley's film engages dialectically with two central, and corresponding, dichotomies: between language and the lived body, and between abstract form and lived space. In the film's triumphant moments, the dominance of the former pair cedes way to the vibrancy of the latter. That the narrative throughout has been crafted around discourse (gossip and storytelling) and abstraction (the various 'deals' that hold two characters in some polar relation, the identity clichés that over-determine their reputations) means that the full effect of the final 'consummation' can be felt and experienced. It is perhaps significant for this reason that Josh is a virgin, as the narrative structure of the film is one of delayed gratification, of a tension produced and heightened by each obstacle placed in the couple's way.

The extended 'space stage' upon which the climactic tracking shot is set (a theatrical mise-en-scène crafted out of a parking lot by the beach) contributes to the peculiar logic of the scene: it does not operate according to a clearly ordered, linear temporality but has a purely spatial syntax. Indeed, the final sequence of the film operates according to what I wish to call a theatrical 'regioning', a spatial progression of dramatic stage entrances and exits in which a series of proximate, face-to-face meetings (rather than abstract 'meetings' in discursive non-space) on 'stage' finally settle the narrative conflict. In order to get there, though, the film must pass through another heavily choreographed sequence, which, put together with the final scene by the beach, contains within its evolution of the mise-en-scène the narrative progression of the whole.

This theatrical sequence begins as an exercise in subterfuge and surveillance in the enclosed but empty space of Josh's house. The house is a spatial corollary to the circular activity of *rumour* in the film, emptied of all but its abstract schema, its narrative components embodied within the major characters. How they are positioned within the house and in relation to the other characters presents one kind of diagrammatic abstraction of the whole, and it is an abstraction in nearly unlivable space (Josh's house is empty except for one or two key props, so that the character relations are the only 'objects' of focus). Audry, Vic and Pearl's admirer Mike (Mark Bailey), still unaware of the development of Pearl's confession to Josh, intrude upon the pair in a sequence of stage entrances through different doors. They enter, essentially, a labyrinth, constructed of little more than additional doors, hallways, walls, corners and apertures.

An architectural metaphor for the way the densities of commerce and discourse obscure relational clarity, in Josh's house one is always shielded from the other by a wall, a door, or at least a window. Even as nearly empty as it is, the house's complex floor plan and narrow spaces produce a prepositional muddle, people behind, above, or around the corner from each other, initially unable to get a clear view of what anyone else is 'doing' there. Beside the single mattress in the unfurnished bedroom in which Pearl is napping, however, is a telephone that establishes the relation between the inside and the outside, and which draws the 'players' out into open space, where like in a Shakespearean comedy all the misunderstandings that drove the plot to this point can be reconciled, all the deals finally dissolved.

The significance of the camera's move into open space, onto an extended 'space stage' by the beach from the cramped mise-en-scène of the house, is that it brings all the central players with it. Then, within a beautifully choreographed sequence without cuts, we hear only the most essential dialogue, stripped of innuendo and rumour; Audry's far more sensible mother Liz (Katherine Mayfield) diffuses any last

Fig. 9.1: Adrienne Shelly and Robert John Burke listen for a sound in the distance *The Unbelievable Truth*

misunderstandings on the part of Vic. Here, a theatrical dance sequence of sorts takes place, albeit one less explicit than is often found in later Hartley films, the two-step consisting of the movement of bodies and the camera in concert. Vic and Liz both enter the dance and exit, leaving the lovers alone in each other's arms for the first time. In the film's final shot, Audry and Josh both listen for a sound in the distance, but one hears only the sound of waves and seagulls as the camera pans up and out to sea and sky (Fig. 9.1). This is not the annihilation of the world as such (one is set up to notice the *absence* of bombs detonating) but the annihilation of a *specific*, insular world, the world of a town on the edge of the ocean. That is, indeed, the final dichotomy of the film: land and ocean, representative perhaps of the boundary between language and uncolonised love and desire. This final movement presents the dissolution of gridded and regulated spatial boundaries, which throughout the film have been imposed on nothing less than the bodies of Audry and Josh.

The Interrupted Dance – Faces
If it seems anachronistic to read the transformation in mise-en-scène at the end of *The Unbelievable Truth* as fundamentally theatrical, as a move toward the body/space relation of the stage, it appears less so once one thinks of Hartley within a strain of distinctly American filmmaking of the late twentieth century. This is not to say, of course, that the commonly cited influence of the French New Wave on Hartley is invalid or unimportant, but that readings of Hartley alongside Godard and Bresson may not give a complete picture. Indeed, with attention specifically turned to spatiality and the way forms of cinematic space mediate the dialectics of language, community, identity and embodiment in characterisation (all key aspects of Hartley's debut feature film), I maintain that one cannot get to Hartley without Robert Altman and John Cassavetes.

Homay King characterises Cassavetes' art as an exploration of 'free indirect subjectivity', a phrase of Pier Paolo Pasolini's, though in doing so she places the former in a line running through Antonioni, Bertolucci and Godard. But what she calls a 'crisis of attribution' in his films, the way they 'exteriorize affect' and 'dispossess the actors of their emotions and to locate their source in a diffuse visual situation' (2009: 50), is another way to describe the logic and movement of *The Unbelievable Truth*, from the limitations of repressed and interiorised affect to the theatrical choreography which unleashes the pent-up and frustrated emotions not in a melodramatic outburst but in the texture of the mise-en-scène and visual-spatial arrangement. '[If] affects cannot be localized', King writes, 'then the characters to whom they ostensibly belong cannot be pathologized in a clear-cut manner' (ibid.). All of the ways in which discursive identificatory practices hem in the romantic-affective potentials of a character, from his dress to his past and from her radical politics to her role as a daughter, thereby lose their power (and do so visibly).

Though the title of *Faces* and Cassavetes' propensity to show a number of close-ups in sequence (for example, when his suburban revelers are together in one of the central living room scenes) suggest that it might be a film about some posited iron-clad link between inner character and affect and the expression of the human face.

But close shots are at most only part of the film's cinematographic strategy. Indeed, though Cassavetes exploits the dramatic range of expressions in Gena Rowlands', John Marley's and Lynn Carlin's performances, on the whole it is a film shot *between* the close-up and middle distance, and it literally turns on a series of 'dance' sequences usually involving more than two characters and the camera itself. And while it is also a film of interiors, groups of characters often stumbling into a house from outside as if making dramatic stage entrances, Cassavetes' mise-en-scène is characteristically designed for maximum mobility on the part of his actors, their movements not rigidly scripted to use the interior spaces according to any pre-determined spatial syntax.[1]

Though *Faces* is not a film about the theatre like Cassavetes' *Opening Night* (1977) of a few years later, the interior sets are 'space stages' in their own right, where, in spite of the solipsistic close-ups that define certain conversational scenes, affective conflict and emotional transformation are allowed to permeate the scene as a whole. This occurs in part because of the wide range of movement achieved between the dancer-actors and the camera within relatively small spaces. In contrast to Hartley's film, the loosely choreographed sequences do not move from enclosed-but-empty stages to expansive exterior planes. Cassavetes' stage is, in this respect, far more cluttered with props. However, this is appropriate, since the affective register of *Faces* is far more subdued and tragic than that of *The Unbelievable Truth*, and the foreshortened and condensed narrative of the former does not allow for the spatial 'opening' that corresponds to the release of pent-up emotional energies in the latter.

In the film's second scene, Richard (Marley), Jeannie (Rowlands) and Fred (Fred Draper) leave a nightclub together and continue drinking in the car on the way to Jeannie's house. As they squeeze through the door and enter the living room, the camera crowds Richard and Fred as they drunkenly spin and sing, contributing to and exacerbating the gracelessness of their dance. In the course of its movement, the camera breaks the 180-degree rule, spinning drunkenly along with them. The camera only stabilises when the men grab Jeannie and dance along with her (to a sloppy rendition of 'Deck the Halls'), as if it has been pushed out of the dance to the side. A series of close-up and low-angle shots then accompany a conversational sequence heavy with psychological analyses of the three characters (Fred and Jeannie even agree that Richard 'looks like Sigmund'). King focuses her attention on the following dance sequence:

> Jeannie emerges from the bedroom and begins to dance with Fred as he sings. In a mobile medium shot, Fred and Jeannie continue to dance, maneuvering somewhat clumsily behind a large table lamp that blocks a portion of the frame and, positioned in the foreground, momentarily intercedes between the dancing couple to form a visual barrier between them. A low-angle close-up shows Fred and Jeannie with their arms above their heads while Jeannie executes a spin. The next close-up shot appears to follow a movement match on Jeannie's turn, but as the figures settle into the frame, we see that Jeannie is now dancing with Richard. (2009: 55)

In King's analysis of the proxemic patterns between the dancers in this scene, the interactions between the characters are not documented by the camera but mimicked by it: the act of 'cutting in' in the dance occurs also in the camera's cuts; the camera spins along with the dancers at one moment and acts as a passive wallflower when pushed out; and 'jumps' as a drunken ballerina might jump. But the significance of these cinematographic techniques is not simply that the camera performs rather than represents bodily movement; the camera is *always* part of the film's action, the 'enunciating position [of the camera] is thus contaminated by and implicated in what it observes: no longer is there a discursive distinction between the camera-reporter and what it reports on' (2009: 59). The viewer is thus not a passive judge of the characters but implicated in and complicit with the way they encounter their particular social world.

For King, this means that Casssavetes' camera takes on the affects of the characters rather than interiorising them in a psychology of the other. On its own, this is a lesson consonant with the movement of Hartley's film, away from a world dominated by rumour, surveillance and regulation. But it is also notable that, almost by definition, this is a theatrical approach to cinema, which frames bodies for an audience *in situ* and constructs a mise-en-scène that grants those bodies relative freedom of motion. The first 'dance' of the film is indeed the first of many. Although *Faces* differs from *The Unbelievable Truth* in significant ways, in the particular social sphere examined, in tone, and in worldview, it turns narratively and philosophically on the moments in which the dance is interrupted (in the scene above, when Fred turns the conversation to Jeannie's status as a prostitute). Audry and Josh's redemption in Hartley's film is achieved because the misunderstandings obstructing it are dragged, literally, into the 'open' – Cassavetes shows us (and indeed makes us feel) what happens when one's milieu prevents that from ever actually occurring. His film works in an almost inverse fashion when compared to Hartley's: various dizzying amalgamations of songs, jokes, fights and dances are frozen by the one phrase that cuts through, the clearly spoken and heard line about sexual desperation or divorce, that cannot be ignored and brings into the 'open' (for the characters as well as the viewer) not a misunderstanding but the repressed truth about what the scene was really about all along. The end, then, is not the dissolution of discursive limitations but their tragic re-imposition.

Sounds of the Casino Stage – California Split
Robert Altman directed several films adapted from American stage plays, including David Rabe's *Streamers* (1983), Donald Freed and Arnold M. Stone's *Secret Honor* (1984) and Sam Shepard's *Fool for Love* (1985). *California Split*, though not an adaptation, provides a milieu appropriate for a theatrical, open mise-en-scène while nonetheless centring its central dramatic action indoors: on the casino floor. Altman's relation to the theatrical aspects of Hartley's filmmaking, though, has less to do with choreography and literal or figurative dance sequences – after all, Altman's characters mostly *talk*. But an examination of the sonic dimension in perhaps the most characteristic (if often neglected) of his dialogic films reveals significant parallels between his narrative style and Hartley's in *The Unbelievable Truth*. In a film about compul-

sive gamblers, the movement on and off the 'stage' of the casino floor foregrounds what Carrie Rickey calls the 'proscenium' aspect of Altman's filmmaking, in which an improvisational atmosphere in a long-take gives the actors freedom to maneuver (if not in movement specifically here, in expression) within a bounded 'arena of action' (1977: 36). However, at crisis-points in his film, Altman modulates the sonic key in which his characters are operating, their bodily gestures at the poker table generally dependent upon it, in order to open up new existential possibilities.

Though a film about gambling addiction, *California Split* is not judgemental in its representation of Charlie Waters (Elliot Gould) and Bill Denny (George Segal). Rather, Altman presents the stages on which that addiction can be adequately fed: the horse track and the casino, and in particular the card table, which is repeatedly shot as an enclosed space with its own written and unwritten rules of conduct around which the larger floor becomes little more than an atmospheric din once the players get in 'the zone' (a psychological term that is also spatial, since it involves blocking out the rest of the surrounding world). Nonetheless, Altman's characteristic use of overlapping sound is the central method of dramatic unification in the film, so that the casino 'proscenium' always (until the climax of the film, when the spatio-auditory logic changes) includes the entirety of the interior space. Since Altman's microphones pick up almost everything within earshot, Charlie and Bill are always members of a larger, public ensemble, enveloped within a sonic blanket that, in another sensory register, stands in for theatrical scenery. They are almost never alone, not even in their own homes; for nearly the entire length of the film, there is the background hum of a potential audience, which perhaps mimics the compulsive 'background' noise in the gambler's head that drives him to take on higher and higher stakes.

According to Philip Brophy in his thorough catalogue of the 'modern' soundtrack, *California Split* contains 'no non-diegetic or extra-diegetic sound' (2004: 51), a technical rarity given the increasingly artificial nature of soundtrack production. That all sounds in the film originate at an identifiable acoustic spatial location within its scenic boundaries (whether directly visualised or not) produces a theatrical effect; the stage properties of the mise-en-scène are reinforced by the radio microphone's roving into the corners of the various interiors. As Brophy notes, '[Gould's] hesitant, fluctuating and mumbled delivery conveys a richness that could not be acoustically recreated' (ibid.). But, as in Hartley's films, Altman's sonic environment ultimately serves a narrative logic. The multiplicity of sound levels that Altman allows to compete with one another, whether in the clash between noise and dialogue or background babbling and foregrounded monologue, also sets up an auditory relation between excessive noise and disturbing quiet. This is a dramatic relation utilised in theatre since antiquity, then commonly established in the movement between chorus and interior monologue (eventually in the soliloquy).

'When there is an excess of sound (the horse track, card games and poker halls)', Brophy notes, 'the narrative conveys a continuum of character action. When there is noticeable silence (as in William's many reflective moments) the narrative signals a change in character orientation' (ibid.). Because Altman's radio microphones routinely pick up all noises and echoes in the scenic horizon, dramatic changes in noise level are by necessity accompanied with changes in location. The film's noisy opening scene occurs in a set built in a dance hall; Altman himself reported that he 'just set up these gambling situations and filmed them happening' (in Altman and Thompson 2006: 86). In Charlie and Bill's progress toward their big score in Reno, a journey that mimics the progress of young actors making it onto the 'big stage', the gambling floors progressively get noisier. But finally, at the film's climax, they enter a small, private room in a Reno casino where a high stakes poker game is already in progress. It is as if, by comparison, they have stepped into a sonic vacuum.

When they enter the private backroom, Charlie and Bill are, for the first time in the film, audience members rather than actor-gamblers on stage. Sitting at the bar before Bill enters the game, Charlie reads the players at the table for his now-silent, meditative partner: the bald guy in the glasses is a 'percentage player, doesn't take many chances, has no flair' while the cowboy – 'Lyndon Johnson definitely his hero' – controls the rhythm of the game, and so on. He reads the wardrobes of the players as if they are stage costumes, their dress suggesting their occupations suggesting their styles of play. Charlie is not even whispering as the game proceeds in front of them, as if the barside is an elevated box from which they have a privileged vantage point on the action. When Bill enters this staged, eclectically cast game with a buy-in of $2,000, he begins a winning streak that takes him from table to table, playing the part of the gambler who cannot lose until, at the craps table, he tells a flabbergasted Charlie that he is done betting. Bill (perhaps like Segal himself, who Altman identified as the only non-gambler on set, who was himself 'in over his head'), in one of his 'reflective moments', realises that his time with Charlie was a temporary role that he must leave behind. 'Charlie, there was no special feeling', he says, 'I just said there was.' Unlike his friend, he was only acting.

* * *

Faces and *California Split* are only two examples, albeit representative ones, of the development of a theatrical mise-en-scène in American art films that influenced (whether directly or as a kind of 'elective affinity' with, I cannot here say with certainty) Hartley's earliest films. This is not to say, of course, that assumptions about Hartley's debt to European art cinema aesthetics is false; one could trace similarities between *The Unbelievable Truth* or Hartley's other films to giants like Godard and Bresson just as I have done with these particular American New Hollywood texts. But it is indeed surprising that in the (admittedly limited) critical literature on Hartley and his first feature there is so little reference to Cassavetes and Altman. Given the dense history of twentieth-century experimental American theatre, it makes at least intuitive sense that filmmakers intent on drawing widely from aesthetic and cultural tropes of their home country (something these three all certainly do) would turn to techniques of staging.

One way to avoid a resulting American chauvinism, though, is to place Hartley's (and his predecessors') spatial syntax in wider context, as part of a general late-twentieth-century aesthetic and theoretical 'turn' toward representations of space as a primary cultural-political battleground. This kind of historical argument is, of course, beyond the scope of this essay. But nevertheless, this problematic extends from Henri Lefebvre's *The Production of Space* (translated into English in 1991), which argued that global capital increasingly depends upon the production of space itself (not just the production of things *in* space), through Jameson's *Postmodernism, or, The Cultural Logic of Late Capital*, which posited that postmodern space 'has finally succeeded in transcending the capacities of the individual human body to locate itself, to organize its immediate surroundings perceptually, and cognitively to map its position in a mappable external world' (1991: 44). Lefebvre and Jameson are representative thinkers of a far wider discourse on the production of space in the postmodern period (or the period of late, informational capital), and while the latter does not posit that filmmakers and other artists are explicitly engaged with this problematic, he does argue that the visual arts present privileged places in which to *see* (and contest) new contradictions in body/space relations. For Jameson, the project of 'cognitive mapping' involves producing the kinds of art that allow us to re-orient ourselves in overwhelmingly complicated spatial configurations, and ultimately to understand them and our place within them.

Still, despite Jameson's extensive work on narrativity in (usually realist) literature, he tends to look to the abstract and avant-garde visual arts in his analysis of postmodern aesthetics. The value of turning to filmmakers like Hal Hartley – experimental but driven by narrative, American but highly eclectic – as possible representatives of a new mode of visual exploration of space and embodiment has yet to be fully acknowledged. Further, a historiography of American cinema that takes Hartley to be a legitimate node in the invention of a post-classical aesthetic has the benefit of crafting a more optimistic picture of this movement, contesting easy claims that ambitious and expansive independent art film, by the 1990s, could only either spin off into the domain of the weird (David Lynch) or admit to co-option by major studios (Martin Scorsese and Steven Soderbergh). If the explosion of special effects in Hollywood cinema has, among other things, diminished the theatrical in popular film, perhaps it has also, by extension, complicated the project of 'cognitive mapping' through the visual arts, of being able to profitably create film that examines the placement, regulation and possible liberation of bodies in discursive and physical space (one does not quite know where actors and bodies really *are* in virtual space). Re-finding, celebrating and thinking *with* Hal Hartley and other contemporary heirs to Cassavetes and Altman is one way to come to terms with this challenge.

Note

1   The improvisation allowed to the actors in their use of domestic space extends even beyond the human. In a late scene, a moth can be seen flying in and out of an open front door. Presumably attracted to the light of the living room set inside, this insect extra performs its own dance for the camera (albeit during one of the more inappropriate times for revelry in the film).

CHAPTER TEN

Parker Posey as Hal Hartley's 'Captive Actress'
Jennifer O'Meara

Speaking at a 2008 retrospective of Parker Posey's work in Deauville, France, Hal Hartley declared that 'Parker was the first actor I ever met whom I recognised as a movie star. And she hadn't made any movies yet' (2009). More recently, Hartley's 2013 'Kickstarter' campaign for *Ned Rifle* (2014) – the follow-up to *Henry Fool* (1997) and *Fay Grim* (2006) – includes a video segment in which Posey discusses the role, with Hartley describing her as a 'captive actress' who must reprise the part of Fay Grim for a third time (2013d). These paratexts point to the enduring nature of the Hartley/Posey dynamic, one which precedes her first film, continues until his latest feature-length project, and includes a total of four shorts and five features: *Flirt* (short, 1993), *Iris* (1994), *Amateur* (1994), *Opera No. 1* (1994), *Flirt* (1995), *Henry Fool*, *The Sisters of Mercy* (2004), *Fay Grim* and *Ned Rifle*. Using close analysis of both textual and extra-textual material, this essay will examine why Hartley has chosen Posey as his 'captive' actress and, indeed, why Posey is content to be held.

In their respective books on Hartley's work, Mark L. Berrettini (2011) and Steven Rawle (2011) identify Hartley's use of a recurring group of actors, including Martin Donovan, Bill Sage and Elina Löwensohn.[1] In this essay I focus on Hartley's collaboration with Posey, in particular, which I partly explain in terms of complementary skills, such as Hartley's sharp precise dialogue and Posey's verbal dexterity and vocal control. I argue that Posey's voice is in keeping with Martin Shingler's description of a voice that is 'rich' for cinema (2010), something crucial to ensuring successful embodiment of Hartley's nuanced dialogue. Expanding on Diane Negra's study of Posey in 'Queen of the indies' (2005), Hartley's casting of the actress is also considered in terms of their respective associations with independent cinema. Posey's work in Hartley's cinema – particularly the role of Fay Grim which she played three times – is used as an entry-point into the filmmaker's broader treatment of complex women who refuse to be constrained to type. Specifically, I link Jean-Luc Godard's use of Anna Karina as muse to Hartley's use of Posey, and suggest it is one parallel by which Hartley has come to be considered the 'Godard of Long Island' (De Jonge 1996). I also consider Posey in respect of Rawle's argument in *Performance in the Cinema of Hal Hartley* that Hartley exposes the performer as a performer. Through reference to interviews and Posey's roles, I argue that her overt theatricality as an actress further motivates their collaboration. In addition to Negra's study, Posey has previously been considered by Susanne Kord and Elizabeth Krimmer (2005) as part of a study on unconventional screen images of women, and by Steven Rybin (2014) in terms of Posey's tendency to depict New Yorkers. Although each study provides important insights into Posey's performance style and/or persona, her work with Hartley tends only to be mentioned in passing. Undoubtedly, some of Posey's defining roles – including Darla in *Dazed and Confused* (Richard Linklater, 1993) and Mary in *Party Girl* (Daisy Von Scherler Mayer, 1995) – have involved other filmmakers. However, since Hartley has frequently cast Posey to significant effect, this essay aims to enrich our understanding of both of their bodies of work.

Hartley's needs as a director and Posey's skills as a performer
Writing on the importance of the voice, Shingler asserts that 'there is any number of stars suitable for vocal analysis, whose persona is largely determined by their idiosyncratic sound and whose popularity rests upon the appeal of their voice' (2006: 16). Shingler identifies distinctive voices from classical Hollywood, but notes that it would be illuminating to compare voices in mainstream cinema to those of other national cinemas, as well as independent cinema (2006: 5). Close analysis of Posey's performances in Hartley's films (as well as in other productions) reveals that her voice is in keeping with Shingler's subsequent description of a 'rich voice' as one that is: 'full-toned, fully rounded, resonant, deep, energized, amplified and projected ... articulate, pure and clear' (2010: 112).[2] Shingler also reminds us that there is a lot more to the voice than speech (2006: 5). While this is undoubtedly the case, Hartley's screenplays can be so dialogue-driven that verbal dexterity is a key criterion that his performers must meet.

Hartley has spoken of his strong preference for words over action, particularly in early films. It was only through talking to other filmmakers that he realised that most directors had a preference for *showing* things happen, unlike his own urge to 'watch the people conversing or struggling with each other' (Hartley in Wyatt 1998: 72). As I will demonstrate, Posey's distinctive vocal qualities allow her to excel in Hartley's often dialogue-driven films. Thus, although Rybin rightly credits Posey with the ability to create interesting performances even without 'an especially good script', Posey both values a good script and can help bring one to life. In *Henry Fool*, Posey uses her vocal skills to load her character Fay Grim's words with extra meaning, as in the following exchange with Simon about Henry's literary advice:

Fay: Simon, wake up, the guy's in a dream world.
Simon: He's afraid that his reputation will prevent people from giving my

> work an honest chance.
> Fay: His reputation as *what*?
> Simon: As a writer.
> Fay: [exhales in disbelief] Give me a break.
> Simon: He's kinda like an exile; marginalised on account of his ideas.
> Fay: If he's such a great big fat genius then why doesn't he write books [pauses] like you do?
> Simon: He has, he's written a book, it's nearly completed, he's been working on it for years, it's just not published.
> Fay: [knowingly] Yeah, I bet; it's probably disgusting.
> Simon: It's a quite difficult and brilliant piece of work, apparently.
> Fay: Have you read it?
> Simon: No, not yet – soon. Certain work needs to be experienced all at once in order for one to appreciate the full force of its character.
> [*very long pause in which Fay looks at Simon sceptically*]
> Fay: [rushing, dismissively] Yeah, well, whatever… [shifting to a more sympathetic tone] Listen, Simon – forget Henry. Go straight up to this Angus James character yourself and make him read your poem. [Fay/Posey straightens her posture and begins to smile proudly] I'm going to apply for a job at the one-hour photo joint, and then I'm going to go over to the mall and see about a job at the bank.

Although less than a minute in length, the sequence exemplifies Posey's intuitive understanding of, and confident execution of, Hartley's material. The scepticism in Fay's question 'His reputation as what?' comes through in Posey's notably drawn out vowel sound in 'what'. Posey uses pauses meaningfully to indicate that her character has just had a new thought, as when she softly adds 'like you do' after asking Simon (James Urbaniak) why Henry, a so-called genius, doesn't write books. Posey then uses her tongue to hiss both 's' sounds in the word 'disgusting'. She also makes good use of varying speeds, as when she conveys that she is unconvinced by her brother's comments with 'yeah, well, whatever'. By rushing the three words together after an extensive pause (ignoring the presumed punctuation), Posey makes the words sound even more dismissive. Her tone suddenly rises when she starts talking about her plans to see about a job at the bank. This gives the impression she is much more interested and optimistic about her *own* endeavours than about Simon's. Furthermore, although Posey is a long-time resident of New York, the uniqueness of her voice is heightened when, momentarily, her Southern accent breaks through. This is the case when she pronounces 'dream world' as '*drayme* world'.

Hartley has singled out Posey's skilled delivery of dialogue as key to their enduring collaboration: As he says, 'Parker hears the rhythm of how I write perfectly well. I think it has to do with the amount of work she had to do being trained as an actress, to enunciate and to listen to poetry. […] So she has an ear for finding it' (Hartley in Avila 2011: 79). Indeed, Posey's voice is briefly discussed by Negra in her study of Posey as a case study of a niche star. Several of the terms Negra uses to describe

Posey – 'caustic', 'blunt' and 'a figure of irony, ambiguity, and truthfulness' (2005: 80, 83) – imply but do not acknowledge the way her speech is written by the likes of Hartley. Negra identifies a contrast between Posey's empowered speech in indie films and the lisp her character is revealed to be hiding in *Josie and the Pussycats* (Harry Elfont and Deborah Kaplan, 2001). The expressive shift highlights Posey's tendency to play verbally empowered roles (as in Hartley's work) and reveals the full extent of her vocal skills, since the performance of a lisp requires considerable vocal control. Posey's voice is therefore in keeping with Shingler's argument that a voice that is well-suited to cinema is distinctive, but not necessarily conventionally pleasing. In fact, in Melissa Denes' interview with Posey she goes so far as to describe Posey's voice as 'full of gravel' (2001). Like Posey's lisp in *Josie and the Pussycats*, her delivery of Hartley's blunt dialogue (using harsh vowels and hissing sounds) is not aurally pleasing.

Posey's association with a distinctive delivery of dialogue is also indicated by the reception of her work, as in a BuzzFeed listicle which foregrounds the 'memorable lines' for each of Posey's ten 'most important' roles (see La Rosa 2013). Author Erin La Rosa uses capital letters to highlight Posey's tendency to raise the volume for specific words. Posey's vocal expression, both in Hartley's work and more generally, thus reveals her willingness to eschew conventions for women to endear themselves to others by speaking softly, sweetly or with a deferential hesitation. A complementary dynamic could be said to exist between Posey's vocal aggression (relative to many female performers) and the kind of dialogue Hartley writes for women, a dynamic which positions Posey's delivery and Hartley's dialogue alongside the fast-talking screwball heroines of the 1930s and 1940s.

Alissa Quart (2002) and Rybin have already compared Posey to characters from this era. Quart puts a pathological spin on the comparison, describing Posey as like 'Katharine Hepburn on *a lot* of methamphetamines' (2002: 42; original emphasis), but Rybin views the screwball heroines (and Posey's update on them) positively:

> the supposedly 'screwy' characters played by Carole Lombard and Irene Dunne in the classic genre of screwball are not irrational, but rather operate with their own nimble intelligence. Posey does much the same, creating moments of dizzy discontinuity not because her characters lack smarts, but rather to allow them to create their own form of continuity within – amounting to a witty possession *of* – their world. (Ibid.; emphasis in original)

Comparisons between Posey and screwball heroines can be strengthened with reference to Hartley's dialogue, Posey's performance of it, and Maria DiBattista's analysis in *Fast-Talking Dames* (2001). In her book, DiBattista celebrates the verbal power of women in the screwball period, contrasting it with female film dialogue post-1950. According to DiBattista:

> Smart girls, wise girls, bad girls, even silly girls who defined themselves by and through their words became increasingly rare apparitions, and indeed their muting has lasted into the twenty-first century. (2001: 332)

I disagree with the extremity of DiBattista's summation, and a survey of Posey's and Hartley's bodies of work (their collaborations, but also more broadly) reveals a wealth of such female characters. Right from the start of Hartley's career, when he cast Adrienne Shelly as Audry in *The Unbelievable Truth* (1989), his female characters have been opinionated and articulate speakers. Through profane language and an unapologetic discussion of their sexuality, Posey's characters in Hartley's films also break with DiBattista's summation that female characters are limited, verbally, in contemporary cinema. Fay in *Henry Fool* tells Henry to 'eat shit and die!', for instance, with explicit language recurring throughout the film; Amy (Diana Ruppe) tells Simon to 'kiss my ass' and Mary (Maria Porter) addresses Henry as 'you bastard'. Typically, the function of cursing in cinema is discussed in terms of the psycho-social performance of *masculinity*.[3] Given that swearing is typically considered to be unfeminine, expletives position Hartley's female characters outside of respectability and allow them to assert power through language. Posey's characters' open discussion of their sexuality is arguably more radical still. Fay speaks candidly about both her sexual desires and her own biology, as when she casually mentions that 'God, I wanna get fucked', and later tells her brother Simon that his poem 'brought my period on a week and half early'. Explicit discussion of menstruation is rarely found in film dialogue and, when it does occur, it is generally discussed among female characters. By making the comment to her own brother, Fay/Posey eschews the norm and enters a territory that is even more taboo.

Posey brings to the role of Fay Grim a history of playing sexually assertive characters, with this intertextual consistency a potential source of pleasure for Posey and Hartley fans alike. Between the making of *Henry Fool* and *Fay Grim*, for example, Posey played the title role in *The Misadventures of Margaret* (Brian Skeet, 1998). As Suzanne Kord and Elizabeth Krimmer identify, Margaret indulges in her sexual fanta-

Fig. 10.1: Parker Posey as the sexually assertive Fay Grim in *Henry Fool*

sies and, importantly, these escapades 'are not followed by repentance and apologies' (2005: 28–9). This is equally the case with Fay who is not ashamed of expressing her sexuality directly – as when she initiates sex with Henry in *Henry Fool* (Fig. 10.1) – or indirectly, as when she comments in *Fay Grim* that she chose only to read the 'dirty parts' of Henry's memoir.

In addition to Posey's confident delivery of Hartley's empowered female dialogue, her ability to signal character interiority is in harmony with Hartley's writing. Jeremy Northam, Posey's co-star in *The Misadventures of Margaret*, eloquently describes how it is as though Posey 'is turned inside out, and we can see the synapses jangling' (Northam in Denes 2001). This is important given the emphasis Hartley places on the thought processes of his fictional characters, with interiority even stressed in Hartley's published screenplays. Lines are prefaced with descriptions such as '*thinks, then...*' and '*realizing*' (Hartley 2002: 78; 82). Posey is skilled at conveying this sense of active thought.

The contrasts inherent in Posey's performance style also complement the contrasts in acting style evident in Hartley's work more generally. Hartley's performers are both minimalist and overblown in their expressions and gestures, with Rawle detailing Hartley's use of choreographed slapstick violence.[4] Similarly, in a 2001 interview for *The Telegraph*, Melissa Denes identifies in Posey's mannerisms a jarring contrast between expressing very little and expressing an excessive amount. Denes asks: 'if Sundance, the *New York Times* and a generation of young film-makers and cinema goers are convinced of Posey's cool, why all this high campery, this let's-put-on-the-show-right-here behaviour?' Thus, although Hartley is frequently associated with a detached, blank style of performance, Posey highlights that there is more to it than this; like Hartley's performers more generally, she can be both minimalist and excessive, both dry and excitable.

Returning to Hartley's comment that Posey hears the rhythm of his dialogue perfectly, his recognition of her rhythm brings comedic timing to mind. Posey's ability to convey the dark humour in Hartley's work often means she has to deliver words deadpan style or under her breath. As a consideration of their collaborative paratexts will now reveal, a shared sense of humour seems to be another harmonious component of their collaborator relationship. Posey introduces Hartley as her 'friend' in the 'Parker Posey – Captive Actress!!!' video made for Kickstarter (Hartley 2013d). This familiarity is conveyed by the playful banter that ensues during the two-and-a-half minute interview. Posey occasionally looks down at notes but, in various dry ad-libs, she feigns annoyance with Hartley for not giving her a larger role in the third film:

> I've been in two of these films by my friend Hal Hartley [...]. He's written a third one which [pause] he *needs* me to be in too [Posey pauses and gives the camera a look of displeasure], but just briefly... [a smile breaks across Posey's face], but in a very good scene. (Ibid.)

At this point in the video, an intertitle appears, assuring us with a similar playfulness that 'she's in a lot of good scenes' (Fig. 10.2). Hartley and Posey's offscreen connec-

Fig. 10.2: Posey and Hartley joke about the significance of her role in a promotional video for *Ned Rifle*.

tion is further established when, flicking through a published book of Hartley's drawings she asks if one of them is of her. Off-camera, Hartley says 'no that's my cousin, Jeanine, but there is a picture of you in it'. He enters the shot and, as he flicks to the page, he explains that it is a picture from after they finished shooting a film in Paris. Posey is visibly pleased that she has made it into the book, while the depth of their connection is revealed by the ease with which Hartley locates and explains the picture. Hartley has previously explained that reusing actors allows him to develop a 'shorthand' style of communication on set (see Avila 2011: 80). Hartley and Posey's easy communication – including their shared jokes – is apparent in the partly-improvised videos they made for *Ned Rifle* and, more broadly, it is likely to be a factor that has contributed to their enduring collaborations.

Posey is equally deadpan in another Kickstarter video, seemingly unscripted, entitled 'Henry and Fay' (Hartley 2013c). Posey and Thomas Jay Ryan (who plays Henry) discuss the first two films while sitting in front of a large screen playing clips. When Ryan refers to Fay Grim and matter-of-factly tells Posey 'that's the part you played', she replies ('I remember') with characteristic dryness. As in the 'Captive Actress' video, Posey alternates between blank humour when 'in character' and expressive warmth, particularly when addressing Hartley offscreen. Furthermore, just as Hartley recognises her skill for delivering language, she refers to his skilled use of language; describing the trilogy with Ryan, she explains that 'there's something about these films that is so … mystical'. At this point, she stops herself, raises her hand and adds with a broad smile as she looks off-camera, 'I don't know if you like that word, Hal'. Her self-correction alludes to the specificity of Hartley's writing style and indicates that, like his characters who often debate definitions, Posey is keenly aware that Hartley might take issue with her choice of words.

Hartley and Posey as 'King' and 'Queen' of the Indies
Despite Posey and Hartley holding different occupations within the film industry, the two share certain similarities in terms of the marginal space they occupy relative to studio productions. Although Posey first appeared in the soap opera *As the World*

Turns (1991–92), she soon earned herself the label of 'queen of the indies' in a slew of independent productions, including *Drunks* (Peter Cohn, 1995), *Basquiat* (Julian Schnabel, 1996) and *The House of Yes* (Mark Waters, 1997). Hartley parallels Posey's indie credibility, in that he is one of the few unquestionably 'independent' filmmakers to emerge from the United States in this period.[5] In contrast to filmmakers like Quentin Tarantino, Wes Anderson and Noah Baumbach – who began with very low-budget productions but increasingly collaborated with studios or specialist subsidiaries – Hartley has continued to work on small budgets and with minimal influence from outside parties. In a similar vein, existing studies on Posey highlight the significance of indie cinema in providing her with roles that are well-suited to her personality and talents. Kord and Krimmer argue that indie cinema and television are the main channels for performers whose body, age or personality 'make them ineligible to play the young, pretty, and perfectly proportioned blockbuster heroine' (2005: 113). In Posey's case, it is her personality rather than her appearance or age that marks her out from the Hollywood norm. As they note, Posey's characters tend to 'inhabit the margins of society, both socially and psychologically' (2005: 124). The same could be said of Hartley's characters, who tend to be alienated from their family or society more generally.

Hartley and Posey not only belong to the same fruitful era of late-twentieth-century independent American cinema, but they are both central figures of what Emanuel Levy refers to as 'The New York School of Indies' (1999: 184–217).[6] Rybin's analysis of Posey's performance style rightly identifies the centrality of New York to Posey's body of work, noting that it is the city 'most fitting for the enchantingly flighty presence she inscribes on film'. Similarly, although Hartley has made various films outside of the United States, including shooting parts of films in Europe and Japan, he – like Posey – remains strongly-associated with New York. In fact, it is partly Posey's attendance at State University of New York at Purchase, where she studied acting, which connected her with Hartley in the first place. Hartley also graduated from the university's filmmaking programme, and he was informed about Posey's talent by his former professor (see Eaves 2005).[7]

Given that Posey was one of the key performers during the indie revival at the end of the century, Hartley's desire to cast her could be viewed, cynically, as part of a broader strategy to distance himself from the mainstream. Indeed, his keenness to associate with notable indie performers extends beyond the film world into independent music, with indie bands like Sonic Youth and Yo La Tengo featured on his soundtracks. Even Hartley's casting of the English musician P. J. Harvey as Magdalena in *The Book of Life* (1998) could be considered in respect of the Hartley/Posey dynamic; if, at the end of the century, Posey was the queen of indie cinema, then Harvey was the queen of indie music. As recently as October 2013, Harvey was referred to as 'queen of indie' by the long-standing music magazine and website, NME (see Jones 2013). Harvey and Posey were also born within a year of one another and share a spirit of protest against cultural norms of acceptable female behaviour, in addition to certain physical similarities (notably, dark hair that contrasts with a pale complexion and a penchant to scowl or glare).

Rather than assuming that Hartley thought he could gain viewers or indie credibility by casting Posey, I would argue that Hartley and Posey share an enduring belief that the market for indie films is substantial and loyal. This shared belief is evident in the 'Ned and Fay' promotional video (2013c), as when Thomas Jay Ryan asks Posey about the possibility that the third part of the *Henry Fool / Fay Grim* saga will not get made. Posey cuts him off with a defiant confidence that 'there will be a third'. She squints at Ryan, as though frustrated that he doesn't have enough faith in the project, and looks off-camera (presumably seeking Hartley's confirmation) that 'this is how it's done now; with Kickstarter'. Posey's expression shifts again when she grabs Ryan's shoulder and, indicating that she is enticed by the prospect of promoting the film at small, independent venues, she looks to Hartley again as she excitedly explains that people will come out to support the production when they travel 'all over the country, to these little festivals'.

Posey's distaste for large studio productions is reflected across her interviews, including one with Andy Greenwald in 2012 in which she laments the current state of both television and film: 'It's sad that only a few people these days get a chance to really create their own material and not have anyone mess with it.'[8] Posey thus shares Hartley's preference for productions that allow the end product to reflect the vision of a small few. Hartley has gone so far as to say that his 'one rule' when raising funding is to accept money that comes with 'minimal strings attached' (Hartley in Fried 1993: 40).

Exposing Posey as a Performer: Actor as Character and Character as Actor
Another harmonious element of the Hartley/Posey dynamic is the way in which, onscreen, Hartley reveals the performative nature of human behaviour and, offscreen, Posey emphasises her own performativity. Negra identifies the perceived fine line between Posey and her characters by situating Posey as a 'picture personality' rather than a conventional 'star' (2005: 72–4). Drawing on Richard DeCordova's conceptualisation of the picture personality, Negra ascribes to Posey the kind of limited extrafilmic discourse that he identifies in pre-1914 cinema: 'Extrafilmic discourse insisted on the personality's real-world identity, to be sure, but in describing that identity it merely referred readers back to the evidence in the films in a kind of tautological loop' (DeCordova 1990: 91). Identifying this kind of limited discourse in media coverage of Posey, Negra notes how 'It is often suggested that Posey is fundamentally indistinguishable from the characters she plays; that she is, in certain essential ways, a personality both originative of film roles and retentive of them after a film has been produced' (2005: 73). Considering things from Hartley's perspective, it is easy to see Posey's appeal. As Rawle details in *Performance in the Cinema of Hal Hartley*, exposing the performer as a performer (and the character as a performer) is a recurring element in Hartley's work. With performance itself a kind of tautological loop in his films, it is unsurprising that Posey (a performer who equally embodies this kind of loop) fits neatly into his world.

Much like Hartley, Posey views the performance process reflexively, often creating a tongue-in-cheek impression of her own overt theatricality. In a diary she wrote for indieWIRE on the set of *subUrbia* (Richard Linklater, 1996), she describes listening to a recording of her lines as she sleeps (2011). In the diary, Posey plays the role of a desperate actress who – quoting Sidney Lumet – insists that 'There are no Small Parts, just Small Actors', before adding that, 'I've written more lines for myself, of course' (ibid.). This diary is an early variation of Posey's joke in the 'Captive Actress!!!' video, when she pretends to be bothered that Hartley didn't make her part in *Ned Rifle* bigger. More generally, Posey's interviews tend to reveal how she views characters conceptually and sees only a fine line between performing in everyday life and performing on-camera.

Rawle argues that Hartley exposes the performer as a performer through repeated use, as well as through scenes that reveal the process through which performance is eventually fixed (2011: 57). This is particularly the case in *The Sisters of Mercy*, a short which Hartley compiled using out-takes from *Iris*, a short made eleven years earlier with Posey and Sabrina Lloyd. Given that Posey embraces performance as a reflexive process, even discussing herself as a character in the third person, it is unsurprising that she allowed Hartley to create a new work – in the form of *The Sisters of Mercy* – by revisiting her decade-old performance. As Rawle explains, 'The film exposes the labour and activity of the performers and the process by which a performance becomes fixed in the final text' (2011: 8). Additionally, just as Posey embraces theatricality in interviews, and discusses herself as a character, Hartley's characters can deliver lines like actors. At one point in *The Unbelievable Truth*, Josh (Robert John Burke) and Jane (Edie Falco) repeat the same lines of dialogue three times. Through their varied deliveries, the rehearsal element of the acting process is thus revealed.

Returning to DeCordova's concept of a tautological loop between the character and the performer in real-life, it is useful to consider the significance of overlaps in Posey's public persona and the blunt women she tends to play in Hartley's films. Consider the following excerpt from a 1996 interview with Christina Kelly for *Index* magazine:

Kelly: Is Parker...
Posey: Yeah, it is.
Kelly: What?
Posey: My real name. (Kelly 1996)

Posey is unconcerned with being polite and instead alludes to the repetitive nature of publicity work when she starts to answer the stock question about her name before Kelly can finish asking it. Posey thus displays the same kind of jaded frustration and impatience with the world as does her character of Fay Grim.

Hartley's public persona also overlaps with the characters that he writes, with his speech in interviews uncannily reminiscent of his characters' dialogue. Hartley uses the kind of circular phrasing that recurs in his scripts when describing explicit sex scenes as 'embarrassing. It's redundant. Redundancy is embarrassing' (Hartley in Fuller 1993: xxxv). There are also overlaps between the content of his characters' speech and Hartley's own biographical details. When the title character of *Henry*

Fool announces that 'a prophet is seldom heeded in his own land', it is difficult not to consider Hartley's personal comments about his following being larger overseas, as well as Hartley's temporary move to Berlin where he received a writing fellowship.[9] Thus, although Hartley does not appear in his own films (save for the occasional cameo), interviews with him can create the impression that he, like Posey, is almost indistinguishable from his own characters. Although the term 'picture personality' (which Negra uses in relation to Posey) is not applicable, since Hartley is not performing onscreen, a looping effect is nonetheless created between Hartley's characters and his extra-filmic persona. In these ways, Posey and Hartley seem to incorporate allusions to onscreen characters during interviews, potentially to satisfy fans of their work who look out for such overlaps.

Posey is to Hartley as Karina is to Godard
The Hartley/Posey dynamic can also be considered in terms of Hartley's status as the so-called 'Godard of Long Island'. Peter de Jonge used the term to describe Hartley in a 1996 article, with similarities between the two filmmakers frequently highlighted in analyses of Hartley's work. While Berrettini notes that, in Hartley's films, Elina Löwensohn bears, 'more than a passing resemblance to [Anna] Karina' (2011: 31), I would instead link Godard's use of Anna Karina as muse to Hartley's use of Posey. Significantly, both Godard and Hartley can make claim to an element of discovery with their respective performers. Godard famously cast Karina, then unknown, after he saw her in a soap commercial and decided he liked her look. Although Posey had appeared in *As the World Turns* before Hartley cast her in *Flirt*, his discussion of their early encounters also highlights that he saw something special in Posey. As noted earlier in this chapter, Hartley declared that she was the first actor that he ever recognised as a movie star, despite the fact that 'she hadn't made any movies yet' (Hartley 2009). The comment is made in the spirit of respect and admiration, but it is also phrased in a way that flatters Hartley's ability to recognise her potential before others did.

Godard's working relationship with Karina accompanied a personal relationship and marriage, a significant difference that means the term 'muse' is not quite right for Posey.[10] When, in 1967, Godard and Karina broke up after a six-year marriage, Karina stopped appearing in his films (see Dixon 1997: 24; 131). By contrast, Hartley and Posey's relationship appears never to have extended beyond friendship, with Hartley married to the Japanese actress Miho Nikaido (who appears in several of his films) since 1996. Leaving this contrast to one side, however, allows for a comparison to be made between Hartley's and Godard's general approach to female characters, which Posey and Karina could be said to encapsulate. For Vlada Petric and Geraldine Bard, Godard is the *nouvelle vague* filmmaker to exhibit 'the greatest concern for female characters' (1993: 98). Similar praise could be levelled at Hartley in relation to independent American filmmakers at the end of the twentieth century. Excluding the work of women like Allison Anders, Nicole Holofcener and Susan Seidelman, this period was marked by filmmakers like Kevin Smith and Quentin Tarantino who tended to foreground male stories. Hartley does centre films like *Henry Fool*, *Simple*

Men and *The Book of Life* on male characters but, ever since casting Adrienne Shelly to play unconventional young women in his first two films (*The Unbelievable Truth* and *Trust*) he has shown a consistent interest in eschewing stereotypical female types. Much as Godard foregrounded Karina and women's issues both in his early and subsequent work, the kinds of women which Posey plays are reflective of Hartley's interest in creating complex female characters. Indeed, my earlier discussion of the uncommonly candid and profane dialogue that Posey delivers in Hartley's work is one component of this.

For Geneviève Sellier, in films like *Vivre sa Vie* (Jean-Luc Godard, 1962) and *Le Petit Soldat* (Jean-Luc Godard, 1963), scenes can amount to 'a fetishistic contemplation of Anna Karina's face' (2008: 154). In Posey's case, Hartley's films could instead be said to fetishise her voice. Writing on *Vivre sa Vie*, Sellier details how multiple changes in lighting, clothing and hair serve to highlight Karina's beauty (2008: 163). With Posey, on the other hand, multiple vocal changes (of speed, pitch and volume) serve to highlight Posey's voice. This is not to say that Posey does not possess range in terms of facial and bodily expression, but that her voice is central to – and is played up in – Hartley's work, while Karina's appearance is central to – and played up in – Godard's work. Given Hartley's distinctive dialogue, it is unsurprising since that he would make the most of Posey's rare vocal skills. At the same time, the distinctiveness of Godard's dialogue has historically been overlooked, with Karina's delivery downplayed as a result.[11]

When one compares the representations of women in Godard's and Hartley's work, Petric and Bard's description of Godard can reasonably be applied to Hartley: 'he focuses on [women's] psychological uniqueness; and he analyses the roles they play as women in society, family, and male-female relationships. [...] These protagonists are seen as equal to, or more powerful than, their male counterparts' (1993: 98). Specifically, both filmmakers have explored the social, political and economic issues that can revolve around the female body, such as prostitution and modelling. In Hartley's *The Unbelievable Truth*, Audry (Shelly) is effectively sold into the modelling world by her father (Christopher Cooke), who sees it as a way to make money. Audry is defiantly nihilistic, and more concerned with nuclear disarmament than a formal education (she refuses to attend Harvard when accepted), but she agrees to model as it provides her with an escape from her parents and small town. As Rawle eloquently describes: 'Audry adopts a typical position of femininity in contemporary society, as an image to be looked at', but she also performs 'as an adult in control of her sexuality in order to negotiate the social structures of exchange and economic relationships' (2011: 91). As with Godard's treatment of prostitutes in films like *Vivre sa Vie*, Hartley creates sympathetic female characters who are cornered, by men, into making money from their bodies. In *Amateur*, Hartley continues to playfully problematise the way that 'sex sells' through the character of Isabelle (Isabelle Huppert); Isabelle is an ex-nun who writes porn, but she is also a virgin who believes she would be a nymphomaniac if she were to have sex. The character has a strong allegorical resonance, since Isabelle embodies the opposing extremes that female characters are often reduced to; the virgin and the whore. Isabelle both defines herself by, and aims to profit from, a sexuality that she has not yet explored. There are thus substantial overlaps between Godard's and Hartley's representation of women's issues. These parallels tend to be overlooked in favour of comparisons made between the two filmmakers on the basis of style.

Hartley's willingness to foreground unconventional female characters extends to his casting of unconventional performers, like Posey, but also to P. J. Harvey who carved out an autonomous career in alternative rock at a time when it was heavily dominated by male musicians, and whose music expresses an independence from conventions such as marriage. One could also trace a line between Hartley's collaborations with Posey and his casting of Aubrey Plaza, sixteen years Posey's junior, in the role of Susan in *Ned Rifle*. Within the next generation of female American performers, Plaza comes the closest to matching Posey as a cynical, reflexive and darkly humorous figure. The actress is best-known for her role as the sarcastic April Ludgate on the popular sitcom *Parks and Recreation* (NBC, 2009–15).[12] Hartley was unfamiliar with Plaza's work until her agency contacted him (see Cohen 2015), but Plaza shares Posey's dryness and a certain sense of overt theatricality; her character on *Parks and Recreation* had an aristocratic alter-ego – Janet Snakebite – who she frequently performs for pleasure.[13] Plaza shares Posey's skill for jaded facial expressions, with both actresses also bringing a sense of knowingness to their various roles.

In his article on Posey, Rybin (2014) describes how she playfully addresses audience members who come to a film purely to see her: she 'darts right past those viewers who have arrived at these films for their plots and their leading stars, all in playful search of those eyes who have arrived at the movie for her'. The description brings to mind one of Plaza's memorable trademarks in *Parks and Recreation*. The show has a faux-reality TV set up, which means the characters often speak directly to the camera. Plaza's character speaks to the camera relatively infrequently, but she often looks to the camera to signal her disdain with unfolding events. This is obviously different to Posey addressing those in the audience who are familiar with her work, but Plaza nonetheless shares Posey's talent for dividing her character's behaviour into i) elements that are directed at others in the fictional world and ii) elements that are directed at the outside world.

As Rybin's description of Posey's playful address suggests, the actress knows that she has a cult following who expect things from her performances that they will not find elsewhere. Hartley equally seems to acknowledge and appeal to his fans through a distinctive auteurial style and intertextual references across his body of work, even explicitly aligning himself with auteur theory when he explains that if the auteur is dead then 'I'm working in a vacuum' (Hartley in Kornits 1999).

* * *

As the components of this essay indicate, there are multiple reasons for Hartley and Posey's ongoing collaboration. Both Hartley and Posey seem keen to ensure that the fast-talking dame, one who speaks her mind, does not disappear completely. Often it is the content and delivery of Posey's dialogue that distances her characters from dominant Hollywood types, as is the case in her collaborations with Hartley, along with many of Hartley's other female characters. Posey's expressive voice and verbal skills ensure that Hartley's dialogue is executed as he intends it to be. Posey also brings her offbeat comedy timing to his work, something which allows his dark humour to seep from the page to the screen. Through reference to interviews, Posey's roles in Hartley's films, and Hartley and Posey's promotional videos, I have also shown that her reflexive approach to performance, including an overt theatricality, further motivates their collaboration. Furthermore, Hartley and Posey can be said to share a self-conscious approach to the construction of their respective personae. A comparison can also be made between Posey as a performer who symbolises resistance to certain Hollywood actress norms, and Hartley as a writer-director who symbolises resistance to Hollywood filmmaking practices, including a tendency to marginalise women or depict them stereotypically. Hartley shares these traits with Godard and, as I have argued, Hartley's recurring use of Posey may partly be inspired by Godard's recurring use of Anna Karina.

With the *Henry Fool / Fay Grim / Ned Rifle* trilogy completed in 2014, it is unclear at the time of writing whether Hartley and Posey have plans to work together again. Given that Posey played the character of Fay Grim three times, it has been central to both her career and Hartley's filmography. But, unlike the period in the late 1990s when they made a variety of shorts together, Hartley and Posey did not collaborate – even on any short projects – in the period between *Fay Grim* and *Ned Rifle*. It is possible, however, that given Hartley's success crowdfunding his last two feature-length productions (with Posey contributing significantly to the campaign for *Ned Rifle*) that the two will use this avenue to finance future collaborations.

It is difficult to overstate the significance of Hartley and Posey occupying a shared peripheral space outside of the Hollywood studio system. At the end of the twentieth century, independent American cinema experienced a resurgence that both benefited, and benefited from, Hartley and Posey. Unlike many up-and-coming performers of this period, Posey did not view her work in indie cinema as a necessary stepping stone into Hollywood. Similarly, unlike other writer-directors who started as 'indies', Hartley did not gradually begin to work with studios, or even specialist subsidiaries. It is perhaps this intangible quality – an embracing of their status as outsiders – that best explains the Hartley/Posey dynamic. Despite their respective work being peripheral to mainstream cinema, each has remained central to American independent cinema since the 1990s and into the new millennium. Hartley and Posey have both shown resilience to the challenges of working independently, as well as showing flexibility in order to work in other media (such as television) and to take advantage of cultural and technological developments in order to make work with the help of digital media platforms like Kickstarter. Given that Hal Hartley and Parker Posey share much in common, their enduring willingness to collaborate is as understandable as it is enduring.

Notes
1 Rawle has also carried out an in-depth analysis of Hartley's collaboration with Donovan in terms of cult stardom (2013).

2   Shingler uses the term 'rich voice' in relation to *The Rich Are Always with Us* (Alfred E. Green, 1932).
3   See Peberdy (2011: 3) and Ging (2012: 111) for a discussion of film profanity and masculinity.
4   Rawle details how Hartley's violence quotes from gestures and movements associated with slapstick comedy and cartoons. By transplanting 'a form of abstract violent movement into a realistic idiom', he argues that Hartley creates a commentary on viewer responses to typical representations of violence (2011: 152–3).
5   Jim Jarmusch is the other quintessential independent American filmmaker from this period. For a more detailed comparison of Jarmusch and Hartley, one based on verbal style, see 'Poetic Dialogue: Lyrical Speech in the Work of Hal Hartley and Jim Jarmusch' (O'Meara 2013).
6   Levy's chapter on 'The New York School of Indie' does not mention Posey, however, since he focuses on filmmakers rather than performers.
7   As Berrettini details, Hartley scouted both acting and cinematography talent at SUNY Purchase, including cinematographer Michael Spiller, and acting graduates Edie Falco, Bill Sake and Robert John Burke (2011: 6).
8   Posey is referring here to comedian Louis C. K., whose show she appeared on in 2012.
9   Hartley received a fellowship from the American Academy of Berlin (see Avila 2011: 85).
10 Karina appeared in Godard's *Une femme est une femme* (1961), *Vivre sa Vie* (1962), *Le Petit Soldat* (1963), *Bande à Part* (1964), *Pierrot le Fou* (1965), *Alphaville* (1965) and *Made in U.S.A* (1966).
11 In an uncommon description of Godard's dialogue in *Vivre sa Vie*, Wheeler W. Dixon notes that Karina's character Nana engages with a philosopher 'in a metaphysical dialogue of considerable length and density' (1997: 31). It should be noted that J. J. Murphy compares Hartley's use of clichéd and aphoristic speech to that of Godard (2007: 103).
12 Incidentally, Posey made a guest appearance on the show in 2011.
13 It should be noted, however that Hartley had to look beyond Plaza's work on *Parks and Recreation* to see the kind of range he wanted when casting Susan. In an interview with Alex Cohen, Hartley explains that only in *Safety Not Guaranteed* (Colin Trevorrow, 2012) did he see Plaza's 'skill, charm, real charisma, [and] breadth' (Cohen 2015).

CHAPTER ELEVEN

The Figure Who Writes: On the Henry Fool Trilogy

Steven Rybin

The propulsive motif of Hal Hartley's *Henry Fool* trilogy – the driving force behind the first film (1997) and its sequels, *Fay Grim* (2006) and *Ned Rifle* (2014) – is writing. There is the writing of a possible madman and confirmed sex offender, Henry Fool, who arrives in a small Queens burgh one sunny morning, carrying a satchel of notebooks, his *Confessions*, a self-professed masterwork. There is also the writing of Simon Grim (James Urbaniak), Fool's protégé, a taciturn garbage man who finds self-expression, and literary fame, through the medium of poetry. And there is the typing of Fay Grim (Parker Posey), Simon's flirty, unemployed sister, who pecks out her resume on a laptop and, later, posts her brother's poem on the internet. There is also the writing Simon's mother reads – Simon's own – a reading that motivates her suicide. More: there is the writing (and the speaking aloud from a written script) of the various pundits, politicians and popes who declare Simon Grim, and his poetry, a pox on society, with its apparent scatological content; the writing of the address on the envelope on which Ned, son of Henry Fool and Fay Grim, finds the address of his reclusive uncle Simon; the re-writing, or interpretation, of Fool's *Confessions*, across countries and continents, as it is taken to contain, in code, directives for various international acts that might harm the security of the United States; the writing of Susan Weber (Aubrey Plaza), a graduate student who is working on a dissertation on Simon's poems; and finally, and not least importantly, there is the writing of Hal Hartley himself, the writer and director of these films, the one who writes the story and the dialogue and frames and composes those who write and read in the frame.

But much of this writing is hard to see. Only dim, high-angle shots of the several volumes of Fool's *Confessions*, in the first film, show us his composition in any sort of entirety. Even then, it is impossible for the viewer (even in a paused frame) to discern any of Fool's scribbling, given both his atrocious penmanship and the camera's distance from his text. Of course, some writing in these films is very much visible: there is, for example, the writing that Hartley places, non-diegetically, onto the unfolding surface of his film, the writing that tells us that Thomas Jay Ryan plays Henry Fool, that James Urbaniak plays Simon Grim, that Parker Posey is Fay Grim, and Liam Aiken Ned Grim, and so on; this extra-diegetic text, in *Fay Grim*, becomes even more salient, serving to signpost the narrative events and complications leading to Fay's vertiginous fall into unwitting international espionage. The presence of such text on the screen stands in contrast to the invisibility of the writing the characters themselves produce. Viewers cannot read the poems that win Simon Grim fame, and are not privy to the *Confessions*; and while Susan speaks at length about her thesis on the poetics of Grim, the camera does not pass over the textual shape her thinking takes. As viewers, what we mostly get, in terms of writing, in the *Henry Fool* trilogy, is visible only on the skin and body of the figures of the frame. These films, I argue, are not about the subject matter of that which is written – the work that is authored – so much as they are about writing's visible affect on the body, the way a piece of read (or written, or shouted, or glimpsed) prose or poetry can drive, spark, tempt, confuse, or somehow otherwise completely untether a body from its moorings. These films are interested more in how the writing of the characters motivates movement, action and consequence in the world, rather than in the subject matter of authorship itself. Even in scenes where writing is present – where we see someone writing, or someone reading – Hartley's focus, again and again, is on the body, and the body's gestural relationship to writing. Hartley's subject in this trilogy is on the way writing moves his characters to thought and action, and the way his characters move and position themselves through or while writing and reading. Writing in these films has a way of coursing through a body – a body that is in turn 'written' by Hartley and his performers, a body that is framed, choreographed and composed.

Of course, the larger tradition of modernism and independent cinema to which Hartley belongs includes many films and auteurs concerned with the relation between writing and onscreen figures. Hartley's preference for deadpan dialogue delivery suggests, for example, Robert Bresson as a key influence. Hartley will show us more than once, in *Henry Fool*, the image of a hand approaching paper with pen or pencil, reminiscent of the opening image of Bresson's *The Diary of a Country Priest* (1951), in which the hand of the titular priest reaches for his journal as he prepares to inscribe his thoughts (Fig. 11.1). André Bazin, reflecting upon Bresson's faithful use of the novel upon which his film is based, suggests that *The Diary of a Country Priest* is 'something like literature multiplied by cinema' (2009: 157). By contrast, it is possible to consider Hartley's trilogy as one which shows us 'life intensified through literature', a cerebral and embodied play of text, one involving onscreen writing but which begins with the writing of Hartley himself and the way this writing is performed. As Sophie Wise has suggested, 'On the page succinct, distilled, very deliberate dialogue calls attention to itself … Hartley's finished films, visualized and embodied, still retain this writerly quality' (1999: 254). This is a vision of life intensified by textuality.

Fig. 11.1: Robert Bresson's *Diary of a Country Priest*

Fig. 11.2: Jean-Luc Godard's *A Woman is a Woman*

Fig. 11.3: Hal Hartley's *Fay Grim*

Other predecessors for Hartley's use of writing and text include Jean-Luc Godard's play with onscreen text across many of his films, perhaps most emblematically *A Woman is a Woman* (1961), in which the viewer is shown onscreen text alerting the viewer to Godard's own cinematic influences and punctuating important plot events (Fig. 11.2). Hartley uses a similar device in *Fay Grim* (Fig. 11.3) to comically underscore intentionally confusing narrative developments. And the atmosphere of paranoia which gradually develops as a result of reading and writing in the *Henry Fool* trilogy recalls Mark Rappaport's cinema, particularly *Chain Letters* (1985), in which a group of New Yorkers are linked by a subversive string of letters, inspiring them to imagine other ways of doing and being. (In one scene, a Vietnam vet smashes his television after becoming enraged by dominant ideological discourse; later, he speaks about a scenario for a movie script or a science fiction novel he might write, a spoken text as convoluted and paranoid as the government plot of *Fay Grim*.)

As this brief rundown of Hartley's influences begins to suggest, there are two interrelated issues at play here. One is how Hartley, as director, blocks and frames these figures who put pen to paper or eye and mind to text. The other is what the figure in the frame does – how the space is changed through further movement – upon reading or writing. Hartley's authorship – his own way of writing, his wielding of what Alexandre Astruc called 'the caméra-stylo', or camera-pen – is often figured as part of a larger intellectual discourse known as 'smart cinema', a phrase coined by Jeffrey Sconce (2002) to designate those directors who position themselves, and their audiences, against the earnest dumbness and vapid accessibility of mainstream films. And to be sure, Hartley's precise visual compositions and rigorous performative choreography act like a cerebral address to the viewer, who must pass through Hartley's graphic approach to filmmaking before any sort of emotional connection to character might be forged. Nevertheless, approaching Hartley purely as a 'smart' director obscures the extent to which, in the films and in our reception of them, writing affects the body. In such moments, Hartley's films, far from having already positioned themselves as either ironic or earnest, or smart or dumb, instead have a more immediate, and at times emotional, impact. Such orchestrations of writing's inscription through and on the moving body in Hartley's films do not confirm a pre-articulated cultural position of 'smartness' but rather set the whole issue of cultural positionality into motion again and again, as if the very ability to negotiate a terrain (which, in the *Henry Fool* trilogy, takes on an increasingly global, political and international shape) were determined by how one moved, gestured and expressed after having read or written a piece of writing.

If Hartley the auteur is, then, the guiding intelligence behind his films, there are nevertheless also nimble intelligences at play within the stories he tells, the characters who write, read and move after the encounter with a text. It is not surprising that figural movement should be shot through with the feeling for writing in Hartley's cinema, for Hartley himself has described his work with actors, particularly at the rehearsal stage, as 'the very furthest stages of writing, where each character that I've written on the page actually takes on a life' (Fuller 1992: xi). Of course, Hartley has also cautioned against reading his films as a polyphony of voices, reminding viewers that 'none of us are really the work. The work is the work ... I don't want anybody's contribution to be so particular as to take away from the guiding aesthetic principle ... There shouldn't be disparate personalities within the piece' (Fuller 1992: xviii–xix). In this sense, Hartley's writing arguably subsumes and 'contains' the writing, and the affects of writing, produced by his characters – even as they move as they write or read, Hartley must be taken as the author of these figurations, despite whatever claims to authorship are made within the story worlds of his films. Hartley, in these terms, discusses his work in ways that place it someone closer to the traditional notion of the pre-novelistic 'epic', wherein, as Mikhail Bakhtin teaches us, 'point of view and evaluation are fused with the subject into one inseparable whole' (1981: 17).

Hartley's insistence on a unified and monological authorship, however, is perhaps only tenable in the films up to and including *Flirt*. What makes the *Henry Fool* trilogy so especially central to the middle period of Hartley's career is the way in which the films not only continue to explore the tensions between authored work and performed text on the level of form, but also how their subject matter complicates Hartley's own conception of his films as works unified by tone, rhythm and authorial point of view. Where Hartley's early films are very much about the achievement of an artistic work by Hartley himself, as *auteur* (these are the films, up to *Flirt*, which are most assuredly responsible for the director's place in the pantheon of 'smart cinema' and independent cinema more generally), the subject matter of the *Henry Fool* trilogy engages more directly with the impact of writing (the pleasure and pain of text) produced by characters in the films and the reception of this writing by figures in the frame. This aspect of the trilogy, then, goes further than the earlier films in placing Hartley's own ongoing formal achievements into dialogue with the strivings of his characters to create their own works and with the larger cultural reception of those works – works which, once they are read (in the case of Henry Fool's *Confessions*) and published (Simon Grim's poetry), are then circulated and felt.

Each character in the trilogy moves across a different trajectory as they find themselves moved by writing. Henry Fool, across the entire trilogy, moves in a largely linear way, lurching forward with gruff brash, a reflection of his misplaced confidence in the importance of his *Confessions*. Simon Grim begins to move with his achievement of highbrow cultural distinction near the end of *Henry Fool* before finding himself marginalised in obscure corners of the internet, by the end of the trilogy, with a lowbrow comedy routine. Fay Grim's journey, meanwhile, is inspired by the use of books in purely physical terms, resulting in a carefully choreographed way of moving that uses the trilogy's world of male authorship as a mere pretext for a more creative way of inhabiting space. As for Ned and Susan in the final film in the trilogy, theirs is a more schizophrenic movement, proceeding along a contradictory trajectory that bounces between religiosity and secularity (in the case of Ned) and monologism and dialogism (in the case of Susan).

Simon's Reading and Writing as a Social Act: Out of the Habitus in Henry Fool
Before the titular character arrives on the scene in *Henry Fool*, it is as if Simon's 'little burgh' had never encountered reading and writing at all. (The town does have a small library, but it and its mostly college-age denizens are cut off from the larger community until Simon's poetry ignites debate and discourse.) This burgh, the city of Queens, is only the ostensible setting of the film, for Hartley's narrative spaces are much more specific and finite in nature: the Grim house; the local convenience store; various alleyways and streets. Taken together, these city blocks form what Pierre Bourdieu (1984) might call Simon Grim's *habitus*, a location determining Simon's position in the world, his habits of doing and thinking and being. Yet Henry's presence, and his inspiration to Simon to begin writing, eventually sets Simon apart from his social surroundings, an idea suggested not only in Urbaniak's and Ryan's performances but also through the way in which Hartley, as Steven Rawle suggests, binds

'gesture with shot' (2011: 211). As examples of this tendency of Hartley's camera to intimately bind itself with characters, Rawle points to moments in *Henry Fool*, such as when Simon Grim first sets pen to paper to begin his attempt at a poem, as examples of the film's tendency to abstract the idea of embodied touch from any notion of individual character psychology, so as to more affectively bind his camera and the viewer to gesture and its open possibilities. This approach continues to distance Hartley's films from conventional notions of character psychology and motivation, while at the same time suggesting an unpredictable affect, elicited by writing, thrusting both character and viewer into an uncertain narrative future. When the figure of Simon Grim first places pen to paper, it is a moment of uncertainty: what he is about to write is not the product of any kind of character psychology (throughout the first part of the film Hartley has taken great pains to demonstrate that precisely what Simon lacks is a coherent psychology and expressivity). Instead, it is a new moment, a moment in which Simon will discover who he might be by putting this pen to this paper: his own writing will affect him as he writes it, propelling him throughout the remaining spaces of *Henry Fool*. And, notably, *against* certain other spaces: before Grim begins to write, he *plunks* the empty notebook Henry has given him onto his mother's kitchen table, standing over it for a moment, approaching the moment of writing with some hesitancy. The sound Grim's notebook makes on the banal kitchen table is itself a sign that whatever words he is about to write will be in some sense *against* this domestic and working-class space, a space which has hitherto stifled his voice. The voice he begins to develop while writing in this notebook on this kitchen table will eventually send him beyond this space, into his apartment in Manhattan, and then into the international intrigue of the later films in the trilogy.

It is worth taking a closer look at how moments of writing and reading are orchestrated in *Henry Fool* before looking at the variations performed on these orchestrations in *Fay Grim* and *Ned Rifle*. The first figure to read Simon's poetry is Henry himself. Hartley cuts from the shot of Simon writing to a shot of Simon sleeping, the next day, after a long night of writing, his head in his arms. The camera pans to Henry entering the front door. Henry's gestures are, here, as banal as the kitchen table upon which Simon writes: the shaking of a coffee kettle; the foraging through a refrigerator for food; asking Simon for money, upon waking him up. Henry, after sitting at the table for a moment, picks up Simon's composition book, and begins to read his poetry, walking with it, moving towards the camera and into a medium close-up. As a moment of performance, this act of reading is convincing: although Henry has been moved to stillness by whatever Simon has written, Thomas Jay Ryan's eyes dart across the page from left to right, imprinting words on retina. 'I thought … I was … I wanted to…' Simon struggles to explain what he has written; but Henry recognises something in these words immediately. He clasps the book shut and turns to Simon, but does not yet share what has moved him about Simon's words. 'I'll correct the spelling', he says, comically detaching himself from the emotion of whatever it is Simon has written. Hartley (and Ryan, in his performance) avoid spelling out the particular internal impact these words have had on Henry as he reads them. In other words, Hartley does not immediately convert the moment of reading into a digestible instance of character psychology, or cause-and-effect. Instead, he draws his figure close to the camera as he reads, creating out of the moment another abstract illustration of writing's impact. And like the earlier moment in which Simon begins to write, this moment in which Henry begins to read serves to propel him into an uncertain future: what will he do with Simon's writing? Beyond correcting the spelling, what will he do to improve Simon's form? As with the act of writing, reading propels bodies in *Henry Fool* to move forward, as if the words themselves became a part of performative rhythm. And the moment also suggests that Henry is himself more of a reader and receiver than an author and a producer: even in the later films, he is responding to a series of events that occur as a result of the transnational circulation of his *Confessions* rather than authoring their words; the *Confessions* are already a very much completed 'work' before the trilogy even begins. If Henry is an author at all, it is as author or origin of a certain international reputation rather than an author of a particular text.

Simon's discovery of himself as reader and author, as *Henry Fool* shows us, happens in a very particular kind of social context, a context with its own cultural tensions and divisions, which Hartley further explores in the next scene. Simon discovers three old books, their pages falling out and their binding cracked and warped, in one of his garbage trucks. Words in the social world of *Henry Fool* are treated, by others besides Simon and Henry, as so much trash. Simon's initial interest with these texts is as objects: he sits down outside with them, on a set of steps, and holds them in his hands, feeling through their pages, his fingers caressing the surface of the text before he pulls out a couple of loose pages. But Simon's body and movements are awkward; when he moves to reach for his beer, the pile of books falls to the cement floor, a gesture that beautifully exemplifies the tension and possible incommensurability between artistic aspirations and the ways of moving and being to which Simon has become habituated. Hartley keeps his distance from this moment of reading, too, as if he as author, some steps ahead of Simon in his own cultural distinction, were now merely observing a figure attempting to contort himself from invisible garbage man to visible and culturally productive reader. Where the camera had been close to Henry as he read Simon's words, here the camera frames Simon reading from a diagonal angle (the railing of the steps slightly distancing us from him as he reads), and in a longer medium shot. (The moment unfolds, as do several in Urbaniak's performances throughout this trilogy, as slightly comic, as if we perhaps laugh, in our detachment, *at* Simon before again becoming close to him.) Yet in the next moment Simon bends down to rescue the fallen and damaged books, gently picking them up and restoring their pages to their spots. It is a moment Hartley frames, like the earlier shot in which Simon first set pen to paper, in a close-up, once again binding gesture to shot in a moving moment that propels the film, again, into an uncertain future. What will Simon do with these books once he puts them back together? How will this reading, and the future writing it will no doubt inspire, propel him out of this habitus? (As if to emphasise how violently the act of reading pits Simon against his social context, after he rescues the books from their fall, two local bullies will knock him over the head with a beer bottle.) A moment like this reminds us that Hartley is not so much interested in creating 'smart cinema' as he is in creating a cinema in which smartness begins to discover itself, when it begins to gently detach itself from previous ways of living after writing and reading spark further gesture and movement.

The subsequent scene, after Simon is savagely beaten by the bullies, is a remarkable orchestration by Hartley of the impact reading and writing has on both author and public. Hartley ends the sequence in an alley with a shot of the two bullies kicking Simon to the ground. From this, Hartley cuts to a bird's-eye high-angle shot of Henry Fool, correcting and revising Simon's epic poem while sitting in the convenience store operated by Mr. Deng (James Saito) and his daughter Gnoc (Miho Nikaido). The shot, framed from above, places Simon's notebook at a diagonal angle, and what the viewer notices are not Simon's words but rather Henry's hands furiously marking up Simon's text, with lines, exclamation points and arrows indicating where he would like to make changes. Henry is Simon's first reader, and he sits here in the social context, Mr. Deng's store, which will soon become a hotspot for poetry and cappuccino once Simon's poems become popular. Cutting from this close-up of Henry's hands marking Simon's text to a medium shot of Henry sitting at a table, the camera frames Simon, briefly out of focus, as he stumbles into the store. He approaches Henry's table and, weak from the beating by the bullies, drops the books he retrieved from the garbage trunk and falls to the ground. 'I was going to tear out their eyes, and I knew I could do it', Simon intones as he slowly begins to get up, the dialogue a direct parallel to words in Henry's earlier story, told to Simon in the Grim basement, about a fight Henry had in a bar in Central America. It is almost as if Simon is imagining himself as the hero of Henry's epic story, projecting himself into the imagined text of Henry's orally communicated myth. The moment is a clear indication of the impact Henry's storytelling has had on Simon, his listener. And Simon's work of imagination, inspired by Henry, has resulted not only in this beating but also in the epic poem that Henry leaves behind in Mr. Deng's convenience store. There, it is found by another reader: a moment after Henry drags Simon out of Mr. Deng's store, Gnoc picks up Simon's poem from the table, reads it and begins singing.

In this scene and in others throughout *Henry Fool*, Hartley is concerned to show the larger emotional and social impact of words on their readers, rather than text itself: how Henry's myth moves Simon to write, and to (try to) fight back against those who might bully his thoughts; how Simon's poem moves Henry to his own furious and inspired act of editing; and how Simon's work moves Gnoc, previously silent, to singing. And this thread continues throughout the film, as Simon's words have both direct and indirect impact on others around him: Henry's continued presence in the Grim household, itself motivated by his sense that Simon has talent and is worthy of mentoring, leads to Fay attempting to seduce him; Simon's words lead his mother, Mary (Maria Porter) to reflect upon her own failed career as a piano player, before her suicide later in the film; the mixed reception of Simon's poetry, once posted in Mr. Deng's store, in the local community, especially among the religious right (who find it offensive) and college students, who respond with either excitement or indifference; and the impact of Simon's writing on the larger culture, once it is posted and circulated on the internet, which turns it into fodder for intellectual comment and popular discourse. This varied circulation across and within both the local community of Queens in the film and the implied global community of the internet parallels Simon's own trajectory and new possession of cultural capital, from humble garbage man to internationally celebrated, award-winning poet. And the larger cultural impact of Simon's words also throws into relief the failure of Henry to find an audience, beyond Simon, as an author: Simon's publisher Angus James (Chuck Montgomery) refuses to publish Henry's *Confessions*, and at the end of the film Henry, having failed to find an audience for his words in America, flees the country on an international flight.

Reading on a Global Scale: Fay Grim Across the Henry Fool Trilogy
Simon and Henry are, of course, not the only writers and readers in *Henry Fool*. Fay does her own reading and writing in the first film of the trilogy. Both Fay's gender and Parker Posey's performance, however, suggest an altogether different inhabitation of the *habitus* Simon tries to write himself out of. At the beginning of the film, Fay defines herself by *not* reading, introduced in the script for *Henry Fool* as someone who watches bad television (always a sign of a character's lack of cultural capital in Hartley's films). Yet Fay ultimately responds with a unique way of inhabiting her surrounding world, a world which, as the trilogy unfolds, becomes more and more inflected by both Simon's and Henry's authorship and the cultural and political contexts in which their texts circulate.

The first time Fay reads anything in *Henry Fool*, it is Simon's poetry. This moment comes after we have seen Fay write for the first time: since Simon has given up his job to focus, full-time, on his poetry, Fay will have to get a job. She types her resume on a laptop, on the same kitchen desk where Simon earlier wrote. Her writing here, however, is distinguished from Simon's work not only by its instrumentality (she is typing her qualifications into a pre-formatted computer programme), but also by its stereotypically feminine inflection: Fay points out, to Simon, not the content of her resume, but the fact that it will be printed on 'scented rose' stationary; and her initial view of Simon's poetry (before having read it) is entirely conventional ('a poem's supposed to be a kind of small kind of delicate thing, kind of feminine, kind of gentle – look at this, you made a fuckin' telephone book'). Yet, after getting over this initial reaction to the sheer physicality of Simon's poem (she is responding, initially, to the simple fact of its size, occupying as it does several notebooks), she begins to read it. In a few moments, she is captivated by these words, leisurely smoking a cigarette (and drawn away, momentarily, from the goal-directed pursuit of her resume writing) as her eyes dart across Simon's verse. At every point from now on, when Fay appears in *Henry Fool*, she will in some way be marked by Simon's efforts to become a poet. She now, effectively, lives in a social world inflected (for both good and ill) by the success of Simon's authorship (and Henry's own ongoing efforts to circulate his *Confessions*), where earlier she was defined by an unfulfilling domestic world.

Initially, Fay's response is to live in this world of male authorship by continuing to assert both her feminine and sexual presence, for she lives in a world in which the men are authors (and publishers) and the women readers (and editors) of texts, readers who respond to words in explicitly physical terms. After she reads Simon's poem in its entirety, she heads to Mr. Deng's convenience store, interrupting one of Henry's monologues and sharing with everyone that Simon's poem has instigated unanticipated menstruation. Later, Fay's relationship to male authorship takes the form of a slightly twisted courtship, one that is marked by a carefully choreographed and aggressive physicality. When Henry, later in the film, spies Fay reading his *Confessions* in the Grim basement, the two of them exchange violent gestures: Fay slaps Henry in the face after he prevents her from leaving, after which Henry grabs her by the throat and pushes her to the wall. These, however, are less naturalistic gestures than others in the film, and are a sign that Fay's intensely physical relationship to male writing might be the beginning of her own performatively distinctive way of moving. It is as if Fay's reading of Henry's text has sparked a new, creatively choreographed way of inhabiting this otherwise banal domestic environment. Of all the sequences in the film, it is this prelude to sex in the Grim basement that most saliently recalls the mannered performance style of Hartley's earlier films, as Ryan and Posey circle around one another as if in a dance (Fig. 11.4). In terms of Posey's performance, this moment, which calls attention to the fact of performance as something constructed and choreographed more than any other moment in the otherwise naturalistic *Henry Fool*, recalls her carefully choreographed way of moving in earlier Hartley films such as *Opera No. 1*, *Amateur*, *Flirt* and *The Sisters of Mercy*, and anticipates her carefully orchestrated movements in *Fay Grim*, in which her character begins to carve out a unique way of inhabiting a world authored by men less through psychology and intention and more through gesture, movement and expression.

For a time, reading the work of the two men in her life leads to something relatively liberating for Fay; for example, after she learns of her brother's newfound fame as a poet (news delivered at her wedding to Henry), she responds by dancing with joy at the reception, a moment in which the intentionally stilted and mannered movements of the basement scene give way to ecstatic, free-flowing gestures. Of course, the ending of *Henry Fool* will find Fay inscribed in the same domestic haunts in which she

Fig. 11.4: Parker Posey and Thomas Jay Ryan perform a twisted courtship in *Henry Fool*

began, struggling to raise her son Ned while Henry gallivants in bars. Nevertheless, in passing, in her own distinctive way, through the world of *Henry Fool* – a world marked by the writing of men – she has arrived at a place quite different from where she began. She spends her final moments in this first installment of the trilogy not watching television but thinking, about her future and Ned's, a sign of the long-term and open-ended affects her encounter with a world of authorship has had on her.

If *Henry Fool* is, however, ultimately about the relationship between Simon and Henry, *Fay Grim*, is the film in which Posey will assume the leading role of heroine and more forthrightly stake her character's claim to moving through a social space marked by the authorship of men. There is, in *Fay Grim*, as with the other films in this trilogy, quite a bit of writing and more than a little bit of reading: in the film's first sequence, Fay visits a church, and there reads a small pamphlet entitled 'How to Pray'; later, FBI Agent Fogg (Leo Fitzpatrick) will jot down Fay's answers to interrogation as FBI Agent Fulbright (Jeff Goldblum) presses her about the content of Henry's *Confessions*; Simon's publisher Angus James will deliver a note to Simon (who sits in prison as an accomplice of Henry's escape from the United States) about the potential political content of Henry Fool's *Confessions*, accompanying volume six of same; Fay will later read the volumes of the *Confessions* at the French Ministry of Security; and so on. What unites all of this writing in *Fay Grim* is that it circulates in an impersonal political sphere in which individual authorship and stated intent counts for little. Where acts of reading sparked Simon's individual creativity in *Henry Fool*, similar acts in *Fay Grim* lead to often potentially deadly consequences beyond the control, or authorship, of individuals: Fogg's notepad leads to Fay's involvement in global espionage; Angus James's discussion of the *Confessions* with Simon in prison leads to the former being gunned down by an assailant; and Fay's reading of two books at the French Ministry of Security, in which she has been instructed to locate covert information (on page 17, second paragraph from the bottom, in blue ink, third sentence in quotations), an act which ultimately puts her life in grave danger. Where writing and reading were means of achieving cultural distinction in *Henry Fool*, in *Fay Grim* these acts of writing and reading become overtly political, increasingly arcane and personally threatening, with distinctive actions emerging in the light of reading or writing now attracting danger and, in some cases, death.

But in addition to these diegetic motifs of writing, which move the trilogy from the local haunts of Queens in *Henry Fool* to the global circulation of prose and poetry in *Fay Grim*, there is also the 'writing' of Hartley himself. *Henry Fool*, as I suggested earlier, is perhaps Hartley's most naturalistic film, and perhaps also his least self-reflexive (see Fuller 1998: xxi–xxii). *Fay Grim*, by contrast, is a film in which the director's authorship explicitly underscores formal and stylistic choices. Nearly every shot in the film, for example, is framed at a canted angle, an unusual formal choice seen only occasionally in *Henry Fool*. Further, Hartley, as previously mentioned, redundantly flags certain narrative events by placing certain large blocks of text onscreen (occasionally using such text, in a kind of comic verbal equation, to reflexively point to the film's convoluted plot line; see Fig. 11.3). Likewise, the film's digital aesthetics involve the blurring of motion and the use of freeze frame at certain junctures, serving, like the use of text onscreen, to underscore important narrative events. Perhaps most strikingly, the performance styles are even closer to the dance-like movements of earlier Hartley films such as *Amateur* and *Flirt* than they are to the relatively naturalistic movements of characters in *Henry Fool*. If the use of non-diegetic text and a self-reflexive digital style of filmmaking attest to Hartley's own reassertion of authorship (as if he were now saliently highlighting his status as the third male author alongside Henry and Simon), the shift in performance style gives Posey room, as a performer, to further develop our ongoing understanding of Fay in her relation to a world heavily marked by the authorship of men. She finds ways of moving through this authored world creatively, finding, above and beyond the machinations of the narrative and the dangers these machinations present to her character, her own pleasure in the text.

Fay's initial reaction to Simon's writing, in *Henry Fool*, is a response to its sheer physicality. In that film, her response to the physical nature of Simon's text is a sign of her naiveté, her character's distance from the cultural distinction Simon is about to achieve. But on the global stage of *Fay Grim*, the character's physical relationship to text evolves, as Posey has Fay approach male writing not as subject matter that might determine her life but rather as an object, an expressive prop that she might use in a creatively original way through her participation in the film's dance-like choreography. After Fay picks up a missing volume of Henry's *Confessions* at the French Ministry of Security, she leaves with the books clutched, in a manila envelope, in her right arm. She has been told to do so, by her contact in Paris, because the choice of arm she uses to clutch the books will convey to secret operatives, closely watching her, what content they contain. But Posey's performance deflects our attention away from the comic density of information burdening *Fay Grim*'s espionage plot, and towards a more purely choreographic orchestration of gestures and movements – a dance in which Henry's text becomes an object used expressively. Shortly after arriving at her hotel in Paris, Fay encounters a trio of spies in a stairwell (lit in high-key and modernist in its architecture style), all of them aiming to retrieve the *Confessions* she cradles in her arms. The scene plays like an adaptation of a Hollywood action scene reimagined, in a more mannerist key, by Hartley and his actors, all of whom eschew naturalistic movement in favour of balletic movements and postures. A spy named Juliet (Saffron Burrows) follows Fay into the stairwell. Posey darts from the right to the left side of the frame, clutching a handrail as Burrows passes by. Burrows, in turn, is surprised by a spy as she turns the corner of the stairwell, who runs up the staircase in the opposite direction. As he approaches, Posey now circles back to the other side of the frame, leaning against the handrail, as this new spy is, comically, stopped short by yet another agent at the top of the steps, who orders him to relinquish the *Confessions*. Ostensibly, Fay is sinking further and further into an increasingly convoluted espionage plot she and the audience of the film barely understand. But Posey's performance dances on the surface of all this narrative information as she elegantly and repeatedly circles around the supporting actors. The way she moves – performance as a kind of authorship of life – is the film's genuine concern. It is as if Henry's words and the thicket of plot emerging in their wake were a mere proscenium for the way

Fay, launched out of the domestic space of Queens and into a global world, bounds across the screen.

Inheriting, and Rewriting, an Authored World: Ned and Susan in Ned Rifle
If Posey's work in *Henry Fool* and *Fay Grim* is to author a distinctively performed inhabitation of an otherwise male-authored world, *Ned Rifle* is, in part, about the boy who does not so much inhabit but rather inherits that world. As the son of Henry Fool and Fay Grim, Ned Rifle – his last name a pseudonym bequeathed him when he is placed in witness protection after his mother, at the end of the previous film, lands in jail – is gifted an enormous amount of baggage. In the very first sequence of the film, he would seem to inherit both narrative and stylistic tropes from the previous two films in the series. He is living in his Christian foster home, and clearly he has taken his new parentage to heart: he is introduced praying (reminding us of the spiritual motifs in the earlier films, when we find both Simon and Fay Grim consulting priests and prayer books to inspire a heavenly course of action for Henry Fool). Depicted kneeling on the ground outside, Ned is framed in a canted frame reminiscent of *Fay Grim*. But his inheritance of both spirituality and a way of being framed in the world are quickly brushed off, as if to suggest he will have to make his way in the world apart from the influence of his mother, father or uncle. In the next sequence, Ned helps a worker erect a cross in front of the church, and Hartley's camera now, for the first time in the series since *Henry Fool*, returns to a level (if slightly low-angle) shot, in a film that will be altogether less self-reflexive than *Fay Grim*. Later, when one of his fellow churchgoers insults his mother as a 'terrorist', he gets visibly angry, rejecting this parishioner's glib moral judgement of a member of the secular world: like Simon and Fay before him, Ned will have to work out his own understanding of all these texts and words which have preceded his existence, texts which, in this case, involve a tension between the religiosity he has inherited from his foster parents and the more secular orbit in which his mother, uncle and father live.

As in the other films in the trilogy, writers and readers populate the world of *Ned Rifle*, the world through which Ned moves. In the earlier films, Ned's association with writing and reading is minimal. In *Henry Fool*, the child Ned locates an envelope with Simon Grim's Manhattan address, allowing him to track his famous uncle down; in *Fay Grim*, he uses his keen intelligence to operate a translation programme, working with Uncle Simon and Angus James to decode the content of Henry Fool's texts. But this world of text in *Ned Rifle* is very much an ironic inversion of what text means and how it circulates in *Henry Fool*. *Ned Rifle*, following on the heels of *Fay Grim*, returns words and their meanings to a less global and more domestic environment. However, it also suggests that the earnest cultural achievements of Simon's poetry and the international intrigue of Henry's *Confessions* texts are less words belonging to their authors and more words to be played with, refused and critically analysed, a world of authorship that might be wrested from their authors in the shaping of a new future. It is perhaps Simon himself who indicates how much the world of writing has changed since the original film in the trilogy. When Ned goes to visit him in his hotel early in the film, he finds his uncle scribbling jokes rather than writing poetry. Where in *Henry Fool* Simon Grim finds cultural distinction through his achieved status as a 'poet laureate and cultural touchstone', in *Ned Rifle* he trades that in for 'good old-fashioned slapstick humour, naughty innuendo, a few well-placed fart jokes' in his new career as a stand-up comedian.

This scene with Uncle Simon is funny – certainly it is difficult to imagine either the actor James Urbaniak or his character, the stoic Simon Grim, headlining a comedy show – but *Ned Rifle* is not content to merely laugh at tropes taken seriously in the trilogy's first installment. Ned, although bemused by his Uncle's efforts to become a comedian, takes very seriously the texts he has inherited. In the first sequence of *Ned Rifle*, the first text the title character encounters is a Bible, a gift from his foster father (Hartley regular Martin Donovan, in priestly garb) on his eighteenth birthday. Inside is a note, signed by his foster parents (Hartley uses a voiceover to convey their good wishes). In a way reminiscent of his mother's approach to Henry's and Simon's texts as physical objects, Ned cradles the book in his hands, feeling its contours; when he opens it to read, he finds not words but a naked picture of the reverend's daughter, Claire (Melissa Bithron). Ned is at once marked by two forms of reading: on one hand, he takes this Bible and its written contents very seriously (throughout the film he will be depicted as piously Christian); but on the other, this book is also a physical object, full of all kinds of physicality.

If this moment points the way towards a synthesis of sex and literature (reminding us that Ned himself was conceived in sex spurned on by the reading of a book), it is notable that the first time anyone writes in *Ned Rifle* it is Susan Weber (Aubrey Plaza), a graduate student who, like Ned, inherits the world of Henry's and Simon's authorship. However, unlike Ned, who throughout the film denies having read a word of Simon's poetry or Henry's notebooks, and who refers for guidance to the authority of a single text (the Bible, which he keeps with him throughout the film), Susan matches the authorship of Simon and Henry with her own sharp voice. She not only

Fig. 11.5: Liam Aiken and Aubrey Plaza discuss a world of words in *Ned Rifle*

interprets the work of Simon to her own ends (she claims it functions as a sign of protest against the commodification of thought in mainstream popular culture) but also blends the authorship of Simon and Henry together. Henry, she says, has been posting caustic comments about Simon's work in the 'comments' section of Simon's comedy stand-up website, textual material that Susan, as an interpreter, takes just as seriously as Simon's poetry. Her dissertation – confidently and forcefully titled *The Poetry of Simon Grim*, and which she clutches near her person throughout nearly the entire film – argues that Simon's and Henry's texts form a dialogical bond, the work of the poet unable to be understood without reference to the texts of the mentor who guided him.

When Ned first meets Susan, she is sniffling and blowing her nose, and waiting patiently for noted poet Simon Grim to emerge from hiding in his hotel room (Fig. 11.5). Her sniffling is reminiscent of the illness that descends upon Fay the first time she reads Henry's words in *Henry Fool*, but where Fay was initially subject to Simon's words, Susan has taken those words as her object, studying them with a critical distance and sharp intelligence. Susan, strikingly, would seem to be the most salient example in the trilogy of a character who takes the world of authorship preceding and surrounding her – a world of text created by the film's primary male characters – and uses these words not as a sign of monological authority but as an opportunity to craft her own voice. But like Ned, who struggles to reconcile the religious world of his foster parents with the secular world of Simon, Henry and Fay, Susan is stuck between two extremes: on one hand, she desires to meet both Simon and Henry, and to discuss with them their work in a dialogical manner befitting her status as an academic (in one scene, in a car, she and Henry collaboratively work together on a new text, debating the finer points of ontology and textuality); but on the other, she desires to kill Henry, to murder the voice of one of the authors who has inspired her, for reasons that become clear as the film goes on. For Susan was already very much inscribed in that world of authorship created by Henry and Simon – she is perhaps even the primary cause of it. As is revealed late in the film, Susan is the 13-year-old girl with whom Henry Fool had sex, prior to the beginning of the trilogy, a crime for which he has served a seven-year prison sentence (during which time Henry writes much of the *Confessions*). Susan's monological desire for revenge (a revenge that would be the ultimate consequence of Henry's authorship in the world) is at odds not only with her status as a distant origin or spark for Henry's *Confessions* (without their fateful meeting, much of the text, it is implied, would never have been written), but with her equally earnest desire to meet these authors who have inspired her (regardless of what connection they seem to have to her personal life) and to talk with them, an action that contributes a significant female voice to what has hitherto been a largely male world of authorship in the trilogy. Susan ultimately rejects her participation in this circulation of discourse, however, through a profoundly monological act, the murder of Henry (which silences his voice, if not the circulation of his texts, in the name of revenge).

Ned and Susan, despite the violent ending that *Ned Rifle* uses to bring the trilogy to a close, are unable to resolve these textual tensions. Ned, dressed throughout the film in a black shirt and white collar recalling the figure of a priest, witnesses the death of his father at the hands of Susan, who kills him with a gun after an evening of drunken sex at a cheap motel. Moments later, Ned accidentally kills, in a sudden moment, Susan, who leaps at him and into the knife he holds outward in helpless self-defence. This surprising act of violence cuts short the life of two distinctive writers, Henry and Susan, the twisted couple that lies at the heart of *Henry Fool*'s entire trajectory. In the film's final moments, rejecting his father's dying words to 'run' (which parallels Simon's identical advice for Henry at the end of the first film), Ned accepts moral ambiguity as he awaits both legal and divine judgement. The end of the trilogy leaves his fate uncertain, but also implies (through his rejection of his father's final word) the beginning of a new authorship through the rejection of past texts. The Grims, for their part, will continue on: Fay, in prison, starting a book club (still marveling at the sheer physicality of text, as she did in the first film, Fay includes only very big books in this club); and Simon, now adrift, floating somewhere between highbrow literature, lowbrow comedy and the scandal of celebrity which lies in-between.

For his part, in the making of this trilogy, Hal Hartley has no doubt authored a series of works unified by his own sensibility and voice. But in his authorship, he has worked to create a world imbued with the writing of works, the reading of text and the clutching of books: a play with words and the physical forms they take, enacted by the characters who live within a world shaped by writing.

FILMOGRAPHY

Below are details on films and shorts Hal Hartley has written and directed. For more information on Hartley's short films prior to 1989, see Hartley and Kaleta 2008 (in the bibliography).

The Unbelievable Truth (US, 1989)
Director: Hal Hartley
Screenplay: Hal Hartley
Production Company: Action Features
Producers: Jerome Brownstein, Hal Hartley, Bruce Weiss
Cinematography: Michael Spiller
Editors: Nick Gomez, Hal Hartley
Sound: Nick Gomez, Jeff Kushner
Length: 90 min.
Cast: Adrienne Shelly (Audry Hugo), Robert John Burke (Josh Hutton), Christopher Cooke (Vic Hugo), Julia McNeal (Pearl), Katherine Mayfield (Liz Hugo), Gary Sauer (Emmet), Edie Falco (Jane), Matt Malloy (Otis), Bill Sage (Gus).

Trust (US/UK, 1990)
Director: Hal Hartley
Screenplay: Hal Hartley
Production Company: True Fiction Pictures/Film Four International/Zenith Productions Ltd.
Producers: Jerome Brownstein, Ted Hope, Scott Meek, Bruce Weiss
Cinematography: Michael Spiller
Editor: Nick Gomez
Sound: Tom Paul, Jeff Pullman, Kate Sanford, Reilly Steele
Length: 107 min.
Cast: Adrienne Shelly (Maria Coughlin), Martin Donovan (Matthew Slaughter), Rebecca Merritt Nelson (Jean Coughlin), John MacKay (Jim Slaughter), Karen Sillas (Nurse Paine), Bill Sage (John Bill).

Theory of Achievement (US, 1991)
Director: Hal Hartley
Screenplay: Hal Hartley
Production Company: Alive from Off Center, Yo Productions Ltd. #2.
Producers: Ted Hope, Larry Meistrich.
Cinematography: Michael Spiller
Editor: Hal Hartley
Length: 18 min.
Cast: Bob Gosse, Jessica Sager, Jeffrey Howard, Bill Sage, Elina Löwensohn, Naledi Tshazibane, Nick Gomez, M.C. Bailey, Ingrid Rudefors.

Ambition (US, 1991)
Director: Hal Hartley
Screenplay: Hal Hartley
Production Company: Alive from Off Center, Good Machine, Twin Cities Public Television.
Producers: Alyce Dissette, Ted Hope, John Ligon, Larry Meistrich, James Schamus, Neil V. Sieling.
Cinematography: Michael Spiller
Editor: Hal Hartley
Length: 9 min.
Cast: George Feaster, Patricia Sullivan, Rick Groel, Chris Buck, Jim McCauley, David Troup, Margaret Mendelson, Julie Sukman, Bill Sage, Larry Meistrich, Michael McGarry, Casey Finch, Adam Bresnick, Elizabeth Feaster, Francie Swift, Lisa Gorlitsky, Mark V. Lake, Bob Gosse, Ernesto Gerona, Nancy Kricorian.

Surviving Desire (US, 1991)
Director: Hal Hartley
Screenplay: Hal Hartley
Production Company: American Playhouse, True Fiction Pictures.
Producers: Jerome Brownstein, Ted Hope
Cinematography: Michael Spiller
Editor: Hal Hartley
Length: 60 min.
Cast: Craig Adams, Dan Castelli, Martin Donovan, Mary B. Ward, Matt Malloy, Hub Moore, Rebecca Merritt Nelson, Julie Sukman, Thomas J. Edwards, George Feaster, Lisa Gorlitsky, Emily Kunstler, John MacKay, James Michael McCauley, Vincent Rutherford, Gary Sauer, Steven Schub, John Sharples, Patricia Sullivan, David Troup.

Simple Men (US/UK/Italy, 1992)
Director: Hal Hartley
Screenplay: Hal Hartley
Production Company: American Playhouse Theatrical Films in association with Fine Line Features, BIM Distribuzione, True Fiction Pictures, Film Four International, Zenith Productions Ltd.
Producers: Jerome Brownstein, Hal Hartley, Ted Hope, Bruce Weiss
Cinematography: Michael Spiller
Editor: Steve Hamilton
Length: 105 min.
Cast: Robert John Burke (Bill McCabe), Bill Sage (Dennis McCabe), Karen Sillas (Kate), Elina Löwensohn (Elina), Martin Donovan (Martin), Mark Chandler Bailey (Mike), Christopher Cooke (Vic), Jeffrey Howard (Ned Rifle), Holly Marie Combs (Kim), Joe Stevens (Jack), Damian Young (Sheriff).

Amateur (US/UK/France, 1994)
Director: Hal Hartley
Screenplay: Hal Hartley
Production Company: Channel Four Films, La Sept Cinéma, True Fiction Pictures, UGC/American Playhouse Theatrical Films, Zenith Productions Ltd.
Producers: Jerome Brownstein, Hal Hartley, Ted Hope, Lindsay Law, Yves Marmion, Scott Meek
Cinematography: Michael Spiller
Editor: Steve Hamilton
Length: 105 min.
Cast: Isabelle Huppert (Isabelle), Martin Donovan (Thomas Ludens), Elina Löwensohn (Sofia Ludens), Damian Young (Edward), Chuck Montgomery (Jan), Dave Simonds (Kurt), Pamela Stewart (Patsy Melville), Parker Posey (Girl Squatter), Dwight Ewell (Boy Squatter).

Iris (video short, US, 1994)
Director: Hal Hartley
Production Company: True Fiction Pictures.
Cinematography: Hal Hartley
Length: 3 min.
Cast: Sabrina Lloyd, Parker Posey.

Opera No. 1 (US, 1994)
Director: Hal Hartley
Production Company: True Fiction Pictures.
Cinematography: Hal Hartley
Length: 8 min.
Cast: Patricia Dunnock, Parker Posey, Adrienne Shelly, James Urbaniak, Lydia Kavanagh, Jeff Howard.

NYC 3/94 (Poland, 1994)
Director: Hal Hartley
Production Company: True Fiction Pictures.
Screenwriter: Hal Hartley
Cinematography: Hal Hartley
Producer: Hal Hartley
Length: 9 min.
Cast: Dwight Ewell, Lianna Pai, Paul Schulze, James Urbaniak.

Flirt (US/Germany/Japan, 1995)
Director: Hal Hartley
Screenplay: Hal Hartley
Production Company: Possible Films.
Producers: Jerome Brownstein, Reinhard Brundig, Martin Hagerman, Ted Hope, Satoru Iseki
Cinematography: Michael Spiller
Editors: Steve Hamilton, Hal Hartley
Sound: Pietro Cecchini, Jeanne Gilliland, Jeff Pullman, Jennifer Ralston, Steve Silkensen.
Length: 85 min.
Cast: Bill Sage (Bill), Parker Posey (Emily), Martin Donovan (Walter), Robert John Burke (Man No. 2), Karen Sillas (Doctor Clint), Dwight Ewell (Dwight), Elina Löwensohn (Nurse), Dominik Bender (Johann), Geno Lechner (Greta), Miho Nikaido (Miho), Toshizo Fujiwara (Ozu), Chikako Hara (Yuki), Kumiko Ishizuka (Naomi).

Henry Fool (US, 1997)
Director: Hal Hartley
Screenplay: Hal Hartley
Production Company: True Fiction Pictures.
Producers: Keith Abell, Jerome Brownstein, Thierry Cagianut, Hal Hartley, Larry Meistrich, Daniel J. Victor
Cinematography: Michael Spiller
Editors: Steve Hamilton
Sound: Daniel McIntosh, David Paterson, David Raphael, Reilly Steele, Karl Wasserman.
Length: 137 min.
Cast: Thomas Jay Ryan (Henry Fool), James Urbaniak (Simon Grim), Parker Posey (Fay Grim), Maria Porter (Maria Grim), Kevin Corrigan (Warren), James Saito (Mr. Deng), Miho Nikaido (Gnoc Deng), Jan Leslie Harding (Vicky), Dianna Ruppe (Amy), Veanne Cox (Laura), Nicholas Hope (Father Hawkes), Gene Ruffini (Officer Buñuel), Liam Aiken (Ned), Chuck Montgomery (Angus James).

The Other Also (US, 1997)
Director: Hal Hartley:
Screenplay: Hal Hartley
Production Company: True Fiction Pictures.
Length: 7 min.
Cast: Elina Löwensohn, Miho Nikaido, James Urbaniak.

The Book of Life (US/France, 1998)
Director: Hal Hartley
Screenplay: Hal Hartley
Production Company: La Sept Arte, Haut et Court, True Fiction Pictures.
Producers: Simon Arnal, Caroline Benjo, Jerome Brownstein, Thierry Cagianut, Pierre Chevalier, Chelsea Fuhrer, Matthew Myers, Carole Scotta
Cinematography: Jim Denault
Editors: Steve Hamilton
Sound: David Paterson, Jeff Pullman, Reilly Steele
Length: 63 min.
Cast: Martin Donovan (Jesus Christ), Thomas Jay Ryan (Satan), P.J. Harvey (Magdalena), Miho Nikaido (Edie), Martin Pfefferkorn (Martyr), D.J. Mendel (Lawyer), James Urbaniak (True Believer).

The New Math(s) (Poland, 2000)
Director: Hal Hartley
Production Company: British Broadcasting Corporation, True Fiction Pictures.
Producers: Jerome Brownstein, Susan Leber, Christian Seidel, Henk van der Meulen, Rodney Wilson.
Editors: Ben Tudhope.
Length: 15 min.
Cast: D.J. Mendel, David Neumann, Miho Nikaido.

No Such Thing (US/Iceland, 2001)
Director: Hal Hartley
Screenplay: Hal Hartley
Production Company: United Artists Films, American Zoetrope, Icelandic Film Corporation, True Fiction Pictures, Monster Productions.
Producers: Willi Baer, Francis Ford Coppola, Fridrik Thor Fridriksson, Hal Hartley, Linda Reisman, Cecelia Kate Roque.
Cinematography: Michael Spiller
Editors: Steve Hamilton
Sound: Kjartan Kjartansson, Andrew Kris, George Lara, Jennifer Ralston, Reilly Steele.
Length: 102 min.
Cast: Robert John Burke (the Monster), Sarah Polley (Beatrice), Julie Christie (Dr. Anna), Baltasar Kormákur (Artaud), D.J. Mendel (Agent), Helen Mirren (The Boss), Miho Nikaido (Beautician), Bill Sage (Carlo), James Urbaniak (Concierge), Damian Young (Berger).

Kimono (Germany, 2001)
Director: Hal Hartley
Screenplay: Hal Hartley
Production Company: P-Kino, Regina Ziegler Filmproduktion, Westdeutscher Rundfunk (WDR), Ziegler Film & Company.
Producers: Thierry Cagianut, Tanja Meding, Matthew Myers, Regina Ziegler
Cinematography: Sarah Cawley
Editor: Steve Silkensen
Length: 28 min.
Cast: Miho Nikaido, Valerie Celis, Ling, Shen Yun.

The Sisters of Mercy (US, 2004)
Director: Hal Hartley
Screenplay: Hal Hartley
Production Company: True Fiction Pictures.
Cinematograph: Hal Hartley
Length: 17 min.
Cast: Sabrina Lloyd, Parker Posey.

The Girl from Monday (US, 2005)
Director: Hal Hartley
Screenplay: Hal Hartley

Production Company: Possible Films, Mad Mad July, Monday Company.
Producers: Steve Hamilton, Hal Hartley, Lisa Porter
Cinematography: Sarah Cawley Cabiya
Editor: Steve Hamilton
Sound: Dan Brashi, Justin Kawashima, Andrew Kris, Inbal Weinberg
Length: 84 min.
Cast: Bill Sage (Jack), Sabrina Lloyd (Cecile), Tatiana Abracos (the Girl from Monday), Leo Fitzpatrick (William), D.J. Mendel (Abercrombie), James Urbaniak (Funk), Paul Urbanski (CEO), Edie Falco (Judge).

Fay Grim (US/Germany, 2006)
Director: Hal Hartley
Screenplay: Hal Hartley
Production Company: HDNet Films, Possible Films, This Is That Productions, Zero Film GmbH.
Producers: Julien Berlan, Mark Cuban, Martin Hagemann, Hal Hartley, Ted Hope, Mike King, Jason Kliot, Mike S. Ryan, Joana Vicente, Todd Wagner, Maren Wölk, Özlem Yurtsever.
Cinematography: Sarah Cawley
Editor: Hal Hartley
Sound: David Jung, Christian Lutz, Paul Oberle, Matthias Schwab
Length: 118 min.
Cast: Parker Posey (Fay Grim), D.J. Mendel (Father Lang), Liam Aiken (Ned), Megan Gay (Principal), Jasmin Tabatabai (Milla), Chuck Montgomery (Angus James), James Urbaniak (Simon Grim), Thomas Jay Ryan (Henry Fool), Jeff Goldblum (Agent Fulbright), Leo Fitzpatrick, (Carl Fogg), Saffron Burrows (Juliet).

The Apologies (US, 2010)
Director: Hal Hartley
Screenplay: Hal Hartley
Production Company: Possible Films.
Length: 14 min.
Cast: Nikolai Kinski, Bettina Zimmermann, Ireen Kirsch.

Implied Harmonies (US, 2010)
Director: Hal Hartley
Production Company: Possible Films.
Editor: Hal Hartley
Length: 28 min.
Cast: Louis Andriessen, Kyle Gilman, Hal Hartley, Jordana Maurer, Claron McFadden, Jeroen Willems, Cristina Zavalloni.

Adventure (US, 2010)
Director: Hal Hartley
Production Company: Possible Films.
Length: 20 min.
Cast: Hal Hartley, Miho Nikaido.

Accomplice (US, 2010)
Director: Hal Hartley
Production Company: Possible Films.
Length: 3 min.
Cast: Jean-Luc Godard, Jordana Maurer, D.J. Mendel.

A/Muse (US, 2010)
Director: Hal Hartley
Screenplay: Hal Hartley
Production Company: Possible Films.
Length: 11 min.
Cast: Christina Flick.

Meanwhile (US/Germany, 2006)
Director: Hal Hartley
Screenplay: Hal Hartley
Production Company: Possible Films.
Cinematography: Daniel Sharnoff.
Editor: Kyle Gilman.

Sound: Michael Feuser, Aleks Gezentsvey, Steve Hamilton, Tom Paul
Length: 59 min.
Cast: D.J. Mendel (Joseph), Danielle Meyer (Wendy), Miho Nikaido (Miho), Pallavi Sastry (Phone Store Clerk), Penelope Lagos (Tuesday), Chelsea Crowe (Woman on Bridge), Lisa Hickman (Bank Manager), Kanstance Frakes (Lori).

My America (US, 2014)
Director: Hal Hartley
Writers: Greg Allen, Bekah Brunstetter, Kia Corthron, Dan Dietz, Marcus Gardley, Kirsten Greenidge, Rinne Groff, Danny Hoch, Naomi Iizuka, Rajiv Joseph, Jeremy Kareken, Neil LaBute, Ferni Lawal, Kenneth Lin, James Magruder, D.J. Mendel, Polly Pen, Lynn Rosen, David Ross, Alena Smith, Gwydion Suilebhan, Lauren Yee.
Production Company: Possible Films.
Producer: Hal Hartley
Cinematography: Michael Koshkin
Editor: Kyle Gilman
Length: 78 min.
Cast: Greg Allen, Jeb Brown, Kathleen Chalfant, John Ellison Conlee, Gia Crovatin, Alvin Epstein, Brian Tyree Henry, Marc Damon Johnson, Femi Lawal, Angelo Lozada, Jefferson Mays, Kelly McCreary, Christy McIntosh, D.J. Mendel, Jennifer Mudge, Cody Nickell, Kristine Nielsen, David Ross, Thomas Jay Ryan, Andrew Weems, Fred Weller, Johnny M. Wu.

Ned Rifle (US, 2014)
Director: Hal Hartley
Screenplay: Hal Hartley
Production Company: Possible Films.
Producers: Sarah Cone, Dave Hansen, Stuart Douglas Harris, Hal Hartley, Regina Katz, Marcus Lovingood, Mark Mohtashemi, Matthew Myers, Aidan O'Bryan, Findlay Parke, Joe Shapiro, Don Thompson
Cinematography: Vladimir Subotic
Editor: Kyle Gilman
Length: 85 min.
Cast: Aubrey Plaza (Susan Weber), Parker Posey (Fay Grim), Liam Aiken (Ned Rifle), Robert John Burke (Chet), Martin Donovan (Rev. Daniel Gardner), James Urbaniak (Simon Grim), Bill Sage (Bud), Lloyd Kaufman (Zach), Jefferson Mays (Dr. Ford), Karen Sillas (Alice Gardner), Gia Crovatin (Olive), John Ellison Conlee (Sheriff), Thomas Jay Ryan (Henry Fool), Quincy Tyler Bernstine (Mary), Bob Byington (Concierge).

BIBLIOGRAPHY

Aird, Elizabeth (1992a) 'Surreal gem brings lost suburban souls to life', *The Vancouver Sun*, 22 November, C1. Available at: LexisNexis.com (accessed 3 June 2015).
_____ (1992b) 'Simple Men is slow, stark, oblique – as you'd expect', *The Vancouver Sun*, 20 November, C5. Available at: LexisNexis.com (accessed 3 June 2015).
Altman, Robert and David Thompson (2006) *Altman on Altman*. London: Faber and Faber.
Andrew, Geoff (1999) *Stranger Than Paradise: Maverick Film-Makers in Recent American Cinema*. New York: Limelight Editions.
Andrews, Tamra (1998) *Dictionary of Nature Myths: Legends of the Earth, Sea, and Sky*. New York: Oxford University Press.
Anon. (1990) 'Art House', *Sunday Herald*, 4 November, n.p. Available at: LexisNexis.com (accessed 3 June 2015).
Anon. (1990) 'Pleasant relief from the norm', *Herald Sun*, 8 November, n.p. Available at: LexisNexis.com (accessed 3 June 2015).
Anon. (2008) 'How we got from 1 to 162 million websites on the internet', *Royal.Pingdom.Com*, April. Available at: http://royal.pingdom.com/2008/04/04/how-we-got-from-1-to-162-million-websites-on-the-internet/ (accessed 26 March 2015).
Anon. (2014) 'How the internet has woven itself into American life', *Pewinternet.org*, Pew Research Center, 27 February. Available at: http://www.pewinternet.org/2014/02/27/part-1-how-the-internet-has-woven-itself-into-american-life/ (accessed 26 March 2015).
Avila, Robert ([2007] 2011) 'Hal Hartley, not so simple', in Mark L. Berrettini (2011) *Hal Hartley (Contemporary Film Directors)*. Champaign, IL: University of Illinois, 77–94.
Baker, Martha (1990) 'Telling the (funny) truth about lies', *St. Louis Post-Dispatch*, 5 October, 3F. Available at: LexisNexis.com (accessed 3 June 2015).

Bakhtin, M.M. (1981) *The Dialogical Imagination: Four Essays* Trans. Michael Holquist. Austin: University of Texas Press.
Bazin, André (2009) *What is Cinema?*, trans. Timothy Barnard. Montreal: Caboose.
Bernstein, Paula (2014) 'Who Needs Theatrical? Why Hal Hartley is Distributing "Ned Rifle" Via Vimeo on Demand', *Indiewire*, 12 December. Available at: http://www.indiewire.com/article/who-needs-theatrical-why-hal-hartley-is-distributing-ned-rifle-via-vimeo-on-demand-20141212 (accessed 29 June 2015).
Berra, John (ed.) (2013) *Directory of World Cinema: American Independent 2*, Volume 16. Bristol, UK: Intellect Books.
Berrettini, Mark L. (2011) *Hal Hartley*. Urbana, IL: University of Illinois Press.
Bourdieu, Pierre (1984) *Distinction: A Social Critique of the Judgement of Taste*, trans. Richard Nice. Cambridge, MA: Harvard University Press.
Bourke, Terry (1990) Untitled column, *Sunday Herald* 22 July, n.p. Available at: LexisNexis.com (accessed 3 June 2015).
Bowen, Peter (1995) 'What's Love Got To Do With It?', *Filmmaker Magazine*, Spring. Available at: http://filmmakermagazine.com (accessed 10 August 2015).
Brinkmann, Ron (1999) *The Art and Science of Digital Compositing*. San Diego: Morgan Kaufmann.
Brophy, Philip (2004) *100 Modern Soundtracks*. London: British Film Institute.
Brown, Joe (1990) 'Offbeat 'Truth' You Can Believe', *The Washingotn Post*, 3 August, N45. Available at: LexisNexis.com (accessed 3 June 2015).
Brzeski, Patrick (2013) 'Cannes: Fortissimo Takes Sales Rights to Hal Hartley's "Ned Rifle"', *The Hollywood Reporter*, 14 May. Available at: http://www.hollywoodreporter.com/news/cannes-fortissimo-takes-sales-rights-522166 (accessed 29 June 2015).
Buñuel, Luis (1994) *My Last Breath*, trans. Abigail Israel. London: Vintage.
Butts, William (ed.) (1990) *Conversations with Richard Wilbur*. Jackson, MS: University Press of Mississippi.
Byatt, A. S. (ed.) (2008) *Memory: An Anthology*. London: Chatto & Windus.
Camus, Albert ([1942] 2005) *The Myth of Sisyphus*, trans. Justin O'Brien. London: Penguin Books.
Canby, Vincent (1992) 'Mismatched brothers on a Godardian road', *The New York Times*, 14 October, C22. Available at: LexisNexis.com (accessed 3 June 2015).
Cardullo, Burt (ed.) (2005) *Jean Renoir: Interviews*. Mississippi: University of Mississippi Press.
Carroll, Noël (2007) 'Vertigo and the Pathologies of Romantic Love', in David Baggett and William A. Drumin (eds) *Hitchcock and Philosophy: Dial M for Metaphysics*. Chicago: Open Court, 101–13.
Casebier, Allan (1991) *Film and Phenomenology: Toward a Realist Theory of Cinematic Representation*. Cambridge: Cambridge University Press.
Clark, Mike (1992) '"Dr. Giggles" – sick laughs; "Simple Men" is plain dull', *USA Today*, 26 October, 4D. Available at: LexisNexis.com (accessed 3 June 2015).
Cohen, Alex (2015) 'Why director Hal Hartley almost passed on Aubrey Plaza for his new film', *Take Two*, 4 April. Available at: http://www.scpr.org/programs/

take-two/2015/04/03/42249/why-director-hal-hartley-almost-passed-on-aubrey-p/ (accessed 2 July 2015).

Colebrook, Claire (2008) *Milton, Evil and Literary History*. New York: Continuum.

Conrad, Joseph (1937) *Conrad's Prefaces to His Works*. London: Duet.

Crayford, Peter (1991) '"Trust" is one of this year's best', *Australian Financial Review*, 8 November, 47. Available at: LexisNexis.com (accessed 3 June 2015).

Cremen, Christine (1993) 'A firm "no thanks" to Hollywood', *Australian Financial Review*, 2 April, 7. Available at: LexisNexis.com (accessed 3 June 2015).

Danielsen, Shane (1993) 'Genre of himself', *Sydney Morning Herald*, 2 April, 3. Available at: LexisNexis.com (accessed 3 June 2015).

DeCordova, Richard (1990) *Picture Personalities: The Emergence of the Star System in America*. Champaign, IL: University of Illinois Press.

De Jonge, Peter (1996) 'The Jean-Luc Godard of Long Island', *New York Times Magazine,* 4 August, 18–21.

Deardorff, Daniel (2009) *The Other Within: The Genius of Deformity in Myth, Culture & Psyche*. Vermont: Heaven & Earth Publishing.

Deer, Lesley (2000) *The Repetition of Difference: Marginality and the Films of Hal Hartley*. Doctoral thesis, Newcastle University.

_____ (2002) 'Hal Hartley', in Tasker, Yvonne (ed.) *Fifty Contemporary Filmmakers*. London and New York: Routledge, 161–8.

Denes, Melissa (2001) 'Striking Posey', *The Telegraph*, 10 March. Available at: http://www.telegraph.co.uk/culture/4722106/Striking-Posey.html (accessed 2 July 2015).

Derryberry, Jil (2002) 'Hal Hartley', in Yvonne Tasker, *Fifty Contemporary Filmmakers*. New York: Routledge, 161–69.

DiBattista, Maria (2001) *Fast-Talking Dames*. New Haven, CT: Yale University Press.

Dixon, Wheeler W. (1997) *The Films of Jean-Luc Godard*. New York: SUNY Press.

Dostoyevsky, Fyodor (2003) *Crime and Punishmnet*, trans. David McDuff. London: Penguin.

Dunphy, Catherine (1992) 'Whimsical Comedy May Grow on You', *The Toronto Star*, 13 November, C8. Available at: LexisNexis.com (accessed 3 June 2015).

Eaves, Hannah (2005) 'Free to Investigate: Hal Hartley', *GreenCine,* 24 April. Available at: http://www.greencine.com/article?action=view&articleID=206 (accessed 27 July 2014).

Ebert, Roger (1995) '*Amateur*', *RogerEbert.com*, 28 April. Available at: http://www.rogerebert.com/reviews/amateur-1995 (accessed 3 September 2015).

_____ (2002) '*No Such Thing*', *RogerEbert.com*, 29 March. Available at: http://www.rogerebert.com/reviews/no-such-thing-2002 (accessed 12 June 2015).

'Editorial' (1971), *Monogram* no 1, April.

Elsaesser, Thomas (1971) 'Reflection and Reality: Narrative Cinema in the Concave Mirror', *Monogram*, 2, Summer, 2–9.

_____ (1996a) 'Spectators of Life: Time, Place and Self in the Films of Wim Wenders', in Roger F. Cook and Gerd Gemünden (eds) *The Cinema of Wim Wenders*. Detroit: Wayne State University Press, 240–56.

_____ (1996b) *Fassbinder's Germany: History, Identity, Subject*. Amsterdam: Amsterdam University Press.

_____ (1997) 'Specularity and Engulfment: Francis Ford Coppola and Bram Stoker's Dracula', in Steven Neale and Murray Smith (eds) *Contemporary Hollywood Cinema*. London: Routledge, 191–208.

_____ ([1999] 2009) 'The Mind-Game Film', in Warren Buckland (ed.) *Puzzle Films: Complex Storytelling in Contemporary Cinema*. Malden, MA: Blackwell, 13–41.

Emerson, Ralph Waldo (1904) 'Memory', in *The Complete Works*. New York and Boston: Houghton, Mifflin, and Company. Available at: http://www.bartleby.com (accessed 6 July 2015).

Fabe, Marilyn (2004) *Closely Watched Films: An Introduction to the Art of Narrative Film Technique*. Berkeley, CA: University of California Press.

Fitzgerald, F. Scott ([1936] 1993) *The Crack-Up*, ed. Edmund Wilson. New York: New Directions.

French, Philip (1991) 'Double trouble – Philip French bemoans a dearth of drama in Little Fool', *The Observer* 20 January. Available at: LexisNexis.com (accessed 3 June 2015).

French, Sean (1991) 'Life stinks but not for the Long Island mists – a Bad Brooks but a Good *Trust*', *The Observer*, 22 September, 56. Available at: LexisNexis.com (accessed 3 June 2015).

Freud, Sigmund ([1917] 2001) 'Mourning and Melancholia', in *The Standard Edition of the Complete Psychological Works of Sigmund Freud: Volume XIV (1914–1916)*, trans. James Strachey. London: Vintage, 237–58.

Fried, John (1993) 'Rise of an Indie', *Cineaste*, 19, 4, 38–40.

Friend, David (2007) *Watching the World Change: The Stories Behind the Images of 9/11*. London: I.B. Tauris.

Fuller, Graham (1992) 'Finding the Essential: Hal Hartley in Conversation with Graham Fuller, 1992', in Hal Hartley, *Hal Hartley: Collected Screenplays 1*. London: Faber and Faber, vi–xli.

_____ (1994) 'Introduction: An Interview by Graham Fuller', in Hal Hartley, *Simple Men and Trust*. London: Faber and Faber, x–xli.

_____ (1995) 'Amateur Auteur', *Village Voice*, 25 April, 56.

_____ (1998) 'Responding to Nature: Hal Hartley in Conversation with Graham Fuller', in Hal Hartley, *Henry Fool*. London: Faber and Faber, vii–xxv.

Gilbey, Ryan (2001) 'Pulling the Pin on Hal Hartley', in Jim Hillier (ed.) *American Independent Cinema: A Sight and Sound Reader*. London: British Film Institute, 142–45.

Gillepsie, Pat (1994) 'Scaring small-town America', *The Age*, 26 May, 25. Available at: LexisNexis.com (accessed 3 June 2015).

Ging, Debbie (2012) *Men and Masculinities in Irish Cinema*. Basingstoke: Palgrave Macmillan.

Goffman, Irving (1990) *Stigma: Notes on the Management of Spoiled Identity*. London and New York: Penguin Books.

Greenwald, Adam (2012) 'Parker Posey talks about her role on Louie, the fine line between sad and funny, and what Louis C.K. looks like in a dress', *Grantland*,

July 27. Available at: http://grantland.com/hollywood-prospectus/parker-posey-talks-about-her-role-on-louie-the-fine-line-between-sad-and-funny-and-what-louis-c-k-looks-like-in-a-dress/ (accessed 2 July 2015).

Griffin, John (1991) 'Cool, deadpan, comedy charts teen angst in suburbia', *The Gazette*, 17 August, D2. Available at: LexisNexis.com (accessed 3 June 2015).

_____ (1992) 'No simple truths in Hartley's "Men" but search strikes resonate chord', *The Gazette*, 14 November, E4. Available at: LexisNexis.com (accessed 3 June 2015).

Grindstaff, Laura (2002) *The Money Shot: Trash, Class, and the Making of TV Talk Shows*. Chicago: University of Chicago Press.

Groen, Rick (1990) 'Film review: *The Unbelievable Truth*', *The Globe and Mail*, 27 July, n.p. Available at: LexisNexis.com (accessed 3 June 2015).

Guilliatt, R. (1990) 'From New York's mean streets, with love', *Sunday Herald*, 3 June, n.p. Available at: LexisNexis.com (accessed 3 June 2015).

Gunning, Tom (1994) *D. W. Griffith and the Origins of American Narrative Film*. Chicago: University of Illinois Press.

_____ (1996) 'Thrice Upon a Time: Flirting with a Film by Hal Hartley.' Preface to *Flirt*, by Hal Hartley. London: Faber and Faber, vii-x.

Hammond, J. M. (2015) 'A Sensitivity to Things: *mono no aware* in *Late Spring* and *Equinox Flower*', in Wayne Stein and Marc DiPaolo (eds) *Ozu International: Essays on the Global Influences of a Japanese Auteur*. New York and London: Bloomsbury, 77–90.

Harmetz, Aljean (1991) 'Big and little buzzes at the Sundance festival', *The New York Times*, 24 January, C15. Available at: LexisNexis.com (accessed 3 June 2015).

Harris, Brandon (2012) 'Indie Filmmaker Hal Hartley Talks Becoming Truly DIY, The "Difficult" Edges Of His Actor D.J. Mendel & His Latest Film "Meanwhile"', *The Playlist (Indiewire)*, 1 March. Available at: http://blogs.indiewire.com/theplaylist/filmmaker-hal-hartley-talks-becoming-fully-diy-the-rough-edges-of-actor-d-j-mendel-his-latest-film-meanwhile (accessed 29 June 2015).

Harris, Christopher (1992) 'Film Review: *Simple Men*', *The Globe and Mail*, 13 November, n.p. Available at: LexisNexis.com (accessed 3 June 2015).

Hartley, Hal (1992) 'Knowing is Not Enough', in John Boorman and Walter Donohue (eds), *Projections: Film-makers on Film-making*, 223.

_____ (1992) '*Surviving Desire*', in John Boorman and Walter Donahue (eds) *Projections: Film-makers on Film-making*, 223–59.

_____ (1994) 'In Images We Trust: Hal Hartley Chats with Jean-Luc Godard', in *Filmmaker* 3, no. 1, 14–18, 55–56.

_____ (1996) 'Actually Responding', in Hal Hartley, *Flirt* (screenplay). London: Faber and Faber, xi-xix.

_____ (1998) *Henry Fool* (screenplay). London: Faber and Faber.

_____ (2002) *Collected Screenplays 1: The Unbelievable Truth, Trust, Simple Men*. London: Faber and Faber.

_____ (2004) *Possible Films: Short Works by Hal Hartley, 1994–2004*. DVD. Possible Films.

_____ (2009) 'Parker Posey Tribute: Deauville France, September 2008', halhartley.com, 5 September. Available at: http://halhartley.com/blog/details/12142/parker-posey-tribute-deauville-france (accessed 30 June 2015).

_____ (2011) Interview with Steven Rawle, Bydgoszcz, Poland, 30 November: portions of the full interview are available in Steven Rawle (2012), 'I'm not that interested in an aesthetic of realism: An interview with Hal Hartley', *WordPress*, 21 March. Available at: https://thegrumple.wordpress.com/2012/03/21/im-not-that-interested-in-an-aesthetic-of-realism-an-interview-with-hal-hartley/ (accessed 29 June 2015).

_____ (2013a) 'OK! About the Distribution Rewards (technical stuff)', *Kickstarter*, 25 November. Available at: https://www.kickstarter.com/projects/260302407/ned-rifle/posts/673620 (accessed 30 June 2015).

_____ (2013b) 'Ned Rifle by Hal Hartley', *Kickstarter*, 22 November. Available at: https://www.kickstarter.com/projects/260302407/ned-rifle (accessed 23 November 2013).

_____ (2013c) 'Henry and Fay', *Kickstarter*, November 8. Available at: https://www.kickstarter.com/projects/260302407/ned-rifle/posts/655860 (accessed 30 June 2015).

_____ (2013d) 'Parker Posey – Captive Actress!!!', *Kickstarter*, 12 November. Available at: https://www.kickstarter.com/projects/260302407/ned-rifle/posts/659257 (accessed 30 June 2015).

Hartley, Hal and Kenneth Kaleta (2008) *True Fiction Pictures and Possible Films: Hal Hartley in Conversation with Kenneth Kaleta*. New York: Soft Skull Press.

Hill, Annette (2005) *Reality TV: Audiences and Popular Factual Television*. London: Routledge.

Hill, Logan (2005) 'Resident Alien: Whatever Happened to Hal Hartley?' in *New York,* May 21, 71.

Hillier, Jim (ed.) (2001) *American Independent Cinema: A Sight and Sound Reader*. London: British Film Institute.

Hinson, Hal (1991) '*Trust*: The cry of suburbia', *The Washington Post*, 16 August, D1. Available at: LexisNexis.com (accessed 3 June 2015).

Holmlund, Chris, and Justin Wyatt (eds) (2005) *Contemporary American Independent Film: From the Margins to the Mainstream*. New York: Routledge.

Hope, Ted (2014) *Hope for Film: From the Frontline of the Independent Cinema Revolutions*. Berkeley, CA: Soft Skull Press.

Howe, Desson (1991) 'Anti-Matter of *Trust*', *The Washington Post*, 16 August, N36. Available at: LexisNexis.com (accessed 3 June 2015).

_____ (1992) 'Hartley craft not so simple', *The Washington Post* 30 October, N42. Available at: LexisNexis.com (accessed 3 June 2015).

Hutchinson, I. (1990) untitled column, *Herald Sun* 1 December, n.p. Available at: LexisNexis.com (accessed 3 June 2015).

_____ (1993) 'Simple style keeping Hal on outside', *Herald Sun*, 8 April, 30. Available at: LexisNexis.com (accessed 3 June 2015).

Indrisek, Scott (2012) 'Cine-File: Hal Hartley', in *Modern Painters*, March, 20–1.

Insdorf, Annette ([1981] 2005) 'Ordinary People, European-Style: or How to Spot an Independent Feature', in Chris Holmlund and Justin Wyatt (eds) *Contemporary American Independent Film: From the Margins to the Mainstream*. New York: Routledge, 27–34.

Iwabuchi, Koichi (2002) *Recentering Globalization: Popular Culture and Japanese Transnationalism*. Durham, NC: Duke University Press.

James, Caryn (1990a) 'Hollywood Tactics Invade the Sundance Festival', *The New York Times*, 5 February. Available at: LexisNexis.com (accessed 3 June 2015).

_____ (1990b) 'Applying 1950s Cool to the 80s,' *The New York Times*, 20 July, C11. Available at: LexisNexis.com (accessed 3 June 2015).

_____ (1992) 'This Director's Characters Have an Attitude', *The New York Times*, 1 November, 21. Available at LexisNexis.com (accessed 3 June 2015).

_____ (1995) 'Critic's Choice: A Survey of Films by Hartley', *The New York Times*, 13 February.

Jameson, Fredric (1991) *Postmodernism, Or, The Cultural Logic of Late Capitalism*. Durham, NC: Duke University Press.

Jillett, Neil (1993) 'With "Simple Men", Hal Hartley does it again, entertainingly', *The Age*, 1 April, 16. Available at: LexisNexis.com (accessed 3 June 2015).

Johnston, Sheila (1995) 'Nun on the run, cowgirls on acid – and morons in space', in *The Independent*, 5 January. Available at: http://www.independent.co.uk (accessed 1 August 2015).

Jones, Kent (1996) 'Hal Hartley: The Book I Read Was in Your Eyes', *Film Comment*, 32, 4, 68–72.

Jones, Lucy (2013) 'Happy Birthday PJ Harvey, Queen of Indie, Perfect Marvel', *NME.com*, October 9. Online. http://www.nme.com/blogs/nme-blogs/happy-birthday-pj-harvey-queen-of-indie-perfect-marvel (accessed June 30 2015).

Kahn, Victoria (2014) *The Future of Illusion: Political Theology and Early Modern Texts*. Chicago: University of Chicago Press.

Karlyn, Kathleen Rowe (1998) 'Allison Anders's *Gas Food Lodging*: Independent Cinema and the New Romance', in Peter William Evans and Celestino Deleyto (eds) *Terms of Endearment: Hollywood Romantic Comedy of the 1980s and 1990s*. Edinburgh: Edinburgh University Press, 168–87.

Kauffmann, Stanley (1995), 'Viewing the Past', in *New Republic*, 24 April, vol. 212, no. 17, 30–31.

Kelly, Christina (1996) 'Parker Posey', *Index Magazine*. Available at: http://www.indexmagazine.com/interviews/parker_posey.shtml. (accessed 15 May 2014).

Kelly, Dierdre (1990) 'Star Turns', *The Globe and Mail*, 11 September, n.p. Available at: LexisNexis.com (accessed 3 June 2015).

Kempley, Rita (1990) '*Unbelievable Truth*': Fresh-Faced Farce', *The Washington Post*, 4 August, G1. Available at: LexisNexis.com (accessed 3 June 2015).

_____ (1992) 'Sheep on the Lam in *Simple Men*', *The Washington Post* 30 October, B7. Available at: LexisNexis.com (accessed 3 June 2015).

King, Geoff (2005) *American Independent Cinema*. Bloomington, IN: Indiana University Press.

_____ (2014) *Indie 2.0: Change and Continuity in Contemporary American Indie Film*. London: IB Tauris.
King, Geoff, Claire Molloy and Yannis Tzioumakis (2012) *American Independent Cinema: Indie, Indiewood and Beyond*. London and New York: Routledge.
King, Homay (2009) 'Free Indirect Affect in Cassavetes' *Faces*', *Maske und Kothurn*, 55, 4, 33–48.
Kirkeby, Ole (2000) *Management Philosophy: A Radical-Normative Perspective*. New York: Springer.
Knelman, Martin (1991) 'An antidote to mindless blockbusters', *The Financial Post*, 26 August, 16. Available at: LexisNexis.com (accessed 3 June 2015).
Kord, Susanne and Elizabeth Krimmer (2005) 'Hidden Alternatives: Judi Dench, Kathy Bates, Parker Posey, Whoopi Goldberg, and Frances McDormand', *Hollywood Divas, Indie Queens, and TV Heroines: Contemporary Screen Images of Women*. Lanham, MD: Rowman & Littlefield, 115–41.
Kornits, Dov (1999) 'Hal Harley – Nobody's Fool', efilmcritic.com, 17 May. Available at: http://www.efilmcritic.com/feature.php?feature=37 (accessed 2 July 2015).
Krell, David Farrell (1990) *Of Memory, Reminiscence, and Writing: On the Verge*. Bloomington, IN: Indiana University Press.
La Rosa, Erin (2013) 'Parker Posey's 10 Most Important Film Roles', *BuzzFeed*,10 May 10. Available at. http://www.buzzfeed.com/erinlarosa/parker-poseys-10-most-important-film-roles#.irnjZ8kgm (accessed 30 June 2015).
Lawrence, D. H. ([1920] 1971) *Women in Love*. London: Heinemann.
Leeming, David (2005) *The Oxford Companion to World Mythology*. New York: Oxford University Press.
Lefebvre, Henri (1991) *The Production of Space*, trans. Donald Nicholson-Smith, Cambridge, MA: Blackwell.
Levinas, Emmanuel ([1946] 2005) 'There is: Existence without Existents', in *The Levinas Reader*, ed. Seán Hand. Malden, MA: Blackwell, 29–36.
Levy, Emanuel (1999) *Cinema of Outsiders: The Rise of American Independent Film*. New York: New York University Press.
Lockwood, Dean (2005) 'Teratology of the Spectacle', in Geoff King (ed.) *The Spectacle of the Real: From Hollywood to Reality TV and Beyond*. Chicago: University of Chicago Press, 71–82.
Lowing, Rob (1993) 'Quirky facets in Hartley sparkler', *The Sun Herald*, 4 April, 102. Available at: LexisNexis.com (accessed 3 June 2015).
Mack, Burton (2008) *Myth and the Christian Nation: A Social Theory of Religion*. London: Equinox.
Malcolm, Derek (1991a) 'The Fool's paradise', *Guardian Weekly*, 27 January, n.p. Available at: LexisNexis.com (accessed 3 June 2015).
_____ (1991b) 'A real underbelly laugh – America's unsmart set supply the laughs for the best (and cheapest) film of the week', *The Guardian*, 19 September, n.p. Available at: LexisNexis.com (accessed 3 June 2015).
Manley, Sebastian (2013) *The Cinema of Hal Hartley*. New York: Bloomsbury Academic.

Martin-Jones, David (2013) 'Foolish Bum, Funny Shit: Scatalogical Humor in Hal Hartley's Not-So-Comedic *Henry Fool*', in Murray Pomerance (ed.) *The Last Laugh: Strange Humors of Cinema*. Detroit: Wayne State University Press, 163–76.
Marvar, Alexandra (2011) 'A Conversation with Hal Hartley', *The Huffington Post*, 15 November. Available at: http://www.huffingtonpost.com/alexandra-marvar/a-conversation-with-hal-h_b_1091650.html (accessed 30 June 2015).
McCarthy, Todd (1992) '*Simple Men*', *Daily Variety*, 13 May, n.p. Available at: LexisNexis.com (accessed 3 June 2015).
McKay, Alastair (1993) 'Getting to the Hartley and soul of the matter', *Scotland on Sunday*, 5 December, n.p. Available at: LexisNexis.com (accessed 3 June 2015).
McQueen, Max (1993) '*Eating* is sheer boredom; *Simple Men* is also a tough one to sit through', *Palm Beach Post*, 23 April, 36. Available at: LexisNexis.com (accessed 3 June 2015).
McNary, Dave (2014) 'Hal Hartley's *Ned Rifle*, Starring Aubrey Plaza, Set for Spring Release', *Variety*, 3 December. Available at: http://variety.com/2014/film/news/hal-hartleys-ned-rifle-starring-aubrey-plaza-set-for-spring-release-1201369493/ (accessed 29 June 2015).
Mietkiewicz, Henry (1990) 'Vivid characters in search of a plot', *The Toronto Star*, 27 July, E6. Available at: LexisNexis.com (accessed 3 June 2015).
Mitchell, Elvis (2002) 'Review: *No Such Thing*', *The New York Times*, 29 March. Available at: http://www.nytimes.com/movie/review?res=9B00E4D71E3BF93AA15750C0A9649C8B63 (accessed 12 March 2015).
Mollick, Ethan R. (2014) 'The Dynamics of Crowdfunding: An Exploratory Study', *Journal of Business Venturing*, 29, 1, January, 1–16. Available at: http://dx.doi.org/10.2139/ssrn.2088298 (accessed 30 June 2015).
Murphy, J. J. (2007) *Me and You and Memento and Fargo: How Independent Screeenplays Work*. New York: Continuum.
Murphy, Peter and David Roberts (2006) *Dialectic of Romanticism*. New York: Continuum.
Myers, Emma (2013) '25 Years of Minimalism to the Max', in *Film Comment* (July-August), 76.
Negra, Diane (2005) '"Queen of the Indies": Parker Posey's Niche Stardom and the Taste Cultures of Independent Film', in Chris Holmlund and Justin Wyatt (eds) *Contemporary American Independent Film: From The Margins to the Mainstream*. New York: Routledge, 71–88.
Nesfield-Cookson, Bernard (1998) *Michael and the Two-Horned Beast: The Challenge of Evil Today in the Light of Rudolf Steiner's Science of the Spirit*. London: Temple Lodge Publishing.
Newman, Michael Z. (2009) 'Indie Culture: In Pursuit of the Authentic Autonomous Alternative', *Cinema Journal*, 48, 3, 16–34.
_____ (2011) *Indie: An American Film Culture*. New York: Columbia University Press.
Nietzsche, Friedrich ([1876] 1999) *Untimely Meditations*, ed. Daniel Breazeale, trans. R. J. Hollingdale. Cambridge: Cambridge University Press.

_____ ([1887] 2010) *On the Genealogy of Morality*, ed. Keith Ansell-Pearson, trans. Carol Diethe. Cambridge: Cambridge University Press.

Nochimson, Martha P. (2002) *Screen Couple Chemistry: The Power of 2*. Austin: University of Texas Press.

O'Meara, Jennifer (2013) 'Poetic Dialogue: Lyrical Speech in the Work of Hal Hartley and Jim Jarmusch', in Marlisa Santos (ed.) *Verse, Voice and Vision: Poetry and the Cinema*. Landham, MD; Scarecrow Press, 165–78.

O'Reilly, Marc (2008) *Unexceptional: America's Empire in the Persian Gulf, 1941–2007*. Lanham, MD: Lexington Books.

Pall, Ellen (1992) 'This Director's Wish List Doesn't Include Hollywood', in *The New York Times*, 11 October.

_____ (1995) 'The Elusive Women Who Inhabit the Quirky Films of Hal Hartley', in *The New York Times*, 9 April.

Peachment, Chris (1992) 'Young, gifted, and frugal', *The Independent*, 1 November, 128. Available at: LexisNexis.com (accessed 3 June 2015).

Peberdy, Donna (2011) *Masculinity in Film Performance: Male Angst in Contemporary American Cinema*. Basingstoke: Palgrave Macmillan.

Perkins, Claire (2012) *American Smart Cinema*. Edinburgh: Edinburgh University Press.

Perry, George (1991a) 'Walt Whitman's shock treatment', *The Sunday Times*, 20 January, n.p. Available at: LexisNexis.com (accessed 3 June 2015).

_____ (1991b) 'Trust, trysts, and trickery', *The Sunday Times*, 22 September, n.p. Available at: LexisNexis.com (accessed 3 June 2015).

Petric, Vlada and Geraldine Bard (1993) 'Godard's Vision of the New Eve', in Marvyel Lock and Charles Warren (eds) *Jean-Luc Godard's Hail Mary: Women and the Sacred in Film*. Carbondale, IL: Southern Illinois University Press, 98–116.

Phillips, Adam (1994) *On Flirtation*. Cambridge, MA: Harvard University Press.

_____ (2013) *Missing Out: In Praise of the Unlived Life*. New York: Farrar, Straus, and Giroux.

Polan, Dana (2001) 'Auteur desire', *Screening the past*, 12. Available at: http://www.latrobe.edu.au/www/screeningthepast/firstrelease/fr0301/dpfr12a.htm (accessed 30 June 2015).

Pomerance, Murray (2013) *The Eyes Have It: Cinema and the Reality Effect*. New Brunswick, NJ: Rutgers University Press.

Posey, Parker (2011) 'From the Vaults: Parker Posey's Diary from the Set of "Suburbia"', *indieWIRE*, 29 July. Available at: http://www.indiewire.com/article/from_the_iw_vaults_parker_poseys_diary_from_the_set_of_suburbia (accessed 30 June 2015).

Quantcast (2014) 'Kickstarter.com Traffic and Demographic Statistics', *Quantcast*. On-line. https://www.quantcast.com/kickstarter.com (accessed 7 January 2014).

Quart, Alissa (2002) 'Who's Afraid of Parker Posey?', *Film Comment*, 38, 6, 42–4.

Rawle, Steven (2009) 'Hal Hartley and the Re-Presentation of Repetition,' *Film Criticism*, 34, 1, 58–75.

_____ (2011) *Performance in the Cinema of Hal Hartley*. Amherst, NY: Cambria Press.

_____ (2013) 'Hal Hartley's "Look-out-Martin-Donovan's-in-the-house!" Shot: The Transformative Cult Indie Star-Director Relationship and Performance "Idiolect"', in Kate Egan and Sarah Thomas (eds) *Cult Film Stardom: Offbeat Attractions and Processes of Cultification*. New York: Palgrave Macmillan, 126–43.

Rickey, Carrie (1977) 'Fassbinder and Altman: Approaches to Filmmaking', in *Performing Arts Journal*, 2, 2, 33–48.

Ross, Matthew (2002) 'Separation Anxiety? Not for Ex-Good Machiners at "This Is That"', in *indieWIRE*, 24 September.

Rothenbuhler, Eric (2005) 'The Church of the Cult of the Individual', in Eric Rothenbuhler and Mihai Coman (eds) *Media Anthropology*. California: SAGE Publications, 91–100.

Rowe, Claudia (1997) 'Film Makers Take Root at Purchase', in *The New York Times*, 2 November.

Rybin, Steven (2014) 'Parker Posey: New York Flight', *The Cine-Files: A Scholarly Journal of Cinema Studies*, 6. Available at: http://www.thecine-files.com/wp-content/uploads/2014/05/Rybin.pdf (accessed May 20 2015).

Saperstein, Pat (2013) 'Hal Hartley Can't Offer Distribution Rights as Kickstarter Reward', *Variety*, 25 November. On-line. http://variety.com/2013/film/news/indie-helmer-hal-hartley-sells-distribution-rights-as-kickstarter-reward-1200884677/ (accessed 30 June 2015).

Saxberg, Lynn (1991) '*Trust*', *The Ottawa Citizen*, 11 October, F3 Available at: LexisNexis.com (accessed 3 June 2015).

Sconce, Jeffrey (2002) 'Irony, Nihilism, and the New American "Smart" Film', *Screen* 43, 4, 349–69.

Sebald, W. G. (2002) *Austerlitz*, trans. Anthea Bell. London: Penguin Books.

Sellier, Geneviève (2008) *Masculine Singular: French New Wave Cinema*, trans. Kristen Ross. Durham, NC: Duke University Press.

Shattuc, Jane (2001) 'The Confessional Talk Show', in Glen Creeber (ed.) *The Television Genre Book*. London: British Film Institute, 84–7.

Shaw, Deborah (2013) 'Deconstructing and Reconstructing "Transnational Cinema"', in Stephanie Dennison (ed.) *Contemporary Hispanic Cinema: Interrogating Transnationalism in Spanish and Latin American Film*. Woodbridge and Rochester, NY: Tamesis, 47–66.

Shenk, David (2003) *The Forgetting: Understanding Alzheimer's*. London: Flamingo.

Shingler, Martin (2006) 'Fasten Your Seatbelts and Prick Up Your Ears: The Dramatic Human Voice in Film', *Scope*, 5, June. Available at: http://www.nottingham.ac.uk/scope/index.aspx (the journal archive is under redesign, with the article received via email on 17 December 2012).

_____ (2010) 'Rich Voices in Talky Talkies: *The Rich Are Always with Us*', *The Soundtrack*, 3, 2, 109–15.

Staiger, Janet (2012) "Independent of What? Sorting Out Differences from Hollywood', in Geoff King, Claire Molloy and Yannis Tzioumakis (eds) *American Independent Cinema: Indie, Indiewood and Beyond*. London and New York: Routledge, 15–27.

Stevenson, Robert Louis ([1886] 2012) 'The Strange Case of Dr. Jekyll and Mr. Hyde', in *The Norton Anthology of English Literature: The Victorian Age*, ninth edition, eds. Catherine Robson and Carol T. Christ. New York: W.W. Norton, 1645–85.

Travers, Peter (2002), '*No Such Thing*', *Rollingstone.com*, 29 March. Available at: http://www.rollingstone.com/movies/reviews/no-such-thing-20020327 (accessed 12 June 2015).

Tzioumakis, Yannis (2006) *American Independent Cinema*, New Brunswick, NJ: Rutgers University Press.

_____ (2012) *Hollywood's Indies: Classics Division, Specialty Labels and the American Film Market*. Edinburgh: Edinburgh University Press.

_____ (2013) '"Independent", "Indie" and "Indiewood": Towards a Periodisation of Contemporary (Post-1980) American Independent Cinema', in Geoff King, Claire Molloy and Yannis Tzioumakis (eds) *American Independent Cinema: Indie, Indiewood and Beyond*. Oxford: Routledge, 28–40.

Upon Reflection: Trust (1999) Prod. Kyle Gilman. *Trust* DVD. Aztec International, the AV Channel.

Vanhala, Helena (2011) *The Depiction of Terrorists in Blockbuster Hollywood Films, 1980–2011: An Analytical Study*. Jefferson, NC: McFarland.

Weber, Bruce (1992) 'Big Movies on Little Budgets', in *The New York Times*, 17 May.

Weimann, Gabriel (2000) *Communicating Unreality: Modern Media and the Reconstruction of Reality*. London: Sage.

Williams, Christopher (1971/2) 'Politics and Production: Some Pointers through the Work of Jean-Luc Godard', *Screen*, 12, 4, 6–24.

Wilner, Norman (1992) 'Hartley keeps it *Simple*', *The Toronto Star*, 13 November, C1 Available at: LexisNexis.com (accessed 3 June 2015).

Winters, Laura (1997) 'For an Art-House Regular, a Wider World' (Interview with Martin Donovan), in *The New York Times*, 13 April.

Wise, Sophie (1999) 'What I Like About Hal Hartley, or rather, What Hal Hartley Likes About Me: The Performance of the (Spect)actor', in Lesley Stern and George Kouvaros (eds) *Falling for You: Essays on Cinema and Performance*. Sydney: Power Publications, 245–75.

Wood, Jason (2003). *Hal Hartley* (Pocket Essentials). Harpenden, UK: Pocket Essentials.

_____ (2006). Interview with Hal Hartley, in *Talking Movies: Contemporary World Filmmakers in Interview*, London: Wallflower Press, 103–15.

Wyatt, Justin (1998) 'The Particularity and Peculiarity of Hal Hartley: An Interview', *Film Quarterly*, 52, 1, 2–6.

Zarrilli, Phillip (2010) *Theatre Histories: An Introduction*. London: Routledge.

Zimmerman, Patricia R. (2005) 'Digital deployment(s)', in Chris Holmlund and Justin Wyatt (eds) *Contemporary American Independent Film: From the Margins to the Mainstream*. New York and Oxford: Routledge, 245–63.

Zupančič, Alenka (2003) *The Shortest Shadow: Nietzsche's Philosophy of the Two*. Cambridge, MA: MIT Press.

INDEX

Accomplice 60–1, 73–5
Adventure 60, 73
aesthetic signature 6
Allen, Woody 31, 58
Altman, Robert 11, 132, 138, 140–3
Amateur 1–2, 5, 11, 33, 41, 47, 55, 57, 60–1, 93n.13, 94–108, 122, 144, 168, 170; reviewers of 98; sexuality in 155 shot length of 29n.5; *see also* amnesia and Huppert, Isabelle
amateur 49, 52, 73–5, 102–3, 105; *see also Amateur*
Ambition 10, 30–1, 35–8, 72, 92n.7
American independent cinema 1, 7, 63, 157
American New Wave 132
amnesia 94–6, 98, 103, 105; amnesia-noir 105; post-amnesia goodness 94; *see also Amateur*
A/Muse 60, 73–4
Anderson, Paul Thomas 29
Anderson, Wes 2, 4, 52, 151
A New Man 94–108
anti-realist filmmaker 5
Antonioni, Michelangelo 18, 25–7, 138
Apologies, The 60, 73–4, 149
Artaud, Antonin 122, 129–31
art-house cinema 50
A Scanner Darkly 57
As the World Turns 154

audience: audience in situ 140; audience online 66; contemporary audience 128; Facebook audience 65; mass-media audience 129
auteur: artistically- motivated auteur 48; auteur desire 66; auteur-ness 48; auteur theory 47, 156; auteur is dead 156; auteurial style 156; auteurist talent 58; classically trained auteur 43; film auteur 4; independent auteur 4–6; not as an auteur 56; potential auteur 47; young auteur 48; would-be-auteur 53
autobiographical pseudo-documentaries 75
avant-garde 129–30, 143
A Woman is a Woman 56, 161

Bailey, Mark Chandler 31–4, 80, 137
Bakhtin, Mikhail 162
Baumbach, Noah 151
Bazin, André 17, 160
Beauty and the Beast 129
Berlin 35, 60, 62, 69, 72–5, 109, 116–17, 154
Big Brother 124
Blade Runner 111
Book of Life, The 1, 3, 11, 15, 35, 72, 75, 121–8, 130–1, 151, 155; medium-range lenses 3, 15; *see also* poiesis, Donovan, Martin, mass media, Ryan, Thomas Jay and post-9/11

Bram Stoker's Dracula 15
Bresson, Robert 2–4, 15, 18, 77, 81, 132, 138, 142, 160–1
Brownstein, Jerome 31
Bubble 75
Buñuel, Luis 14, 95–6
Burke, Robert John 3, 17, 35, 68, 78, 82, 87, 127, 13, 137, 153, 158n.7; *see also Simple Men* and *Unbelievable Truth, The*
Burrows, Saffron 68, 170

Cahiers du cinéma 14
California Split 132, 140–2
Camus, Albert 96–7, 100–1
Captive Actress 11, 144–153
Cassavetes, John 11, 132, 138–43
Chain Letters 161
Choose Me 29
Christie, Julie 129
Cineaste 38, 92n.7
cinephilia 2, 9
Cinéthique 14
Confessions 159–60, 163, 165, 167–71, 173; *see also Henry Fool*
Coutard, Raoul 56
crowdfunding 61–8, 75, 76n.5, 157; *see also* independent cinema and *Ned Rifle*
Cuban, Mark 2
cultural odors 61

Dazed and Confused 44, 57, 145
Deleuze, Gilles 9
dependent cinema 4
Diary of a Country Priest, The 160–1
diegetic: diegetic continuity 41; diegetic motifs 169; diegetic universe 121; diegetic world 124; extra-diegetic 160; non-diegetic 141, 160, 170
digital: digital filmmaking 8, 73; digital video aesthetic 123; self-reflexive digital style 170
Disney 61, 66, 68, 128
DIWO 66–9, 76
DIY 30, 66–9, 76
Do-It-With-Others *see* DIWO
Do-It-Yourself *see* DIY
Donnie Darko 111

Donovan, Martin 3, 31, 38, 40–1, 56, 58, 68, 83–5, 94, 115, 121, 144, 172; *see also Book of Life, The*
Dostoyevsky, Fyodor 38, 41
Double Indemnity 97

early films 3, 44–7, 51, 58, 59n.3, 62, 77, 91, 145, 163
editing: elliptical editing 77; give-and-take editing 18; non-linear editing 57; rapid editing 17, 29n.5; realist editing 83
Elsaesser, Thomas 13–15, 29, 110–12
European art cinema 3, 77, 142
European cinema 14, 20
European modernism 9–10
Everyday, The 71; *see Meanwhile*
Ewell, Dwight 109, 117

Facebook 2, 63, 65, 76n.4
Faces 132, 138–42
Fandor 2, 62
Fay Grim 1–3, 6, 11, 33, 60–2, 68–9, 71, 75, 93n.13, 144–5, 148–9, 150, 152–3, 157, 159–64, 167–71; *see also* screwball comedy, Posey, Parker
female: female American performers 156; female body 155; female characters 87, 148, 154, 155–7; female dialogue 149; female film 147; female performers 147; female protagonist 83, 85; female speaker 80; female voice 173; stereotypical female types 155
Fight Club 111–12
Fine Line Features 51, 54, 64
Flirt 1, 6, 8, 11, 15, 57, 60, 70, 93, 102, 109–20, 144, 154, 163, 168, 170; shot length of 29n.5; *see also* Posey, Parker and puzzle-film
Fool for Love 140
Forgetting, The 105
French New Wave 138
From Here to the Station 2
Full Frontal 57

Game of Thrones 44
Girlfriend Experience, The 57
Girl from Monday, The 1, 60, 68, 72, 75, 93n.13, 122

Godard, Jean-Luc 2, 4, 8, 14, 18–20, 27, 29, 32–3, 56, 74, 75, 77, 102, 132, 134, 138, 142, 145, 154–7, 158n.11, 161
Goldblum, Jeff 68, 169
Good Machine 31, 35
Griffith, D. W. 121, 124–126
Grim, Simon 43, 159–60, 163–4, 171–3

Hail Mary 19
Harvey, P. J. 123, 151, 156
Haynes, Todd 102
Heart is a Muscle, The 2
Henry Fool 1–8, 11, 33, 35, 43–4, 57, 68, 71, 144–5, 148–9, 152, 154–5, 157, 159–174; shot length of 29n.5; *see also* Posey, Parker and Ryan, Thomas Jay
Herald Sun 50
hero 44, 56, 94, 96–98, 111, 142, 166; blockbuster heroine 151; heroine 83, 128, 130, 147, 169; noir hero 97; superheroes 44; unmotivated hero 15; *see also* screwball comedy
Hollywood: American New Hollywood 142; anti-Hollywood 7; Classical Hollywood cinema 3, 14, 145; Hollywood blockbuster 123; mainstream Hollywood 6, 7, 9; Off-Hollywood 67
Hope, Ted 31
Howard, Jeffrey 31, 38, 40
Hughes, John 51–2
Huppert, Isabelle 55, 57, 94, 155; *see also Amateur*

Implied Harmonies 60, 73
Independent 55
independent cinema 2, 61, 63–5, 68, 71–3, 131, 144–5, 160, 163; *see also* American independent cinema.
indie: American indie cinema 7; indie actors 10; indie authorship 63; indie cinema/films/movies 7, 11, 15, 54, 61, 76, 147, 151, 152, 157; indie credibility 151–2; indie distributor 54; indie epic 8; indie filmmakers 7, 29, 62, 66; indie music 15; Queen of the indies 144, 150–2; true indieness 67; US indie scene 15

Indiewire 62–3, 68
Indie 2.0 62–3
Indie 2.0 (book) 73
indieWIRE 153
Indiewood 7, 61, 64, 67, 75
internet 43, 68, 73, 159, 163, 166–7

Jameson, Fredric 5, 132–3, 143
Jarmusch, Jim 102
Josie and the Pussycats 147
Joyce, James 70
Jude the Obscure 86

Kafka, Franz 97, 99, 100
Kafka 57, 154
Karina, Anna 154–5, 157, 158n.11
Kickstarter project 7, 62, 65–8, 76n.n.3,6, 144, 149, 150, 152, 157
King, Geoff 7, 62–3, 66, 73
Komákur, Baltasar 130
Kuleshov effect 17, 23

Lefebvre, Henri 143
Lindenhurst 51–2, 60, 88
Linklater, Richard 2, 44, 57, 59n.4, 145, 153
little death 97, 99
living biography 45
Long Island 46, 49, 51, 53, 54, 57–8, 61, 88, 108, 133, 145, 154
Long Island trilogy 1, 5, 60, 61, 70, 108
low budget 7, 8, 10, 30, 49, 63, 67, 75–6, 151
Löwensohn, Elina 31–2, 34, 88, 95, 144, 154
Lynch, David 2, 50, 52–4, 112, 143

Magnolia (distributor) 75
male: male authorship 163, 167–8, 170; male desire 79, 87; male dominance 90; male self-sufficiency 78
Malloy, Matt 31, 38
mass media 122–3, 125, 127–31; *see also Book of Life, The*
Meanwhile 1, 60–4, 68–75
melodrama 14–15; *see also Trust*
Memento 105, 110, 112
Mendel, DJ 1, 64, 69–72
Merritt Nelson, Rebecca 31, 39

MGM 2, 8, 61, 68
micro-budget 61, 63, 69, 72, 76; micro- and low-budget 63; micro-budget filmmaking 69, 76
middle-class 10, 30–4, 51
Miramax Films 48
Mirren, Helen 44, 122, 125, 127–9, 131
Misadventures of Margaret, The 148–9
mise-en-scène 4, 10, 35, 111, 123, 132, 136–42
modernism 9, 10, 160
Monogram 13–5, 20, 29
monster movie 2, 4, 8, 44; see also *No Such Thing*
moving imagery 78
musicals 115; non-musical film 40; see also *Simple Men* and *Surviving Desire*
My America 1–2
myth 127–31, 166

narrative: causally-propelled narrative 19; narrative conflict 136; noir narrative 98; non-narrative 2; romantic narratives 78–9, 82, 91
Ned Rifle 1, 7, 8, 11, 61–3, 67–9, 76, 144, 150, 153, 156–7, 159, 164, 171–3; see also crowdfunding, Plaza, Aubrey and Posey, Parker
Ned Rifle (pseudonym) 2, 34
Neumann, David 64
New Line Cinema 51, 54
new man 11, 23, 97, 99, 101, 105, 107–8
Newton Boys, The 57
New York 30, 35–6, 39–40, 45, 51, 54, 60–2, 64–5, 69–71, 73, 75, 79, 81, 88, 108–9, 117, 122, 133, 145–6, 151, 161
New York Times 48, 55, 149
Nietzsche, Friedrich 102, 104–6
Nikaido, Miho 35, 69–71, 109–10, 119, 125, 154, 166
9/11 attacks 131; before 9/11 122; post-9/11 44, 122; see also *Book of Life, The*
Northern Exposure 52–3
No Such Thing 1–2, 4, 6–8, 11, 31, 44, 60–1, 93 121–2, 125, 127–131; shot length of 29n.5; see also monster movie and 9/11 attacks
nouvelle vague 154

Ode 108
Other Also, The 72
Opening Night 139
Opera No. 1 7, 73, 144, 168
Ozu, Yasujiro 70

Parks and Recreation 68, 156, 158n.13
personal cinema 7
petite mort see little death
Petit Soldat 155
PF2 69, 73–5
Phillips, Adam 11, 112–14
Picket Fences 52
plasticity 105
Plaza, Aubrey 7, 68, 156, 158n.13, 159, 172; see also *Ned Rifle*
poiesis 11, 121–31; see also *Book of Life, The*
Polley, Sarah 128
pornography 94
Posey, Parker 3, 11, 73, 109, 115, 144–57, 159–60, 167–71; Posey's voice 144, 146–7, 155; see also *Fay Grim*, *Henry Fool*, *Ned Rifle* and *Flirt*
Possible Films: Short Works by Hal Hartley 1994–2004 72
Possible Films 2 see PF2
post-classical aesthetic 143
postmodernism 2, 4, 8, 9, 131–3, 143; postmodern aesthetics 143
poststructuralism 9, 13
Pretty Woman 79, 82
pre-digital age 46
Professional, The 102
Punch-Drunk Love 29
puzzle-film/game films 11, 110–14, 120; anti-puzzle film 11, 109–20; razzle-dazzle puzzle films 112; unlock puzzles 120; see also *Flirt*

Raising Arizona 52
Rappaport, Mark 3, 161
regional identities 61
Reservoir Dogs 3
romantic comedy 8, 11, 15, 77–91, 93n.13, 109; see also *Unbelievable Truth, The*
Rowlands, Gena 139
Rudolph, Alan 29
Russell, David O. 4

Ryan, Thomas Jay 1, 3, 35, 123, 125, 150, 152, 160, 164, 168; *see also Book of Life, The* and *Henry Fool*

Sage, Bill 31–2, 34, 68, 87, 109, 144
Sauer, Gary 31, 38, 80, 83, 133
Sauve qui peut (la vie) 19
Sayles, John 102
Schamus, James 31
Scorsese, Martin 143
Screen 8, 13–14, 20
screwball comedy 3, 8, 147; screwball heroines 147; *see also Fay Grim*
Secret Honor 140
sex, lies, and videotape 44, 48–9, 82–4, 133, 137
Shelly, Adrienne 3, 73, 79, 148, 155; *see also Trust* and *Unbelievable Truth, The*
Sillas, Karen 17, 68, 87, 89
Simple Men 1–4, 10, 15, 17, 20, 26, 28–9, 33, 35, 38, 41, 44, 46–7, 50, 53–7, 61, 64, 71, 77–8, 87–9, 91, 92n.n.n.7,8,11, 93n.13; *see also* Burke, Robert John and musicals
Sisters of Mercy, The 7, 144, 153, 168
Sixth Sense, The 110
Slacker 44, 52, 59n.4
smallness 64, 67, 69–76
smart cinema 8–10, 162–3, 166
Soderbergh, Steven 2–4, 44, 49, 57, 64, 75, 143
Sony Pictures Classics 2, 8, 61–2, 64, 68
Soon 73
space stages 132, 139
Spiller, Michael 31, 49, 56, 158n.7
spoiled identity 106
Stranger than Paradise 102
Streamers 140
subUrbia 153
Surviving Desire 4, 10, 29n.5, 30–1, 38–42, 71–2, 77–8, 85–8; shot length of 92n.7; *see also* Donovan, Martin and musicals

Tarantino, Quentin 2, 3, 151, 154
Texas 46, 54, 73

Theater of Cruelty 129
Theory of Achievement 10, 29n.5, 30–5, 40, 72
Three Shorts by Hal Hartley 72
Times 49
Trial, The 97
Trouble in Mind 29
Trust 1, 2, 15, 30, 33, 41, 46–7, 50–6, 59n.6, 61, 64, 71, 77–8, 82–5, 90, 91, 155; *see also* melodrama and Shelly, Adrienne
Trust Me see Trust
Twin Peaks 49, 52–4
Twin Peaks: Fire Walk with Me 54
2000 Seen By 122

Unbelievable Truth, The 1–2, 5, 11, 15, 30, 33, 46–53, 55, 57, 61, 66, 77–8, 82–3, 85, 90, 132–43, 148, 153, 155; *see also* Robert John Burke, Robert John, Adrienne Shelly and romantic comedy
United Artists 62
Urbaniak, James 73, 146, 159, 160, 163, 172
US JOBS (Jumpstart Our Business Startups) 68

Variety 55, 63, 68
vis-à-vis 42
Vivre sa Vie 155

Waking Life 57
Ward, Mary B. 38, 41, 85
Washington Post, The 49, 51, 54, 56
Weinstein, Harvey 48
Weiss, Bruce 48
Welles, Orson 16
Wenders, Wim 15
West Side Story 39, 40
Wyler, William 16

Zero Dark Thirty 44
zero point 83

GPSR Authorized Representative: Easy Access System Europe, Mustamäe tee 50, 10621 Tallinn, Estonia, gpsr.requests@easproject.com